Gregory T. Moore
Beyond the Voting Rights Act

Democracy in Times of Upheaval

Edited by
Matt Qvortrup

Volume 2

Gregory T. Moore

Beyond the Voting Rights Act

—

The Untold Story of the Struggle to Reform America's
Voter Registration Laws

DE GRUYTER

ISBN (Paperback) 978-3-11-074231-2
ISBN (Hardcover) 978-3-11-078273-8
e-ISBN (PDF) 978-3-11-074247-3
e-ISBN (EPUB) 978-3-11-074256-5
ISSN 2701-147X
e-ISSN 2701-1488

Library of Congress Control Number: 2022936625

Bibliographic information published by the Deutsche Nationalbibliothek
The Deutsche Nationalbibliothek lists this publication in the Deutsche Nationalbibliografie;
detailed bibliographic data are available on the internet at http://dnb.dnb.de.

This book is dedicated to the memory of Bernice Moore, Lanie Moore, Sr., Marilyn Moore Hardy, Lanie Moore, Jr., and my many other family and friends who have departed this earth and contributed to my spiritual, personal, and professional development as a voting rights advocate.

Acknowledgements

The combination of legislative reforms and voter mobilizations recounted in this book were undertaken by a wide spectrum of advocates, organizations, contributors, and coalitions that are too numerous to name here. However, I would like to sincerely thank all those persons and entities referenced below for their long-standing contributions to the struggle for voter reforms highlighted in this book —and to the expansion of our democracy overall.

First and foremost, I want to acknowledge the arduous work and commitment of the "Motor Voter Coalition," made up of over thirty organizations who worked for over 4 years to pass the landmark National Voter Registration Act of 1993, (NVRA). While the coalition received little notoriety, it was effective in plowing through years of partisan gridlock and resistance on Capitol Hill to pass one of the most comprehensive voter reform bills in US History. The original members of the Motor Voter Coalition included: *The League of Women Voters, the NAACP, the Leadership Conference on Civil and Human Rights, the NAACP Legal Defense and Education Fund, the American Civil Liberties Union the Lawyers Committee for Civil Rights Under Law, ACORN, Project Vote, Human Serve, People for the American Way, the Citizenship Education Fund and Rainbow/Push Coalition, the Center on Policy Alternatives, the AFL-CIO, the National Coalition on Black Civic Participation, the A. Phillip Randolph Institute, the National Urban League, the Mexican American Legal Defense and Education Fund, the United States Student Association, Disabled Veterans of America, Black Veterans of America, Disabled-But Able to Vote, Rock the Vote, Common Cause, the US Public Interest Research Group, the Midwest and Southwest Voter Registration Projects, the Committee for the Study of the Electorate, the Center for Constitutional Rights, the American Jewish Committee, the League of United Latin American Citizens, the National Disabilities Rights Network, the Paralyzed Veterans of America, and the United Methodist Church-General Board of Church and Society.*

After NVRA's passage, there were major institutions and organizations who undertook research and analysis of the NVRA's impact in the years after its passage. Within the federal government, the U.S. Election Assistance Commission, and Department of Justice led the oversite and enforcement respectfully. Among the leading advocacy groups were DEMOS, the Advancement Project, Pew Charitable Trust, Project Vote, the Brennen Center for Justice at NYU, the ACLU, the NAACP LDF, the Mexican American Legal Defense and Education Fund, the Democracy Fund and scores of foundations and advocacy organizations. Without their constant monitoring and fierce advocacy of NVRA's full im-

https://doi.org/10.1515/9783110742473-001

plementation and enforcement, the law's impact would have been greatly diminished.

Many prominent members of the civil rights, labor, faith-based and human rights community played a significant role behind the scenes to advance NVRA and the many voting rights crusades highlighted in this book. They include Motor Voter Co-chairs NAACP Attorney Eddie Hailes and League of Women Voters, lobbyists Mary Brooks and Lloyd Leonard; Human Serve leaders Richard Cloward and Francis Fox-Piven, JoAnne Chasnow, and Hulbert James; Disability Activists Jim Dixon and Justin Dart; Mort Halpern, Judy Goldberg-Crockett, and Laura Murphy Lee of the ACLU; Elaine Jones, Penda Hair, Lani Gunier, Ted Shaw, Judith Brown-Dianis NAACP-LDF, longtime NAACP Washington Bureau Chief Hillary Shelton, the Advancement Project's the National Coalition on Black Civic Participation's Directors Gracia Hillman, Atty. Sonya Jarvis, and Melanie Campbell; Marsha Adler and Melanne Verveer with People for the American Way; Wallace Williams, with Black Veterans of America, the Mexican American Legal Defense Fund's Steve Carbo, DEMOS founder and former Connecticut Secretary of State Miles Rappaport, National Urban League's Bob McAlpine, and Ron Jackson; Patrick Lippert and Steve Barr with Rock the Vote; Mary Francis Berry, U.S. Commission on Civil Rights; Ralph Neas, Wade Henderson, Gene Karpinski, U.S. Public Interest Research Group, Nancy Zirkin, Bill Taylor and Ellen Buchman with the Leadership Conference on Civil and Human Rights.

The NVRA could not have been enacted into law without key Congresspersons and congressional staffers. They include the NVRA lead sponsors, Congressman Al Swift's staffers Karl Sandstorm, Herb Stone; Rules Committee Chairman Wendall Ford and lead counsel Jack Sousa; House Judiciary Committee's Chairman and NVRA co-sponsor Congressman John Conyers, Jr.; Staff Directors Julian Epstein, Perry Applebaum, and Committee Counselors Ron Stroman, Keenan Keller, Ted Kalo, and Stephanie Moore; House Leadership staff Lorraine Miller, Steve Chapman, and Cassandra Butts. Special recognition must be given to Republican Members of Congress and their staff who supported voter reform in defiance of their party leadership: Representatives Bill Thomas and Jim Sensenbrenner; and Senators Mark Hatfield, Jim Jeffords, and Dave Durenberger in the Senate.

Finally, I want to pay tribute to many of the fallen warriors who were champions of the NVRA and have left their indelible mark on our nation's voting rights history. They include Althea Simmons, of the NAACP, Professor Richard Cloward, a pioneer of agency based voter registration; Attorney Frank Parker, Lawyer's Committee for Civil Rights Under Law; Ron Brown, the first Black Democratic National Committee Chairman; Patrick Lippert of Rock the Vote; Willie Velasquez and Antonio Gonzales of the Southwest Voter Registration Project; Attorneys Lani Gunier and Counsel Director Julius Chambers with the NAACP-LDF; Curtis Gans with the Committee for the Study of the Electorate; and Equal Employment Opportunity Commission Chairperson Jaqueline Berrien. In the US Congress, Representatives John Conyers, Jr. Al Swift, John Lewis, Bill Gray, Stephanie-Tubbs Jones; and Senators Wendall Ford, Mark Hatfield, and Paul Wellstone in the US Senate.

And finally, a special thank you to the editors and production crew at De Gruyter Publishing: Matt Qvortrup who first invited me to be part of the *Democracy in Times of Upheaval* series, Michaela Göbels, Gerhard Boomgaarden and Katharina Ehlgen who guided this manuscript to its final edits and production. Thank you for your patience and your continued encouragement to bring this decades long research and writing project to fruition. Special thanks to Shelly Wilsey who led me to the ILA international convening and Matt Qvortrup. Thanks to Jennifer Lawrence and copy editors at American Manuscript Editors; to Anitra Merritt and Dr. Denise Wright for the initial word processing and research of my earlier manuscript drafts. Thanks to the academics, peer reviewers, researchers and readers who critiqued multiple versions of the manuscript including: led by my devoted wife and life partner Jean (JB) Moore who has been by my side during much of this journey, Dr. David Descutner, Gillian Berchowitz and Richard Hurd of Ohio University Press; Professor James Steele, Medgar Evers College, (CUNY), Dr. Keith Jennings, Atlanta-Clark University; Dr. Carl Levan, American University, and Dr. Clarence Lusane, Howard University. My sincere thanks to all the above for your commitment to expanding the right to vote and for making this book possible. Most importantly I want to thank God for allowing me to be a part of and bear witness to all of the historical experiences detailed in this book.

Table of Contents

About the Author and the Series Editor

About the author
Gregory T. Moore, a native of Cleveland, Ohio, is a leading national voting rights advocate in the United States with a long and distinguished history of promoting voting rights and the mobilization of African American voters. He has served in several leadership positions and devoted over thirty years to democratic reform initiatives including legislative and grassroots advocacy to secure passage of the landmark National Voter Registration Act.

Moore has served as a Congressional Chief of Staff in the US House of Representatives, Executive Director of the NAACP-National Voter Fund, and Director of the Democratic National Committee's Voting Rights Institute, where he led the party's efforts to establish election protection program operations in all 50 states. He is currently President of the Promise of Democracy Foundation, and serves as Chair of the US Election Assistance Commission's Board of Advisors.

About the series editor
Dr Matt Qvortrup is editor of the series Democracy in Times of Upheaval. Since 2014, he has been Professor of Political Science at Coventry University. He is author of more than a dozen books on democracy, comparative politics, and political theory, including Death by a Thousand Cuts (De Gruyter 2021), Referendums and Ethnic Conflict (University of Pennsylvania Press 2014), and A Comparative Study of Referendums (Manchester University Press 2005). He is a frequent commentator on BBC and writes a regular column for the magazine Philosophy Now. Dr Qvortrup has received several prizes, including the Oxford University Law Prize 2012. Trained as a lawyer and a political scientist, he earned his doctorate at Oxford University.

https://doi.org/10.1515/9783110742473-002

Foreword

Fulfilling Democracy's Broken Promise

For well over a decade from the mid-1980s through 1993 there was a quiet and little noticed movement of voting rights advocates and organizations who fought to reduce barriers to voting through the reform of the nation's voter registration laws. For many years following the passage of the Voting Rights Act of 1965 (VRA),[1] there was a general misconception that the voting rights movement had ended with no need for additional federal legislation. The passage of the Act had taken place following a long-fought battle in the civil rights movement throughout the 1960s. After the bill was passed by Congress and signed into law by President Lyndon B. Johnson on August 6, 1965, many of the mainline leaders and newly elected Black officials shifted their attention to other pressing issues related to the political and economic empowerment of African Americans and disenfranchised citizens.

The tumultuous Student Movement of the 60s and 70s bled and led into a progressive movement made up of activists who moved from waging a campaign to end the draft and Vietnam War to one that pushed for the ratification of the 26th Amendment to the Constitution, (ratified in 1971) that gave young people (18 – 21-year-olds) the right to vote.[2] Prior to that time young men could be drafted into the Army at age 18 but could not vote until they turned twenty-one. Tens of thousands of 18, 19 and 20-year-olds were coming home in body bags having never reached the age where they could vote in a democracy that they were giving their lives to preserve. Like the 19th amendment to the US Constitution that gave women the right to vote,[3] this change would have a major impact on the political composition and makeup of our national electorate. But it would take several decades before young people exercised their full political strength to impact a presidential election.

Meanwhile the voting rights movement continued into the 1970's and early 80s producing significant, but little noticed legislative victories with the reautho-

---

1 "Congress and the Voting Rights Act of 1965," National Archives, (n.d.) accessed March 22, 2022, https://www.archives.gov/legislative/features/voting-rights-1965.
2 Jocelyn Benson and Michael T. Morley, "The Twenty-Sixth Amendment," National Constitution Center, (n.d.) accessed March 22, 2022, https://constitutioncenter.org/interactive-constitution/interpretation/amendment-xxvi/interps/161.
3 "19th Amendment," History, last modified March 9, 2022, https://www.history.com/topics/womens-history/19th-amendment-1.

https://doi.org/10.1515/9783110742473-003

rization and amendments to the Voting Rights Act in 1975, 1982 and 1992.[4] After passage of these amendments the battle to expand voting laws beyond the landmark act was fought in state legislatures across the country for many years with varying degrees of success. In the late 1980s efforts began to shift toward developing comprehensive federal legislation to modernize voter registration laws that could be applied to all fifty states. Even into the early 1990s there were states that restricted voter registration to the handful of county registrars who were seldom mobile and often inaccessible to the people most disenfranchised.

In the late 1980s good government advocacy groups emerged joining some of the more traditional civil rights and civic groups to form new coalitions for expanding voter participation. By the early 1990s these coalitions began to wage a national legislative campaign at the federal level to expand the right to vote by reforming voter registration laws. Their strategy was primarily to outlaw restrictive voter registration laws at the state level and set one national standard that would be conducted uniformly across the country. The ultimate goal was to reverse the growing trend of declining voter participation by expanding the pool of eligible voters who could not vote due to their lack of being registered. It was an ambitious goal for its time.

The Reauthorization of the Voting Rights Act in 1975 was amended by adding bi-lingual provisions requiring the use of multiple language ballots in jurisdictions with minority communities with significant foreign language speaking citizens.[5] In 1982 VRA amendments were added that promoted increased minority representation in congressional and legislative redistricting. Specifically, the 1982 Amendment to Section 2 of the act extended federal voting rights protections related to legislative redistricting by providing that majority-minority districts can be created to prevent the dilution of minorities' voting strength.[6] This extension of the Act paved the way for increased minority representation among Black, Hispanic, Native and Asian Pacific elected officials in the US Congress and in state legislative districts. It would take a full decade after the 1982 VRA amendments before the nation saw the full effects of the act after the 1991 redistricting and 1992 elections. During that ten-year period efforts were focused on enforcing the new provisions that were already on the books and identifying new barriers to voting.

---

4 "Amendments to the Voting Rights Act of 1965," Wikipedia, last modified February 13, 2022, https://en.wikipedia.org/wiki/Amendments_to_the_Voting_Rights_Act_of_1965.
5 "Minority language," Wikipedia, last modified March 3, 2022, https://en.wikipedia.org/wiki/ Minority_language.
6 "Majority-minority districts," Ballotpedia, (n.d.) accessed March 22, 2022, https://ballotpedia. org/Majority-minority_districts.

In 1983 civil rights leader Jesse Jackson, Sr., President of Operation PUSH (People United to Save Humanity) and one of Dr. Martin Luther King's top Lieutenants, launched a historic campaign for president of the United States. Jackson's campaign mobilized millions of minority voters across the US for the first time since passage of the VRA in 1982 amendments. His 1983 "Southern Crusade" and subsequent presidential campaigns in 1984 and 1988 brought the issue of voting rights and electoral disenfranchisement to the forefront of the nation's attention. His campaign's platform demands included calls to end barriers to voter registration and for reform of primary election rules within the Democratic Party that made it hard for African Americans and minority candidates to be fairly competitive in presidential and congressional elections.

In the spring of 1989, a coalition of voting rights, civil rights and civic organizations formed what would become known as the "Motor Voter Coalition." It began what turned out to be a four-year effort to pass the *National Voter Registration Act*, (NVRA) which became commonly known as the "Motor Voter" Bill. This law for the first time in US history set national standards for registering voters to vote in all 50 states.

Beyond the Voting Rights Act provides first-hand accounts of behind the scenes work that led to the landmark NVRA's passage. The manuscript intersects these developments with this author's own personal journey as a national student leader and later a voting rights activist. It is a personal account of the intersection into the voter registration and electoral reform movements of the 1990s and the pro-democracy movement of today. The recounting of the many steps toward voting reforms would come to symbolize the institutional resistance against efforts to liberalize (democratize) the archaic and restrictive voter registration procedures that governed most states throughout the 20th century.

Beyond the Voting Rights Act also recounts the impact of several presidential elections from 1984 through the present that helped bring full awareness of the many barriers to full participation that still exist well into the 21st century. These little noted voting rights crusades unveiled a painful truth: that the nation's archaic registration system was designed to limit, rather than expand the right to vote for many segments of our society. The extensive and ongoing legislative battles served as the genesis of the author's now three decades long personal crusade to reform restrictive voting laws, and to help develop civic and voter mobilization programs to empower students, African Americans, formally incarcerated people, and other traditionally economic and politically disenfranchised voters across the US. By recounting the intersectionality between the multi-decade struggles, these stories provide the context for the ongoing battle against state sponsored voter suppression that continues through this very day.

Beyond the Voting Rights Act tells a story that places in context the Modern-Day battles against voter suppression that are still underway at both the state and national level. Many of the key players who both advanced and fought the battle to reform the nation's voter registration laws are still on the scene fighting today. Many others have departed having left their indelible mark on the effort to expand our nation's democracy. Hopefully, this book can serve as an important study for advocates engaged in the ongoing struggle to pass new federal legislation to restore the protections of Section 4 of the Voting Rights Act of 1965 that were struck down in the landmark Shelby vs. Holder US Supreme Court decision on June 25, 2013.

The NVRA expanded many of the yet unfulfilled promises of the Voting Rights Act, adding the largest number of new voters to the rolls in American History. In a comprehensive report marking the 20th anniversary since its passage, the advocacy group DEMOS reported that over 100 million citizens were registered to vote through the various provisions of the NVRA in the first 15 years since its implementation.[7] NVRA would help swell voter registration rolls that would lead to historic voter turnouts beginning in 2000. The massive turnouts also revealed a democracy that had serious capacity deficits in administering its elections. The election debacles in 2000 in Florida and Ohio in 2004 would usher in a heightened commitment to election protection programs and would lead to the enactment of another major federal initiative to set national standards for election administration through passage of the Help America Vote Act of 2002 (HAVA).[8] Both NVRA and HAVA laid the foundation for the historic registration and mobilization of African American and young voters who played a decisive role in the election of the nation's first African American President, Barack Obama in 2008. NVRA also established the nation's first active federal role in utilizing government's public service agencies to register U.S. citizens. The DEMOS report also revealed the ongoing shortcomings and challenges taking place in states to ensure that agencies are carrying out all of the promises of NVRA and HAVA.

Beyond the Voting Rights Act is the story that bridges historic legislative battles for voting rights, while decades apart, into one ongoing struggle for the basic principle: *one person, one vote* and the fight to protect it. The hard work to implement and carry out the new reforms and provisions of the NVRA after passage

---

7 Mijin Cha, "Registering Millions: The Success and Potential of the National Voter Registration Act at 20," Demos, last modified May 20, 2013, https://www.demos.org/research/registering-millions-success-and-potential-national-voter-registration-act-20.
8 "H.R.3295 – 107th Congress (2001–2002): Help America Vote Act of 2002," Congress.gov, last modified October 29, 2002, https://www.congress.gov/bill/107th-congress/house-bill/3295.

would become its own voter reform movement that continues well into the 21st century.

Beyond the Voting Rights Act provides the back story for how these historic advances were achieved amidst fierce opposition in Washington and in state legislatures across the US. It recounts the genesis of this new era of voter suppression that has grown prevalent in the US since the election of Barack Obama and intensified after his reelection in 2012. The U.S. Supreme Courts' Shelby v. Holder decision in 2013 that eviscerated the Voting Rights Act's pre-clearance provisions would further intensify this battle as states were now free to impose more voting restrictions.[9] The new battle to save our democracy now rests in the development of new national standards for protecting and de-politicizing the administration of U.S. elections.

This manuscript that was over 25 years in the making, is not a historical textbook or a legal or even scholarly analysis of this topic. Rather it is simply a personal narrative into the mind and heart of a voting rights activist who helped expand this advocacy into a broader Democracy movement in the US over 3 decades. It is a movement that has become a lifelong journey and struggle to help fulfill our Democracy's Broken Promise to all its citizens. It is written from that perspective, which is only one perspective from among the scores that might exist from other advocates who also contributed to this extensive legislative battle. This is just one story—my story, from one perspective—my perspective. Most importantly it is a story that has been largely untold until now.

Statement on Proceeds from the book

The authors' proceeds from sales of Beyond the Voting Rights Act will be donated to the Promise of Democracy Foundation, Inc., (PDF) a non-profit organization committed to breaking down barriers to full participation in American Democracy. PDF supports programs that promote voting rights, non-partisan election administration, and initiatives that empower disenfranchised communities. To learn more and support our ongoing work, visit http://www.promiseofdemocracy.org.

---

9 "Shelby County v. Holder," Brennan Center for Justice, last modified August 4, 2018, https://www.brennancenter.org/our-work/court-cases/shelby-county-v-holder.

Chapter 1
The Promise of Democracy

The concept of American Democracy "One Man (Person), One Vote" was one of the first tenets of our Declaration of Independence, written so vividly by Thomas Jefferson and enshrined within the U.S. Constitution and its amendments over the years. The failure to fully embrace these words and ideas has been, and continues to be, the broken promise of our American Democracy. Through all the years of our nation's history, political leaders seemed to get away with breaking this promise, generation after generation. The one guaranteed right in the Bill of Rights (that was inadvertently tied to their own political careers) was the hardest to fulfill. The resistance to expanding full voting rights to all Americans regardless of race or class has been ongoing throughout U.S. history.[1] The same forces that have resisted these reforms to expand our democracy have passed their resistance from political generation to generation. They have never stopped resisting.

It would take the United States 128 years from the adoption of the Constitution to grant women the right to vote;[2] 167 years to grant all African Americans the right to vote;[3] 174 years to grant the right to 19- to 21-year-olds;[4] and 177 years to guarantee rights to bi-lingual Americans.[5] It would be 197 years before the United States set one national standard for registering all Americans, with the passage of the National Voter Registration Act of 1993. Even after the passage of the Voting Rights Act in 1965, state and local political leaders continued to use gerrymandering, role purges, and dual registration systems to maintain their electoral and political advantage. For all our talk of 50 United States and America being the cradle of modern democracy, America, unbelievably, was still operating only as an *Emerging Democracy* through most of the 20th century.

---

1 "The Expansion of the Vote: A White Man's Democracy," U.S. History Online Textbook, (n.d.) accessed March 22, 2022, https://www.ushistory.org/us/23b.asp.

2 "19th Amendment to the U.S. Constitution: Women's Right to Vote" National Archives, last modified August 3, 2021, https://www.archives.gov/historical-docs/19th-amendment.

3 "Voting Rights for African Americans" Lobrary of Congress, (n.d.) accessed March 22, 2022, https://www.loc.gov/classroom-materials/elections/right-to-vote/voting-rights-for-african-americans/.

4 "Suffrage for 18-Year-Olds," History, Art & Archives, U.S. House of Representatives, (n.d.) accessed March 22, 2022, https://history.house.gov/Records-and-Research/Listing/c_016/.

5 Angelo N. Ancheta, "Language Accommodation and The Voting Rights Act" in *Voting Rights Act Reauthorization of 2006*, ed. Ana Henderson (Berkeley Public Policy Press: University of California, Berkeley, 2007).

https://doi.org/10.1515/9783110742473-004

This may be a hard pill to swallow for some, but it is the only realization that could describe the resistance that we witnessed as a society as this new democracy movement began to unfold.

In 1954, in the face of growing racial intolerance and resistance in major parts of the South, the U.S. Supreme Court, then a common blanket of nine white male justices, concluded in the *Brown v Board of Education* decision that America's laws regarding racial segregation, separation, and long-accepted inequality were unconstitutional.[6] It would take the U.S. nearly 12 years after that ruling to pass the Voting Rights Act of 1965; it would take 18 more years to pass the 26th Amendment granting the right to vote to 18-year-olds in 1971; it would take 21 more years to pass the bi-lingual provisions in 1975; and it would take a full 39 years after the 1954 decision and 28 years after passage of the Voting Rights Act of 1965 to pass a law that liberalized and standardized America's voter registration procedures with the passage of the National Voter Registration Act of 1993.

This new law, for the first time, allowed the power to determine how a person is registered to be expanded from the exclusive domain of state and county registrars to non-profit, community-based organizations and individual advocates. It also made provisions for other federal and state-funded entities like Motor Voter agencies, public welfare, and social service agencies to be used to register recipients to vote.[7]

To understand and fully appreciate this story of the movement to pass landmark federal voter registration legislation in 1993, it is important to step back and develop a perspective on the historical aspects of voting status among African Americans that took place for over one hundred years leading up to the Voting Rights Act of 1965. Before the NVRA's passage, it had been less than 30 years since African Americans had been given full access to the ballot. Before the Voting Rights Act of 1965, history reveals a basic flat line of voting activity among African Americans from the 1880s through post-World War II.[8] This period in the American chronology highlights the continued ebb and flow of political changes that took place in that era. It set the stage for the modern-day "voting rights movement." From the post-Reconstruction era through 1965, various

---

6 "History – Brown v. Board of Education Re-enactment," United States Courts, (n.d.) accessed March 22, 2022, https://www.uscourts.gov/educational-resources/educational-activities/history-brown-v-board-education-re-enactment.https://www.uscourts.gov/educational-resources/educational-activities/history-brown-v-board-education-re-enactment
7 "National Voter Registration Act of 1993 (NVRA)," U.S. Department of Justice, last modified March 11, 2020, https://www.justice.gov/crt/national-voter-registration-act-1993-nvra.
8 Ibid.

means were used to systematically exclude major segments of the U.S. population from political participation.[9] This era was also characterized as the time of demobilization; when the political elite had the ways and means to institute laws controlling the democratic process and used those laws as an instrument to maintain their political power.

* * *

The promise of our democratic principles had not been honored for major sectors of the American population in 1965. The nation had grown weary of the challenge to its longstanding traditions of political exclusion. The growing unrest in the Black community in cities and towns across the nation was growing more violent and more insistent on real political and social change. America was at war with itself—unable to reconcile its worldwide reputation as the cradle of democracy and the growing demands of Black people for full democratic rights in the political and social fabric of the nation. Once again, there were demonstrations in the streets, sit-ins, boycotts, rallies, and endless hearings in local courts as well as landmark decisions at justice's highest level. Now the nation faced yet another major decision to extend fundamental citizenship rights to Blacks. The civil rights movement had already effectively pushed through a major civil rights bill in 1964 after a series of non-violent demonstrations led by Dr. Martin Luther King, Jr., and other civil rights leaders. Supporters of the Voting Rights Act of 1965 had been greatly inspired by the movement in Selma, Alabama and throughout the south.[10]

Despite the highly visible confrontation between the civil rights movement, the southern all-white entrenched power centers controlled most of the state and local government's political and economic decision-making. Even before Dr. Martin Luther King, Jr. and the Southern Christian Leadership Conference came along, the NAACP had been demanding more voting and economic rights for Black citizens throughout the South. Against the backdrop of this emerging movement lay largely invisible Black political representations that were mere afterthoughts to the predominantly white ruling structures. These informal Black representatives were largely ministers, lawyers, small businesspeople, and community-based leaders. They were also local elected officials, mayors and council members of small townships, and token members of zoning boards and school

9 Danyelle Solomon, Connor Maxwell, and Abril Castro, "Systematic Inequality and American Democracy," Center for American Progress, last modified August 7, 2019, https://www.americanprogress.org/article/systematic-inequality-american-democracy/.
10 "Confrontations for Justice," The National Archives, (n.d.) accessed March 22, 2022, https://www.archives.gov/exhibits/eyewitness/html.php?section=2.

boards. Outside of politics, many more were schoolteachers, sports coaches, and Black college professors. In many small towns, they were frequently the presidents of Historic Black Colleges or high-level academic officials at the universities—often the most prestigious Blacks in the county.

The ruling white structure in any given southern town consisted of the city or county sheriff, the mayor or powerful elected officials, the safety commissioner, and the local big business community. Just beneath that level of control was another layer of line authority. These were the operatives, the administrators of the major functions of a city—a tight community consisting of judges, heads of local lodges, property owners and landlords of multiple apartment dwellings and multi-family dwellings, and real estate companies. They worked together to maintain control of the major decision-making apparatus of most local and state political structures. This relatively small-knit group, composed almost entirely of white men, was the political structure that controlled nearly every aspect of local business and commerce throughout the South. Their power often superseded that of any legislative body. Through imposition of "Black Codes," they found creative ways to evade federal regulations, court orders, and new federal environmental mandates.[11] Anybody who had a point of view "outside" their small circle was an "outside agitator." Politically, there were few competitive nominating conventions or wide-open primaries. Quite often, major political decisions could be made over a card game, during a round of golf, in the judge's chambers over a few drinks, or at a lodge or hunting range.

Against this backdrop, the civil rights movement began to mount its demands for more political participation for Blacks. This push was particularly threatening to the power structure when African Americans numerically dominated towns and counties. While white entrenched power brokers fought tooth and nail against federally imposed efforts to open up public accommodations, new federal laws forced them to relent and desegregate those institutions that were, in fact, in the public domain. However, as long as clusters of Blacks remained pocketed in the lower economic communities, confined to their side of the track, the unpleasant conditions of desegregated schools, sub-standard public education, and public housing buildings continued. Blacks in the Deep South and Hispanics in Texas and other Southwestern states were not a threat to the power broker economically or even socially. Low wages, limited employment opportunities, economic disinvestment, and inferior education formed a guarantee

---

11 "The Black Codes and Jim Crow Laws," National Geographic, (n.d.) accessed March 22, 2022, https://www.nationalgeographic.org/encyclopedia/black-codes-and-jim-crow-laws/.

that no matter what federal laws were passed, their control of political and economic power would remain firm.

By 1965, after the signing of the 1964 Civil Rights Act, the movement looked for the next level of struggle to bring down the walls of segregation and discrimination. Now that the federal government and the courts had backed public accommodations, it was all over but the shouting by local power bases. "What next?" they pondered. That answer would come soon, this time not in Birmingham but in Selma, a small town in Southeast Alabama. Dr. King lent his support to local efforts there to register Black voters. The issue was inaccessible registrars. Emerging Black Leaders, led by Selma activists Rev. C. T. Vivian, F.D. Reese, Amina Boykins, Albert Turner, and a young activist named John Lewis from Troy, Alabama, had been turned away when they brought large numbers of Blacks to the registrar's office. Once again, the nation saw the sight of a southern law enforcer standing in the doorway—this time, the doorway to the right to vote, guaranteed but never operationally granted to all Americans since the passage of the 14th and 15th Amendments to the U.S. Constitution.[12]

The right to eat a hamburger at a lunch counter was one thing. Granting the right to vote to Blacks and even disenfranchised poverty-stricken poor whites was quite another. A quality education could be debated. The right to public accommodations was limited to the most public of places. But the right to vote was quite a different demand. The federal bill that would come to be known as the Voting Rights Act sought to give Blacks the same political power that whites enjoyed in all 50 states, with a special emphasis on correcting the problems in the Deep South. One person, one vote would give Blacks a majority of the vote in major political and business centers throughout the south. Such a move would change the South's power structure.

Black leaders and the college students who sympathized with them were already making plans to vote in the upcoming elections. The landmark events that etched the permanent symbol of resistance to this movement were the brutal murders of freedom fighters conducting voter registration drives in the south. The most notable was the murder of NAACP Field Secretary Medgar Wiley Evers, who was struck down by a bullet from a long rifle in Jackson, Mississippi in June 1963 while leading a major voter registration and economic empowerment program.[13] Another milestone was the murders of three student voter reg-

---

12 "Civil War Amendments," Senate.gov, (n.d.) accessed March 22, 2022, https://www.senate.gov/artandhistory/history/common/generic/CivilWarAmendments.htm.
13 "Civil rights leader Medgar Evers is assassinated," History, last modified June 10, 2020, https://www.history.com/this-day-in-history/medgar-evers-assassinated.

istration activists, James Chaney, Mickey Schwerner, and John Goodman, who journeyed to the south to support the Mississippi Freedom Summer voter registration drive. The three workers went missing for weeks while conducting door-to-door registration drives in small rural communities in Mississippi. Their bodies were later found in an earthen dam in Philadelphia, Mississippi.[14] Even later, in 1965, Jimmie Lee Jackson from Marion, Alabama, as well as Rev. James Reeb and Viola Liuzzo, a housewife from Detroit, Michigan, were killed while supporting the voting rights march from Selma to Montgomery.[15] Their deaths symbolized the dangers of organizing voters around this power structure and the consequences that often befell those who supported the registration drives, marches, and sit-ins.

The siege of Selma on "Bloody Sunday" brought the issue to a head when marchers were met by white law enforcement wielding tear gas and clubs at the foot of Edmund Pettis Bridge. Despite opposition to its passage throughout the south and in the U.S. Congress, the landmark Voting Rights Act was passed and subsequently signed into law by President Lyndon B. Johnson on August 6, 1965. This measure outlawed racial discrimination at the voting booth, eliminated poll taxes, outlawed literacy tests, and sent federal examiners into the South to ensure its enforcement. It also required the U.S. Justice Department to "preclear" new state or local election laws, primarily in states with a history of racial discrimination. A formula was developed that singled out the southern states with the most egregious violations regarding denying the right to vote to Blacks and other racial minorities. This became known as section 4 of the Voting Rights Act.[16]

The first test of the Voting Rights Act in national elections was the election of 1968. This marked the first time that the Black vote could be maximized in the south. President Johnson and the Democratic Congress had launched a series of "Great Society" programs in response to the civil rights movement. These would come to be known as the "War on Poverty."[17] However, the escalating Vietnam War was draining the funding for these program initiatives. In the years following the VRA, a significant amount of other anti-poverty legislation was enact-

---

14 "Aug. 4, 1964: Civil Rights Workers Bodies Found," Zinn Education Project, (n.d.) accessed March 22, 2022, https://www.zinnedproject.org/news/tdih/civil-rights-workers-found/.

15 "James Reeb and the Call to Selma," Unitarian Universalist Association, (n.d.) accessed March 22, 2022, https://www.uua.org/re/tapestry/adults/river/workshop5/175806.shtml.

16 "Voting Rights Act of 1965," History, last modified January 11, 2022, https://www.history.com/topics/black-history/voting-rights-act.

17 Aaron Cooley, "War on Poverty " Encyclopedia Britannica, last modified February 18, 2020, https://www.britannica.com/topic/War-on-Poverty.

ed that established well-known government institutions; these included the Higher Education Act, the Equal Employment Opportunity Commission, (EEOC), the U.S. Civil Rights Commission, Medicaid, and other programs designed to eradicate poverty and to quiet the unrest that was engulfing the nation.

Like most Americans, African Americans had grown weary by November 1968. Dr. Martin Luther King, Jr. had been assassinated on April 4th followed by Senator Robert Kennedy two months later on June 4, 1968. Dr. King and Kennedy were gone and with them much of the spirit and energy that had kept the movement alive. The law-and-order campaign pushed by Richard Nixon was sure to attract many white Democrats in addition to the independent campaign of Alabama's segregationist governor, George Wallace. The odds were stacked against the party presidential nominee, Hubert H. Humphrey. Humphrey, who was Johnson's vice president, spent much of his campaign defending Johnson's Vietnam War. The war had long since lost the support of the American people, and that unpopularity plagued Humphrey's campaign until Election Day.

The growing revolt against the Vietnam War that had come to symbolize the Johnson-Humphrey administration cut deep into liberal support for the Humphrey campaign. The Black vote could have been more decisive in the race except for two factors. First were the civil rights movement's vocal criticisms of the lack of adequate funding for Johnson's War on Poverty. This was dramatized by the Poor People's Campaign initiated by Dr. King before his assassination and carried out by his lieutenants, including Ralph Abernathy, Andrew Young, and a young aide named Jesse Jackson, who was symbolically chosen as the "Mayor of Resurrection City." March organizers gave this name to the plot of land on the National Mall where the March and sit-in were held.[18] Heavy drenching rains over a number of days dampened morale and helped contribute to the perceived failure of the week-long event as demands to "end poverty now" were met by police orders to disburse and clear the ground. The momentum to end poverty and restart the civil rights movement slowed to a crawl, and the despair and lack of to hope within the Black community was carried into the 1968 election. In November, 58.5% of Black voters turned out and voted, according to the U.S. Census. It was the first presidential election since the passage of the Voting Rights Act of 1965, marking a dramatic increase in turnout since the 1964 election (be-

---

18 Damien Cave and Darcy Eveleigh, "In 1968, a 'Resurrection City' of Tents, Erected to Fight Poverty," The New York Times, last modified February 18, 2017, https://www.nytimes.com/2017/02/18/us/martin-luther-king-resurrection-city.html.

fore the passage of the Voting Rights Act), in which only 44% of southern Blacks participated.[19]

In the end, the Black voter turnout that year was up from 1964, but lower than predicted. Former Vice President Richard Nixon defeated Lyndon Johnson's vice president, Hubert Humphrey, by just over 511,000 out of 73.1 million votes cast—less than one vote per precinct. [20]In that election, millions of eligible Black voters were still unregistered, or had registered but chose not to vote. A marginal increase in Black turnout in key states could have affected the outcome of the 1968 election and essentially changed the course of history.

The Right to Vote: Youth and Universal Voting Rights 1975 – 1980

The escalation of the Vietnam War in 1971 increased the number of American soldiers who were killed or critically injured. Tens of thousands of 18-, 19-, and 20-year-old men were drafted, served, and in many cases died in a war that many of them did not understand or support. Anti-war protests on college campuses and inner cities added more fuel to the fires already set ablaze by the civil rights movement. President Nixon remained leery of anti-war protesters and civil rights agitators[21].

At the same time, the civil rights movement had shifted to the north, where leaders were now concentrating on increasing Black political power. Local Black political groups began to organize at the ballot box, electing mayors, council members, state legislators, and members of Congress. In the aftermath of these victories, President Nixon and an increasingly threatened reform-weary Congress reacted by passing tight federal restrictions on the political participation of non-profit and civil rights organizations. An effort to pass a constitutional amendment allowing 18-year-olds to vote began to grow, largely out of the opposition of many young people to the Vietnam War in 1971 and unrest among urban youth. Although first pushed by youth and anti-war radicals, the measure gained widespread support across the country. In Washington, it was viewed as a way to rein in much of the student unrest. Violent confrontations between student pro-

---

19 "United States presidential election of 1968," Encyclopedia Britannica, last modified October 29, 2021, https://www.britannica.com/event/United-States-presidential-election-of-1968.
20 Ibid.
21 Kenneth J. Heinemann, "Students and the Anti-War Movement," Bill of Rights Institute, (n.d.) accessed March 22, 2022, https://billofrightsinstitute.org/essays/students-and-the-anti-war-movement.

testers and state police had led to the killings of 4 students at Kent State University in Ohio on May 4, 1970[22] and 11 days later at Jackson State College in Mississippi where two student protesters were gunned down by law enforcement.[23] While the Student Nonviolent Coordinating Committee (SNCC) remained active throughout the early 1970s, its key leaders were growing up and moving on to prominent roles in civil rights organizations and elected political leadership. Much of the energy of the student movement shifted from the anti-war effort to the fight to give 18-year-olds the right to vote.

The pressure grew to pass the 26th Amendment as the most expedient way to end student unrest—next to ending the Vietnam War, which had no end in sight. In 1970, Congress passed a constitutional amendment to lower the voting age from 21 to 18. By the summer of 1971, the necessary 38 states had ratified the constitutional amendment. On July 1, 1971, the 26th Amendment to the U.S. Constitution became law, which was a major victory for student activists across the country.[24] Despite the enormous potential of the passage of this constitutional amendment, the era of student political involvement did not immediately impact the political process and did little to calm the unrest among many anti-war protesters. Hopes for a new era of political involvement did not dramatically increase among young people, as many had predicted.

The re-election of Richard Nixon in 1972 and his landslide defeat of Senator George McGovern, (winning 49 of 50 states) [25] was a clear reminder to African American, young, and progressive voters that they had not yet made an impact sufficient enough to determine the outcome of a national election. Nixon did not attempt to repeal the Voting Rights Act, but his Justice Department dragged its feet in fully enforcing all its provisions. It also took no steps to fully implement the 26th Amendment granting 18- to 20-year-olds the right to vote. Nixon viewed them as his biggest critics and made only token gestures to encourage young people to become politically more involved. Millions of Black Voters remained unregistered throughout the South and in many now-decaying northern urban centers. By the mid-1970s, campuses that had once buzzed with anti-war and

---

22 Jerry M. Lewis and Thomas R. Hensley, "The May 4 Shootings at Kent State University: The Search for Historical Accuracy," Kent State University, (1970) accessed March 22, 2022, https://www.kent.edu/may-4-historical-accuracy.

23 "May 15, 1970: Jackson State Killings," Zinn Education Project, (n.d.) accessed March 22, 2022, https://www.zinnedproject.org/news/tdih/jackson-state-killings/.

24 "The 26th Amendment," History, last modified April 23, 2021, https://www.history.com/topics/united-states-constitution/the-26th-amendment.

25 "1972 United States presidential election," Wikipedia, last modified March 19, 2022, https://en.wikipedia.org/wiki/1972_United_States_presidential_election.

civil rights protests began to calm down and shift their focus away from politics. Some campuses even abolished student governments, as was done at Kent State and Ohio University. The turnout of young voters, once predicted to be the new driving force in American politics, was only 48% nationally.[26]

The youth strategy now moved toward building a stronger presence in the nation's capital to lobby Congress and the president for a stronger voice in the nation's education, civil rights, and foreign policy. Groups like the National Student Association (NSA) and the National Student Lobby (NSL) began to pick up the mantle of social change through legislative battles rather than street protests. These two rival national student groups had worked for years alongside mainstream student governments on campuses and were allied with predominantly white activist groups like Americans for Democratic Action, welfare rights groups, and labor unions representing garment workers, farmworkers, teachers, and service employees. In 1978, the NSA and NSL would merge to form the United States Student Association, which became the largest and most powerful student organization in the country.

The most-cited reason for the low turnout among African Americans and youth was low registration. Just over 50% of all Blacks were registered, while the percentage of young people who were registered was well under 45% according to the U.S. Census. In most federal and local elections, turnout among the 50% that were registered ranged from 25% to 45%. Civil rights groups joined predominately white citizens' advocacy groups to call for less restrictive laws, thereby encouraging the more hands-on voter registration being undertaken by state and local affiliates. One of the most important reforms was a national postcard registration that would more effectively allow them to use a powerful tool to register and organize their communities around their issues of importance. In the handful of northern states that experimented with this, there was a marked increase in voter registration among Blacks, Hispanics, and mostly young white voters. While federal laws to create post card registration was introduced and received strong support for years in both legislative chambers of Congress, it failed to gain the votes needed to be passed into law.

---

[26] "Voting and Registration in the Election of November 1968," U.S. Bureau of the Census, (1969) accessed March 22, 2022, https://www.census.gov/library/publications/1969/demo/p20-192.html.

Carter's Election Reforms

In his first 100 days as president, Jimmy Carter introduced a sweeping election reform package to Congress. The centerpiece of the legislation was a bill (HR 5400) to establish Election Day Registration. Carter's proposal received a chilly reception on Capitol Hill. The plan would have permitted any eligible person to register to vote on Election Day with proper identification or a witness. [27]The concept would also be referred to as universal registration or same-day registration. Experts estimated that the act would register a minimum of 50 million voters who remained unregistered and disenfranchised. The plan was immediately attacked by Republicans in the House and Senate. Several southern Democrats and even big-city Congressmen also opposed the bill. They claimed that opening the doors of the election to any American citizen was an invitation to fraud. Opponents also claimed that the current voter registration system was working just fine. The system they claimed was "working fine" was an electoral system in which over 70 million voters had not voted in the last election. Only 53% of Americans bothered to vote in the 1976 presidential election.[28] The levels for congressional and local voter turnout were even worse. For the last congressional election in 1974, only 39% of people voted. Local elections ranged from 70 to 85% of the population declining to vote in municipal elections, based on US Census data.[29]

The Carter bill provided for grants to states to assist in the registration effort on Election Day and to pay for outreach programs for unregistered voters. The formula for providing funds to states was 20 cents for every voter who voted in the last presidential election. An additional 20 to 40 cents per voter would be provided to states that conducted outreach programs for traditionally unregistered voters. The response among congressional Democrats was not much warmer than that of the Republicans despite the strong support of the popular vice president, Walter Mondale. To build support among moderate Republicans, Sen-

---

27 Rick Perlstein, "Jimmy Carter Tried to Make It Easier to Vote in 1977. The Right Stopped Him With the Same Arguments It's Using Today," Time, last modified August 20, 2020, https://time.com/5881305/president-carter-election-reform/.
28 "1976 Presidential General Election Results," USA Election Atlas, (n.d.) accessed March 22, 2022, https://uselectionatlas.org/RESULTS/national.php?year=1976.
29 https://www.census.gov/library/publications/1976/demo/p20-293.html   -   :~:text=The%20voter%20turnout%20in%20the,off%2Dyear%20election%20since%201946"Voting and Registration in the Election of November 1974," U.S. Bureau of the Census, (1976) accessed March 22, 2022, https://www.census.gov/library/publications/1976/demo/p20-293.html#:~:text=The%20voter%20turnout%20in%20the,off%2Dyear%20election%20since%201946.

ate leaders made several amendments to the bill to appease southern senators. The first was to make the entire bill voluntary. The second was to have it apply only to primary elections.

Republicans created a litany of amendments designed to reverse the purpose for which the bill was originally intended. They included a national prohibition of voter registration drives targeted at a particular bloc or class of voter. This provision would have made it illegal to target Blacks in conducting voter registration. Another was to abolish the Electoral College in exchange for Election Day Registration. This was due in some part to the fact that President Gerald Ford had won more states and lost to Carter by a much slimmer margin than the Electoral College vote reflected. The heavy Black turnout had allowed Carter to win the election despite winning only a single state west of the Mississippi River. The point person on Carter's bill was Vice President Walter Mondale. As a Minnesota native, Mondale had seen the Election Day Registration system work well, with Minnesota being one of only four states that had Election Day Registration (EDR). After sensing the widespread opposition on Capitol Hill, Mondale and his staff determined that the national postcard registration bills that had been introduced in the past Congress had no chance of passing during the first year of the new administration.

As hopes faded of passing an EDR registration bill, the administration reluctantly accepted several Republican amendments that weakened the bill's impact. Even after the bill was made voluntary for states, it did not gain the votes needed to pass. The universal registration bill met the same fate as past efforts to pass postcard registration legislation. This time, the bill failed despite the strong support of a Democratic president and Congress. The new administration experienced its first major legislative defeat. This would lead to a series of other legislative intra-party struggles between the White House and Congress and set the tone for the early challenges to the new president and the old guard in Congress.

America in the late 1970s was a place where economic decline overwhelmed every aspect of American society. The nation's unemployment rate was in the double digits, over 10%. Interest rates were close to 20%. [30]Small and even many large companies went out of business. It was the beginning of the decline of the manufacturing industry that had carried America's prosperity for the entire post-World War II period. Suddenly, cities were falling into fiscal collapse, and federal and state governments facing record deficits were forced to cut

---

30 Paul Volcker, "What Led to the High Interest Rates of the 1980s?," PBS News, last modified May 29, 2009, https://www.pbs.org/newshour/economy/what-led-to-the-high-interest.

vital social programs. There was a sense of "malaise," a phrase coined by critics of President Carter after he gave a televised speech to the nation that he viewed as a reality check. The word "malaise" would come to characterize his only term in office.

Carter's presidency ushered in the end of the civil rights and voting rights movement, as it had come to be known. Political support for anti-poverty big government programs began to fade. The Democratic tide that had swept Lyndon Johnson back into office in 1964 had all but dissipated. The anti-Watergate sentiments that had helped sweep Carter into office began to fade. The country's economic condition was also a major factor in the 1980 campaign. With record-high interest rates and double-digit unemployment rates, the country had slid into a major recession, further boosting Carter's unpopularity, as did the Iranian revolutionary government's holding of over 50 American hostages in 1979. Carter's failed attempt to rescue them or negotiate a release was a major issue fostering the perception of the Carter administration as incompetent.[31]

Carter had been further damaged by a strong intra-party struggle led by Senator Ted Kennedy, who launched his long-awaited campaign for president by challenging an incumbent Democratic president during the primaries. It was a spirited but ultimately unsuccessful campaign that turned ugly and caused bitter divisions within the Democratic Party. California governor and retired Hollywood actor Ronald Reagan rode the conservative anti-tax and anti-Carter sentiment into a sunny "Morning in America" presidential campaign in 1980.

The divided Democratic Party and Carter's unpopularity created a perfect storm that resulted in the election of Reagan in November 1980. Reagan was elected president in a landslide, winning 44 out of 50 states, and 489 electoral votes.[32] The major voter registration and electoral reforms that Jimmy Carter proposed when he was elected in 1976 would be stalled throughout the Reagan administration and the Bush administration that followed. Sixteen years would pass before Congress took up any major voter registration reform legislation that had any chance of passing.

---

31 "Jimmy Carter and the Iran Hostage Crisis," BIll of Rights Institute, (n.d.) accessed March 22, 2022, https://billofrightsinstitute.org/essays/jimmy-carter-and-the-iran-hostage-crisis.
32 "1980 United States presidential election," Wikipedia, last modified March 19, 2022, https://en.wikipedia.org/wiki/1980_United_States_presidential_election.

Chapter 2
"Our Time Has Come!" – Jesse Jackson and the Historic 1984 Campaign

In 1982, after relatively moderate political bickering, Congress passed an Amendment to the Voting Rights Act of 1965. The Voting Rights Act of 1975 and 1982 had been passed, on a bipartisan basis without major opposition on Capitol Hill and even signed into law by President Reagan who had opposed other electoral reform measures. The newly reauthorized and updated VRA established a series of remedies to combat Black and minority voter disenfranchisement by deconstructing barriers that made it harder for Blacks and Hispanics to be elected to Congress, state legislatures and local offices. Among the many revisions, the Voting Rights Act of 1982 required federal and state governments to develop political jurisdictions during the redistricting process which offered racial and language minorities an opportunity to elect one of their own to elected office through the drawing of "majority-minority Congressional districts."[1]

Voting rights litigators had fought for and won cases that had called for the expansion of the same standards in state legislative and local elected "single member districts" as opposed to "at large districts." Under this new Voting Rights Act of 1982 Minority candidates had a better chance of electing members of their community than elections that were determined by at-large districts where higher number of minorities were concentrated. The 1982 VRA provisions required states, especially those covered under the original 1965 Act (mostly southern states) to create districts through the redistricting process which took place every 10 years following a US Census. [2]

During this period there was a re-emergence of engagement by many grassroots organizations that were centered in already existing community-based structures. Many voting rights advocates began to work with grassroots groups like *ACORN, Human Serve and Project Vote* to design and develop community empowerment projects to help advance the new act. Indeed, the largest pools of Black voters were concentrated in large urban centers in the North. It was here that community-based organizations began to develop political empower-

---

1 Thomas M. Boyd and Stephen J. Markman, "The 1982 Amendments To The Voting Rights Act: A Legislative History " *Washington and Lee Law Review* 40, no. 4 (1983): 1347–1428.
2 "About Language Minority Voting Rights," U.S. Department of Justice, last modified January 4, 2022, https://www.justice.gov/crt/about-language-minority-voting-rights.

https://doi.org/10.1515/9783110742473-005

ment program within faith-based institutions, community action agencies, and tenant organizations.

1983 began to show the first signs of the impact of the new law that saw Black political power and awareness coming of age. Suddenly the number of Black elected officials had almost doubled since 1973.[3] Additionally, an increasing number of White Democratic elected officials were winning large majorities of the Black vote; some as high as 90 % of the Black vote. This vote would become the margin of victory in close contests while Republicans were winning over 60 % of the White vote but less than 10 % of the Black vote.

1983 saw the election of African American mayors in many of the largest and most influential cities in the U.S. There were the historical campaigns of Harold Washington for Mayor of Chicago, Wilson Goode in Philadelphia, Richard Arrington in Birmingham, and Harvey Gant in Charlotte North Carolina. These victories broke decades of strong political control of central cities by white controlled political machines that had for the most part disenfranchised Black voters. In these and other major cities like Los Angeles, Newark, Detroit, Cleveland, and Atlanta, Blacks were able to exert greater influence over community and economic development projects, push for more equal funding for public education, and expanded employment opportunities for the chronically unemployed in the urban centers. Eventually multiple cities would elect Black mayors and majority-minority city councils as they moved into the 1990's.[4]

At the same time an economic recession was moving across the country. Unemployment, inflation, and interest rates were still in double digits and stagnant. With dwindling resources, many of the formally working-class families became officially classified as poor. Mixed with teenage pregnancy, high school drop-out rates and the greater availability of drugs and guns, many Black youth who lived in poverty in the 1980's began to develop the characteristics of an abandon child. With over 63 % stripped of their fraternal support base, and single mothers forced to work full time, they would become the breeding ground for the crime and deadly drug culture. The economic circumstances

---

3 "Social and Economic Issues of the 1980s and 1990s," Amistad Digital Resource, (n.d.) accessed March 22, 2022, https://www.amistadresource.org/the_future_in_the_present/social_and_economic_issues.html.

4 "Black Politics," Amistad Digital Resource, (n.d.) accessed March 22, 2022, https://www.amistadresource.org/the_future_in_the_present/black_politics.html.

under which many young Black urban dwellers lived would produce a situation where young people had more access to guns than the ballot box.[5]

It was in this political and economic environment in 1983 that Reverend Jesse Jackson, Sr., a noted civil rights leader would begin discussions around the country with African American leaders about the prospects for a national African American led progressive movement through a serious campaign for the Democratic nomination for President. It was in response to many of these same conditions that Jackson had formed Operation PUSH in the early 70's. Formally Operation Breadbasket, PUSH was an offshoot of the Southern Christian Leadership Conference, led by Dr. Martin Luther King, Jr. With a strong Black church base, he formed a new coalition of progressive whites, environmentalists, peace activists, labor unions, students, Asian Americans, Native Americans, gay and lesbian advocates, Black and Latino leaders, and a cadre of liberal elected officials.

Through Operation PUSH Jackson had gained his notoriety by challenging corporate giants to re-invest in Black communities; he had led economic boycotts against Coke-A-Cola, Southland/7–11, Revlon, Burger King, and many others. In response corporations established hundreds of new Black and minority owned franchises in many major cities, with many new partnerships being established through the annual *Black Expos* that pulled together Black businesses, major corporations, and local political leaders who gathered in large convention centers primarily in the Midwestern states. The Black Expos would gather thousands of entrepreneurs and civic leaders who would hold forums and seminars and trade shows focusing on developing a strong economic base for jobs and small minority businesses ownership and franchises. Coupled with his powerful base within Black churches, Jackson was building a strong political base well beyond Chicago. He set up similar programs in cities like Cleveland, OH, Detroit, MI, Gary and Indianapolis, Indiana, Philadelphia, PA and Atlanta, Ga.[6]

Jackson soon turned his attention to the electoral arena; leading major voter registration drives in cities and throughout the south through his "Southern Crusade: Atlanta, Ga., Birmingham, Ala. Columbia, SC, Charlotte, NC, Tidewater, Virginia, New Orleans, and Baton Rouge, La, Louisville, Ky. In 83 his rallying cry, *"Our Time has Come"* and the hands-on voter registration groups collectively reg-

---

5 "Social and Economic Issues of the 1980s and 1990s," Amistad Digital Resource, (n.d.) accessed March 22, 2022, https://www.amistadresource.org/the_future_in_the_present/social_and_economic_issues.html.

6 D. L. Chandler, "Little Known Black History Fact: Operation Push Boycotts," Black America Web, (n.d.) accessed March 22, 2022, https://blackamericaweb.com/2014/08/10/little-known-black-history-fact-operation-push-boycotts/.

istered 2 million new African American voters, the largest increase in Black Voter registration since the passage of the 1965 Voting Rights Act.[7]

The registration efforts of the Southern Crusade came to a climax at the end of the summer of 1983 as the traditional civil rights "Coalition of Conscience" led over 250,000 marches for a March on Washington to commemorate the 1963 march.[8] It was the first major and largest civil rights march since the first 1963 march. District of Columbia Delegate and former SCLC Legislative Director Walter Fauntroy led the coalition. The other major leaders were current SCLC president Rev. Joseph E. Lowery, Mrs. Coretta Scott King, Ben Hooks of the NAACP, Dr. Dorothy Height of the National Congress of Negro Women, Delegate Walter Fauntroy and Lezi Baskerville of the Black Leadership Roundtable, Norm Hill of the A Phillip Randolph Institute, Bill Lucy of AFSCME and the Coalition of Black Trade Unionist along with the heads of the AFL-CIO and United Auto workers. Also key to the march was the Congressional Black Caucus under the leadership of the Chairman Representative Ron Dellums from California and the CBC Dean John Conyers, Jr. who was also the sponsor of the legislative effort to make Dr. King's birthday a national holiday. The march also brought together an array of student leaders from the 1963 sit-in movement who had all gone on to continue their activism including future congressman John Lewis, James Foreman, Ga. State Senator Julian Bond, DC Mayor Marion Barry, Children's Defense Fund President, Marion Wright Edelman, Eleanor Holmes Norton, and a host of others who had not marched together under one banner since 1963.

African Americans' opposition to the Reagan Administration's conservative policies helped drive even more Black voters to the Democratic Party. Jackson's insurgent campaign for president also brought attention to the party's practices that he believed systematically diluted the Black vote. They were 1) second primaries, 2) at-large elections, 3) In assessable registrars, [4) winner take all primaries, 5) extremely high threshold for securing delegates, and 6) ballot access barriers.]

1. *Second Primaries* were instituted in many southern jurisdictions. They were rules which required a candidate who did not receive over 50% in a primary to run one-on-one against the top two vote getters. Blacks would many times place first in a primary with several white candidates. However, in second

---

7 Milton Coleman, "Jackson Begins Crusade For More Black Voters," The Washington Post, (1983) accessed March 22, 2022, https://www.washingtonpost.com/archive/politics/1983/05/11/jackson-begins-crusade-for-more-black-voters/85322183-0622-4a49-815a-4a8ac97d2fae/.

8 Robert Green II, "The 1983 March on Washington and the Age of Reagan," Society for U.S. Intellectual History, last modified June 29, 2014, https://s-usih.org/2014/06/the-1983-march-on-washington-and-the-age-of-reagan/.

primaries, the same winning candidates would lose when white voters in many jurisdictions *block voted* for the white candidate. Block voting by Blacks for a white candidate would often lead to victory. But when Blacks block voted for their own candidates in second primaries, Black candidates would often be defeated due to lower Black turnout in a second election and White voters voting en block for the White candidates.[9]

2. *At-large elections* were used as a tool to dilute heavy concentration of Black voters. For example, if a county had 6 city commissioners; 3 elected at large and 3 by single member districts; governing boards would increase the at-large seats to 4, with two elected by districts, making it easier for whites to maintain control the seat. These changes often occurred when long serving office holders died or retired. At-large positions would be passed through local ordinances which had the effect of making it difficult for Black candidates to emerge victorious. The NAACP Legal Defense Fund (NAACP LDF) described the process as one where "votes of voters of color often are drowned out or submerged by the votes of a majority of white voters who often do not support the candidates preferred by Black voters.[10]

3. *In-accessible registrars* were often the result of stringent registration laws that restricted the time, place, and venue for registrars to sign up new voters. This included a) limited hours for registering, 2) restrictions on where registration could take place, and 3) the restriction on the number of forms distributed to registrars. In many southern states, the voter registrar was located at the county courthouse which was many miles from the poor rural communities disburse throughout the large often rural counties. Deputy registrars were the only certified assistants authorized to register voters on site or in the absence of the registrar. Many counties restricted the number of registrars and restricted their abilities to easily move through the communities to register voters.[11] The Brennen Center for Justice describes "many states required that state or local officials designate citizens registering voters as "deputy registrars." These mandates left those registering voters at the mercy of government officials, who could withhold

9 "Primary election: Background," Ballotpedia, (n.d.) accessed March 22, 2022, https://ballotpedia.org/Primary_election#Background.

10 "At-Large Voting Frequently Asked Questions," NAACP Legal Defence and Educational Fund, INC., (n.d.) accessed March 22, 2022, https://www.naacpldf.org/wp-content/uploads/At-Large-Voting-Frequently-Asked-Questions-1.pdf.

11 Ibid.

the official imprimatur from groups they did not favor. This discretion was vulnerable to abuse.[12]

4. *Winner-take-all presidential primaries* were prevalent in many southern and northern states. To Jackson and his supporters, it was often used in part to prevent Black voters from exerting too much influence over the primary election contests for governor and other statewide contests. The process was used to dilute the delegate strength of Black voters by refusing to give them proportional voting representation in statewide contests. To the party's longtime supporters of winner take all primaries, a high turnout of Jackson supporters could create an election of a candidate who would appear "too sympathetic" to Black voters, thereby reducing their chances of picking up more moderate white voters in the general election. To them, the worst-case scenario would be if a Black candidate were to win a plurality of votes while receiving a majority of their votes from Black voters rather than White voters. A winner takes all primary was simply the best way to prevent that scenario. Jackson, his southern crusade and ultimately campaign challenged all these schemes and for the first time boldly spoke outwardly about them publicly—a rare occurrence within the Democratic party. Local Jackson supporters who challenged the rules would also cause a big stir in most of the small southern towns and even some of the larger northern urban centers.[13]

On issues of social justice, Jackson again forthrightly revealed many of the feelings of African Americans for the first time publicly within the democratic party. What had previously only been whispered in the backrooms and in private homes was now being shouted from the rooftops by Jackson. A growing number of his supporters began to express their dissatisfaction with the Democratic Party elected leadership at the state and national level who they felt had kept Blacks included in their process but only from a distance. Jackson's unabashedly progressive views struck a sensitive nerve within the democratic establishment both Black and white in Washington and in several states that he visited. His painful but true assertion in 1984 that "We (Black Voters) can win without the Democratic Party, but the Democratic Party cannot win without us" outraged party leaders by acknowledging the possibilities of Blacks defiantly working to win elections without the support of white Democrats. It also shined a spotlight on the many instances where Blacks had been the margin of victory for white Democrats in southern statewide contest—a point often downplayed and rarely

---

12 Diana Kasdan, "State Restrictions on Voter Registration Drives," Brennan Center for Justice, 2012, https://www.brennancenter.org/media/310/download.
13 Ralph Smith, "The 'Winner-Take-All' Primary: Rationale and Strategy for It's Abolition," *National Black Law Journal* 2, no. 2 (1972): 130–149.

referenced by winning Democratic candidates in victory speeches on election night. Even post-election analysis by the pundits in the media often downplayed the role of the Black vote in electoral victories—even when clearly evident.

Such talk in 1983 was considered revolutionary. Jackson was labeled an extremist, radical and a spoiler by mainstream newspaper columnists and political pundits. To most Black leaders he was the spark that increased demands on party leaders for more than good promises and good intention. African Americans wanted representation that was made up of their community who shared their interest and concerns and would fight for their interest without hesitation. Jackson's efforts were seen as a threat to many Democratic Party leaders who feared that his high visibility voter registration drives would alienate white Democrats. At the same time White Democratic elected officials had been receiving the support of anywhere between 85% to 90% of the Black Vote even while failing to deliver on promises of jobs, economic development, better housing, and equal funding for inner cities schools. Jackson would reference this fact often in his speeches with proclamations that Blacks were not getting their fair share influence within the party or Congress given their support at the ballot box.

While Jackson was drawing thousands to his events, the media instead concentrated on questions of his internal interparty political struggle rather than his message of economic reform and social justice. While this debate raged in Washington, grassroots activists in the "movement" were beginning to mobilize. They included environmentalists, peace and justice and anti-apartheid activists, labor leaders, gay and lesbian support groups, and student organizations. Their mobilizing efforts around Jackson's presidential candidacy led to the formation of new coalitions all across the country. This "mobilization" would become the largest and most broad based progressive political activism to take place in the south and urban centers since the 1960's civil rights movement. These new local coalitions would come to be known as "Rainbow Coalitions." Their leadership was multi-racial, made up of the same constituencies who were being mobilized: Blacks, progressive whites, Latinos, Asian-Americans, Native Americans, students, and young activists, as well as veteran civil rights leaders.

Meanwhile, the collective efforts of civil rights, voting rights groups, Black churches, and labor began to expand on Jackson's Southern Crusade and presidential campaign. Jackson's church rallies, voter registration bus tours, matched with the NAACP and the National Coalition on Black Voter Participation's Operation *Big Vote* began to mobilize African Americans in both urban and rural areas. The collective efforts of Voter registration groups registered over two million Black voters between 1982 and 1984.[14]

Despite the success of the national registration and mobilization campaigns, there were several obstacles still in place which prevented Jackson's movement from having as much impact as its true potential. Many registrars in Louisiana, Virginia and southern Georgia would refuse to deputize Rainbow activists and remained inaccessible to a large body of voters. Many established political leaders in both the south and northern cities resented Jackson's razzle-dazzle registration drives that would fly into town, arouse their local grassroots community, and then leave town the next day. Registrars were leery of the registration drives led by Jackson and carried on for weeks by local Jackson supporters—many were new organizers who were also new to the election process and had never conducted registration drives before.

Many state and county Boards of Elections complained of the dramatic increase in paperwork from the sudden and ongoing influx of new "uninformed" Black and young voters who were now being registered for the first time in the large and small cities and towns. Blacks began to register in record numbers in many rural communities in southern states like Alabama, Louisiana, Southern Georgia, North Carolina, Tennessee, Florida and even Mississippi. Besides Black Churches, students at Historical Black Colleges and Universities, community colleges and even Ivy League schools began to actively register and organize their campuses. Jackson would draw much of his volunteer base from students who often boarded greyhound buses and mini vans to organize rallies in cities and towns through the south.

After months and months of rallies and chants of "Run Jesse, Run," on November 3, 1983, Jackson finally convened his core supporters from each constituency area of his "Rainbow" of supporters at the Convention Center in Washington, D.C. It was here that he officially announced his candidacy for the Democratic Nomination for President. The convention center was full to the rafters with thousands of supporters from across the country and hundreds of media outlets from across the country and literally across the world.[15] Jackson became the first major African American candidate for president since the 1972 campaign of Shirley Chisholm who was there on stage to give her full sup-

---

14 Coleman, "Jackson Begins Crusade For More Black Voters," The Washington Post, (1983) accessed March 22, 2022, https://www.washingtonpost.com/archive/politics/1983/05/11/jackson-begins-crusade-for-more-black-voters/85322183-0622-4a49-815a-4a8ac97d2fae/.

15 Milton Coleman, "Jackson Launches 1984 Candidacy," The Washington Post, (1983) accessed March 22, 2022, https://www.washingtonpost.com/archive/politics/1983/11/04/jackson-launches-1984-candidacy/3a977116-21c5-4516-9f9e-15bb5798173b/.

port to the campaign along with scores of Mayors, members of the Congressional Black Caucus, business leaders, labor leaders and a few noted celebrities. It would be the beginning of a campaign that would see him participating in televised debates and actually winning primaries in the south and a number of southern and even New England states. The campaign would garner 3.28 million votes, 358 delegates and gave Jackson and his supporters actual influence over some of the party's platform adopted at the 1984 convention.[16] This was unprecedented for a Black candidacy that went beyond a symbolic gesture. It would be the beginning of a major shift within the Democratic party to take the Black vote and its leaders much more seriously than they had in the past.

Uncovering the Barriers to Voter Registration

Throughout 1985 and 1986 there were several meetings around the country convened by voting rights activists and organizations who sought—not always successfully—to bring any national attention to the issues of voter registration barriers and the need for reform. While most meetings were held in Washington and New York, two of the most important gatherings were held in San Antonio, Texas and New Orleans, Louisiana. San Antonio had been chosen primarily for the work that had been done by the Southwest Voter Registration and Education Project, led by its President, legendary Hispanic leader Willie Velasquez, Southwest Voter had registered over a million new Latino voters in Texas, California, New Mexico, Colorado, and Arizona and stood out as one of the most successful and powerful Hispanic organizations in American history.

There were also several other coalitions formed by voting rights and civil rights groups to fight for passage of voter registration reforms. A coalition of over 100 organizations led by Representative John Conyers Jr. and ACORN, pushed for universal same day registration; another coalition led by Project Vote, and Human Serve, the New York based social welfare rights organization, fought for public agency-based registration at welfare offices. Voting Rights litigators, led by the NAACP Legal Defense Fund (LDF) and ACLU, and the NAACP sought to end discriminatory voter purges. Yet another coalition of "good government groups" led by the League of Women Voters and People for the American Way fought for passage of a bill that would allow motor voter registration at Department of Motor vehicles.

---

16 Ibid.

For his part, Jackson formed the Citizenship Education Fund, (CEF) as the Rainbow Coalition's official non-partisan organization to conduct ongoing registration and education programs. It was headquartered in Washington, D.C. while Jackson continued to run his coalition out of his home base in Chicago. CEF supported the registration and reform efforts led by longtime Jackson aides Rev. Tyrone Crider, Rae Lewis, Craig Kirby and later Hubert James, a voting rights activist from the New York based Human Serve who was pushing hard for agency-based registration and against voting barriers.

Opponents of the voter registration reform resisted calls to impose new unfunded federal mandates even if they would make registration easier and more accessible. As the push for voter reform began, the Republican Party in Congress opposed virtually all legislative efforts to change the existing laws through federal statute. They primarily opposed the principle of the federal government setting national standards for registration, list cleaning and other election procedures. They saw it as federal intrusion on something that was largely at their own discretion at the state level.

New Orleans had been chosen to host the convening of voter reform organizations to highlight the many problems of Louisiana's registration laws. The Registrar of voters had been appointed by Parrish leaders to a position that amounted to a virtual lifetime appointment. His appointment was a major factor in his policies and particularly the registrar's office hostility to Black activist's efforts to conduct targeted registration in Baton Rouge and New Orleans. In New Orleans voting rights litigator Attorney Marc Morial, son of the Mayor Dutch Morial led the Louisiana Voter Registration Crusade, an affiliate of the National Coalition on Black Voter Participation, commonly known as "Operation Big Vote". The Crusade had been trying to register African Americans throughout the state in hopes of one day electing an African American to Congress from one of the major Black population centers in either Baton Rouge or New Orleans. In the spring of 1986, the Louisiana Crusade had filed suits in Federal Court against the Registrar of Voters in Orleans Parish who for years had a reputation of being hostile to Black voter registration drives. His registrars were among the most inaccessible, often turning down requests from the Crusade to register students at campus rallies held at Xavier University, Dillard, and other community events.

The pre-election Louisiana purges were only part of a national "voter caging" scheme that had been orchestrated by the Republican National Committee (RNC) in 1986 to dilute Black Voting strength in targeted states prior to the midterm elections. GOP operatives utilized party mailers to Black voters to trigger return mail that were then compiled into voter challenge lists. The federal lawsuit revealed that a majority of 31,000 voters who were purged from Louisiana voter rolls were black voters. The lawsuit ended in a federal consent decree with the

RNC that prohibited the Republican party from engaging in vote caging anti-fraud initiative that target minorities in order to compile voter challenge list.[17]

The overly frequent "cleaning" or "updating" of voter registration lists were often used as a smoke screen for the massive purging of African Americans from the lists of registered voters. Thousands of Black voters often found themselves turned away on Election Day after discovering that their failure to vote in previous local elections had cost them their right to vote—even in federal elections. This occurred under the laws in Louisiana, and other states that allowed election officials to purge voters from the list of eligible voters simply for not voting.[18] With no national standards, voter purges could take place at the discretion of local election officials.

The New Orleans gathering discussed various ways to break down the barriers to Black voter registration that had been so graphically demonstrated in 1984. Leadership of the group shifted among the NAACP Legal Defense fund, Human Serve, the Southwest Voter Registration and Education Project, the Center on Policy Alternatives, the ACLU among other organizations. The meetings were chaired by Hulbert James, the Director of Human Serve and later the Director of the Citizenship Education Fund, Rev. Jackson's non-partisan voter registration organization.

Throughout 1985 the Mayor of Bolton Mississippi, Bennie Thompson and longtime Mississippi community activist Alvin Chambliss had been traveling throughout the south exposing virtual horror stories about actions officials in the Mississippi Delta had undertaken to undermine their efforts to elect Mike Espy to Congress. Their stories from the Delta left even the most seasoned rights activists from the north spellbound. The problems in the deep south, especially Mississippi and Louisiana were much more severe than even meeting planners had anticipated. These same organizations had held a hearing and press conference in June of 1985, billed as "An Emergency Mobilization on the Right to Vote." The groups were trying once again the bring attention to voter registration barriers. The Jackson Campaign for President had readily identified many potential infractions of the law by local officials. The coalition however was not yet poised to go one step further and demand federal legislation to remedy the many abuses. With Ronald Reagan as president, it was a long shot. But with a Democratic Congress, the chances of conducting hearings would at least give the issue a national platform.

---

17 "Voter caging and purging," Ballotpedia, (n.d.) accessed March 22, 2022, https://ballotpedia. org/Voter_caging_and_purging.
18 Ibid.

There were many opinions on when to launch a national campaign. By June of 1985 the presidential campaign was long over, but so much attention had been on the second Reagan term, it was next to impossible to get the press to focus on what seemed like a very minor story. Finally, the date of June 5 was chosen. A congressional hearing was followed by a press conference which featured many of the leading voices in the voting rights community. Among the members of Congress present were John Conyers, Jr., of Michigan, Representatives Parren Mitchell, from Maryland, Louis Stokes, from Ohio, Harold Ford, Sr. of Tennessee, John Lewis of Georgia, Harold Washington, of Illinois, Charlie Rangel of New York and Walter Fauntroy, the Delegate from Washington, DC. From the U.S. Senators Al Cranston of California, Arlen Specter, of Pennsylvania and Ted Kennedy of Massachusetts joined the coalition having been the lead sponsors of S. 675 in the Senate, which would establish Election Day voter registration for federal elections in all 50 states.

Joining them were voting rights litigators and activists from around the country. Among them, Lani Guinier, Julius Chambers, and Elaine Jones, with the NAACP Legal Defense Fund, Judy Goldberg-Crocket and Mort Halprin with the ACLU, Al Raby, a Chicago Community Activist who served as chairman of Project Vote, Willie Velasquez, President of the Southwest Voter Registration and Education Project, Althea Simmons, of the NAACP Washington Bureau, Professor Richard Cloward and Francis Fox Piven, of Human Serve, Curtis Gans, of the Committee for the Study of the Electorate, Farley Peters, with the Center for Policy Alternatives, Melanne Verveer People for the American Way, John Dean, Gracia Hillman and Sonia Jarvis with the National Coalition on Black Voter Participation, Steve Kest and Zack Paulette of ACORN, Jim Dixon, a disability activist from *Disabled but Able to Vote*, Ralph Neas of the Leadership Conference on Civil Rights, Bob McAlpine and Ron Jackson of the National Urban League, and myself as President of the United States Students Association, (USSA), I had been asked to speak at the hearing on behalf of students and their barriers to registration.

I waited my turn from the endless litany of speakers including many members of congress who showed up unannounced to lend their voice to the effort. The hearing had gone well past its appointed time, and I was beginning to believe that they would never get to the segment of the population that was (I believed) among the most disenfranchised of all. With the time running way over I was asked by the chairman of the hearing to keep my comments to less than 3 minutes. I had to speak rapidly to get through my seven minutes of prepared testimony. Before getting through even half of it, in what seemed like only a minute, I was asked to wrap up. I summarized with the following statements.

"Young Americans in general and young Blacks in particular have the lowest registration rate and the lowest turnout of any other sector of American society. Through this lack of empowerment young people also find that they have the highest poverty rate, and the highest unemployment rate, (over 50% in many of our inner cities). Young people have been accused of being the greatest purveyors of violence but in fact, they are the greatest victims of crime; they are the most effected by cuts to jobs programs, education funding cuts and suffers from the least access to quality health care."

"There is a rarely seen or acknowledged chain reaction that is a direct result of this erosion of our democracy. When people, especially young people, do not participate in the electoral process, they lose touch and gradually lose respect for the government and its lawmakers. They lose respect of law enforcement and ultimately, they lose respect for the law itself. It is here where crime really begins. If you have no respect for the law or law enforcement, you can easily turn to guns and drugs as a means for gaining what you all call 'economic opportunity.'"

I looked around the room and it had suddenly gotten completely quiet. I thought it was because my three minutes were up, not to mention the fact that I had gone way off the topic. I had lost my place and didn't know where to pick it back up. The chairman of the committee promptly thanked me with a tight smile for testifying and called for the next witness. I suddenly felt that my testimony ended with no real mention of the need for voter registration reform.

I asked the Chairman could I just add one thing before I left the witness table. He reluctantly nodded yes.

"It just seems to me that young people have more access to guns and drugs than they do the voter registration forms and the ballot box. Unless we as a society do something to redirect young people into the political process, we may lose forever a generation which feels compelled to take on any responsibility for anything."

"Let's just hope that never happens," he said hurriedly and with a condescending smile. I was ushered off and another speaker was standing behind me ready to take my seat. The testimony gave me assurances that this new drive for voter reform would now include provisions to remove those barriers that I had faced for years starting in Athens, Ohio. It began my long relationship with a new coalition; a long 6-year protracted struggle that in my eyes was now a voting rights crusade.

Closing the press conference was Rev. Jackson who recounted a litany of registration horror stories from his campaign. The testimonies collectively described mountains of evidence of voting rights abuses and barriers. "The Disenfranchised" was a term frequently used at the press conference to describe the estimated 70 million unregistered voters. Among the most alarming findings:

- Voter registration workers from Project Vote had been arrested in Pennsylvania for trying to register welfare applicants in line.
- In Alabama voter registration organizers were arrested for allegedly conducting fraudulent registration drives led by then US Attorney Jeff Session.
- In New Orleans the Registrars refused requests of activists to designate sites to conduct registration. Even when large numbers of the unregistered were organized to go down to the courthouse, they found the office closed–at the discretion of the registrar.
- In Chicago, voters were purged from the list every 6 months for non-voting in local elections when the percentage of voters turning out to vote would drop to less than 30%. If they were found to have also failed to vote in the most recent elections, they were automatically removed from the list.
- In California, letters from third party organizations were sent around to targeted voters with Hispanic surnames warning them of felony charges that could be brought against anyone who was not a legal resident of the U.S.

Attempts to contest the results and many of the other abuses were rejected by the local election officials, local judges, and most cases the Reagan Justice Department. The antidotes revealed the very arbitrary rules throughout the south for ballots security and the inconsistent procedures for conducting recounts. From coast to coast the barriers were laid out one by one, painting a picture of a nation with multiple laws at state, county and even local levels that were a hodge-podge of procedures that provided no true protections for a voter attempting to register to vote—even in states covered by the Voting Rights Act and states in the north and west where voting rights abuses were not well known or documented until then.

These and other "list cleaning" schemes including mailings and roll purging cost millions of tax dollars spent for the sole purpose of removing legally registered voters from the rolls. At the same time meager resources were spent on voter outreach programs to re-register voters. Non-partisan voter registration and education groups scrambled for the resources to fund registration drives in targeted minority and low-income communities. Despite all of the hearings, press conferences and regional meetings in Texas and Louisiana, the fact remained that there was little hope of any major voter registration reform bill passing even with a Democratic Majority in both the House and Senate as long as Ronald Reagan or any Republican was president.

Chapter 3
Keeping Hope Alive and Breaking Barriers to Voting

After all the excitement surrounding the 1984 Jackson campaign had ended, many of the Jackson activists continued their advocacy work locally and pushed for a formal structure to continue their efforts under one national banner. In the spring of 1986, Jackson convened all his former supporters from the 1984 campaign as well as a growing number of new supporters including labor, farmers, gay and lesbian advocates, and other liberal elements of the Democratic Party establishment. This gathering drew thousands of activists to Raleigh, North Carolina where they convened to formally establish the new "National Rainbow Coalition." It was chartered as a 501(c)4 organization with a national governing board and state affiliates in several states where Rev. Jackson had gained strong support during the 1984 campaign.

I had been a highly active national student organizer/volunteer who supported Rev. Jackson and the Rainbow movement on college campuses across the U.S. However, I was now the former president of the U.S. Student Association and was also looking to stay involved in this new multi-racial and growing progressive movement. With the help of close Jackson outreach coordinators Rev. Tyrone Crider, Rae Lewis, and personal aide Craig Kirby, I was selected by Rev. Jackson's team as one of the National Rainbow Coalition's national board members (again) representing students.

Jackson also formed the Citizenship Education Fund (CEF) as a companion 501(c)3 non-profit organization to support the non-partisan education and voter engagement components of the Rainbow's work. CEF was chaired by the legendary Percy Sutton from New York. Although chartered in Cleveland Ohio, CEF operated out of Washington, D.C. to coordinate voter registration, education, and training programs separate and apart from the Rainbow Coalition and the Jackson campaign's more political apparatus. Other seasoned and diverse CEF advisors and consultants included inside-the-beltway Democratic party strategists Yolanda Carraway and Lucia Green as well as outside-the-beltway activists including Hurbert James, a welfare rights organizer from New York, and Pan Africanist leader and scholar, Professor Ron Daniels from Youngstown, Ohio.

One night in early May, I received a call from Ron Daniels asking me to meet with him and Rev. Jackson to discuss a more concentrated effort to conduct a youth voter registration campaign in the fall of 1987, leading up to the 1988 presidential primaries. Although I had worked closely with the Rainbow Coalition

https://doi.org/10.1515/9783110742473-006

and its staff, this would be my first one-on-one meeting with Rev. Jackson. He was speaking at the University of the District of Columbia (UDC), and after the speech I was led back to his green room. He said that he had admired my work over the years mobilizing students and for becoming the first Black President of the United States Student Association. He had heard that I had "a passion for voter registration." He said that he needed my energy for what promised to be a very grueling 1988 campaign season in which he was all but assured to be running for president. But unfortunately, there was no job offer to work with the campaign (which I thought would be coming). It was a campaign with a rich message but a poor budget. There was little money and only a handful of campaign slots.

I thanked Ron for setting up the meeting but let him know that I needed to get back to the work I was undertaking to find a real job and start getting serious about either a career in the federal government or going back to school to get my master's degree. In May of 1987, I received a call from CEF Director Yolanda Caraway, who let me know that a vacancy had opened up. Ron Daniels had abruptly left CEF and they now wanted to create the position of Director of the Student Leadership Development Program. CEF would provide me with a modest salary, but an opportunity to resume most of my voter registration work from student organizing. It soon became clear to me that Ron had given up his job to open up a slot for me. It was a major gesture that was much appreciated at the time for its generosity. However, I had no idea that it would lead to a long and sustained engagement with Rev. Jackson and the historic voter mobilization movement he was leading across the U.S.

As a non-partisan organization, CEF could not coordinate with the 1988 Jackson campaign, although it could conduct research, non-partisan voter registration drives, voter education, training, and get-out-the-vote campaigns. With extremely limited funds, I focused on writing voter registration proposals, and developing student leadership programs to help train a new generation of youth organizers who could go into the states in 1988 and begin taking advantage of the energy of the presidential campaign to bring in new voters. Although the staffing was limited to interns and volunteers, we kept the organization thriving, conducting research, engaging in leadership training, and developing new communication tools, non-partisan public service announcements, posters, and flyers that helped spread the message about the importance of voting.

CEF 1) researched voter registration demographics, 2) researched state and local voting barriers, 3) tracked voter reform legislation, and 4) conducted a series of electoral training seminars. While Jackson was the founder of the organization, there was a fervent desire to not do anything that would jeopardize the tax status of the organization or his campaign. Most non-partisan voter registration organizations had already decided to not organize any voter registration drives while the primary campaigns were being conducted. This was a result of a growing list of foundations that withheld major donations to voter registration groups until after the primaries. It was ironic that the lack of funding for traditional registration drives was occurring just as Jackson had spurred more interest in voting by African Americans than ever before.

The Citizenship Education Fund also had skeleton staff and little money to conduct any nationwide drives on the ground. We operated on shoestring budgets, but the program work that we undertook, though under-resourced and modest, gave us a better understanding of the overly complicated election procedures state by state and a bird's eye view of the voter disenfranchisement that was taking place across the country. The information that we gained during this research period proved invaluable in the coming years during our struggle to reform voter registration and election laws in the U.S.

CEF worked in conjunction with Dr. Eddie Williams and his team at the Joint Center for Political and Economic Studies to take a closer look at the administrative procedures *and* political ramifications behind the numbers of voters being purged from the voter registration rolls. We soon came upon information revealing that thousands of voters were being purged from the rolls in states throughout the South. We first discovered that many states had purged tens of thousands of voters from the list for non-voting in late December, following the 1987 local elections. We began to check Southern states to see if, in fact, there was a pattern. Our findings were shocking: Many of the southern states were just the tip of the 1988 voter purge iceberg. Massive voter purges had taken place in North Carolina, South Carolina, Tennessee, Georgia, Florida, Alabama, Mississippi, and Louisiana.

It soon became clear that in any given state, there were more people who were being taken off the list annually than those who were being added. The eight southern states were systematically removing voters from the list at an alarming rate. For every one person that was registered, many more were being taken off. No matter how long a voter had been registered, if they missed voting in 3 or more elections in a row—they could be targeted for being purged— most times without much prior notice. Low turnout local elections would usually trigger the purge process. If you were to miss a primary election—*strike one;* miss a local election for sheriff; *strike two.* Miss another election when you were just not inspired to vote, *strike three!* You are now tagged to be "cleaned" off the registration list or at best be moved to a list of purged voters whose vote could now be challenged.

This process of cleaning voter rolls grew more intense right before a presidential election. Since most politicians relied on the voter registration lists to mail and call voters, there was a lot of pressure on local boards of election to have "clean" or accurate lists throughout the election cycle. Many campaigns would even delay their launch until the voter list had been cleansed. Pressure to clean voter lists often came from campaign operatives who wanted to ensure their hard raised dollars were not being wasted on voter lists that were 20% or more inaccurate. The most current lists of registered voters were a hot commodity for any campaign in that era. The more people were purged, the more accurate the list and the less expensive the purchase of the list. The exchange of voter registration lists and data by political parties, campaigns, vendors, and election boards was big business, and a clean list was key to the price tag of the purchases. Concern for re-enfranchising voters and restoring voting rights—especially from infrequent voters—was nowhere near to the top of the priority list for most campaigns—Republican or Democratic—when it came to managing election data.

Suddenly the claims being made that Black and young voter were apathetic or lazy begin to ring hollow to me. We did not vote more than 50% in any national election because we were systematically and deliberately being disenfranchised and demobilized! Legally registered voters, who may had felt no inspiration to vote in previous elections, were now having their right taken away from them in the name of efficiency and good government. In reality there was no interest in adding such a large unknown element to the political landscape. Civil rights leaders had vehemently opposed the many state-sponsored voter purges. It was clear that the purges were at least partly responsible for much of the decline in Black voter participation that they were tracking.

Many of the voter purge laws were being challenged by Attorneys Lani Guinier and Penda Hair of the NAACP Legal Defense Fund, but without much success in the state or federal courts. The purges were taking place under a barrage of different state and local laws that would have to be challenged jurisdiction by jurisdiction. This would prove to be a painstakingly time-consuming and costly undertaking. To address these growing litigation challenges, a series of emergency coalition meetings were convened by Ralph Neas, president of the Leadership Conference on Civil Rights at their DuPont Circle offices. Lani Guinier and Penda Hair were often joined by NAACP-LDF General Counsel Elaine Jones and Attorneys Judith Brown and Ted Shaw, who would spell out to coalition partners their findings and legal strategies before most of the big cases in Alabama and other cases throughout the South. There was no shortage of passion or good lawyering. However, the federal courts (filled with Reagan appointees) and an increasingly conservative Supreme Court gave little comfort to those who sought a legal remedy to the disenfranchisement struggle.

* * *

The *Super Tuesday* primaries took place during spring break in many of the Historical Black Colleges in North Carolina, Virginia, Georgia, and other Southern states. To combat this, we established a March-March 1st Absentee Ballot Program, which would encourage students to "march" to the board of elections to vote absentee. This was a scarcely used method that allowed voters who would be out of town on Election Day to vote early. To combat the issue, we considered calling on all students who had ever been registered to vote to show up to vote despite their purge status. Even if their votes were rejected, we would be raising awareness of the disenfranchising law. We felt that their showing up at the polls, demanding their right to vote, would make a dramatic point that the purge for non-voting needed to be repealed through federal statute.

We attempted a public awareness effort to expose the system of purging that had taken place all over the South. However, as we traveled across the southern states, many of the local voting advocates and Black elected officials declined to speak out on the issue. This was hard for me to understand until a close friend, the Progressive Black Student Alliance President Keith Jennings, an activist from Fisk University in Nashville arranged a meeting with me and Ed Brown (the brother of SNCC's Rap Brown), who led the Southern-based Voter Education Project (VEP) headquartered in Atlanta, Georgia. Brown explained it to me in plain English: "Any public official who came out and said the purge was illegal and illegitimate would be admitting that their own election was illegitimate and invalid, and no politician, no matter how progressive, wanted to admit that in the deep south."

At one of our southern regional training and strategy meetings, I advocated for registered voters who were not on the voter rolls to cast "challenged ballots" to demand their constitutional right to vote in a "federal" primary election in accordance with the Voting Rights Act. I argued that we could use the Voting Rights Act of 1965 as our legal rationale for a new round of litigation against the voter purges. However, many local Jackson supporters did not want to risk being accused of "stealing the election" if thousands of "ineligible" voters were allowed to vote. Dr. Gwen Patton, an educator and leader of an affiliated Southern Rainbow Coalition from Montgomery, Alabama, objected to the strategy, arguing, "They'll steal Jesse's victory right from under him and accuse *us* of voter fraud! The ballot box is not the place to wage this fight. They put Black folks in jail in Alabama for voter fraud. It's gonna have to come through the courts or new federal legislation."

As the calendar moved closer to the 1988 presidential election, the outcomes of most pending legal challenges to local and county purge procedures had not been very successful. Judge after judge ruled that officials had the right to systematically purge their lists to remove voters whom they referred to as "dead wood." The voters were still being systematically purged for non-voting, albeit legally and properly within the current law. Under the existing state statutes, most of the purged voters were low-income, students and frequent movers who lost their eligibility to vote for simply failing to update their address voting records when moving from the last address where they last voted. The impact that the widespread voter purges could have on African Americans' turnout on Super Tuesday was astounding. The majority of the hundreds of thousands of purged voters were African American, young people, and low-income voters. They were concentrated in big cities and clusters of Black voters in rural counties throughout the South. Most of the 8 states were all part of the "Super Tuesday" band of 1988 primary elections. The 1988 "Super Tuesday" had been developed in 1987 by "moderate" and "conservative" factions within the Democratic Party to give Southern states and moderates in general more influence in the presidential primaries.[1] Privately, many anti-Jackson democratic political strategists had calculated that a second Jackson campaign would not have the resources to effectively compete in 12 Southern states simultaneously.

At CEF we began devising voter turnout models that would offer local nonprofits, Black Churches, and student organizations an opportunity to register or re-register their communities to participate in the primary and general elections. We focused most of our outreach efforts on the Southern states where over 50% of the Black population was still located and where most of the roll purging that we studied had taken place. Since most legal challenges had not been successful, the only remedy to break this cycle was turning out as many voters as possible.

Many other, more blatant political strategies were designed to neutralize the Black and progressive forces within the party that were being led by Rev. Jackson. Coupled with this were the "superdelegate" rules which gave the party leaders 350 to 400 extra delegates beyond what was being elected by the voters during the primaries. In a close contest for the nomination, these superdelegates would ensure that party leaders could continue to choose the nominee and control the platform.[2]

---

1 Lily Rothman, "The Failed Strategy That Created Super Tuesday," Time, last modified March 1, 2016, https://time.com/4234474/super-tuesday-history/.
2 "superdelegate," Merriam-Webster, (n.d.) accessed March 22, 2022, https://www.merriam-webster.com/dictionary/superdelegate.

Rev. Jackson stayed at the forefront of the Presidential campaign, often over-shadowing the other contenders for president in the candidates' debates: Sena-tor Al Gore (TN), Representative Dick Gephardt (MO), Governor Mike Dukakis (MA), and Senator Paul Simon (IL) saw a different Jackson campaign, one that was no longer just symbolic but now competitive. On the speaking stump, while they were drawing hundreds of party faithful to their events, Jackson was electrifying huge crowds of thousands with his bold and empowering mes-sage. Rallies were attended by tens of thousands of African Americans, students, rank and file laborers, Latinos, environmentalists, and peace activists. Even in predominantly white cities and states, Jackson drew tens of thousands to his ral-lies. In Wisconsin, 35,000 showed up to hear Jackson speak at a family farm. We witnessed cars parked for miles on the shoulder of the interstate exits, with peo-ple of all races coming to hear the message. The progressive movement, which was focused on peace and justice issues, now began to pay attention to electoral politics. The Jackson rallies would inspire many progressive groups that once shunned voter registration, door-to-door canvassing, and phone banking to begin doing outreach to their community of supporters.

With all these efforts in play, Jackson went on to win the primary elections in the states of Virginia, South Carolina, Georgia, Alabama, Mississippi, Louisiana, and Delaware, as well as the majority of delegates in Texas. He would lose the state of North Carolina (by less than 10,000 votes) to fellow Southerner Al Gore. Senator Gore would win his home state of Tennessee, as well as Arkansas and Kentucky. Dukakis would win only Florida, Massachusetts, and Maryland but the heavy concentration of delegates in those states and his previous victo-ries would catapult him into frontrunner status over both Gore and Jackson, who were the only other candidates remaining in the race.

Rev. Jackson next took his primary challenge to the industrial North. Due in large part to Michigan's caucuses, which allowed same-day registration, Rev. Jackson won the primary, soundly defeating Massachusetts Governor Mike Duka-kis in a stunning upset. In the week that followed, Jackson was the frontrunner for the nomination, having won more popular votes and more delegates than all other Democratic candidates seeking the nomination. It would be the first time in U.S. history that an African American was the frontrunner in the race for the nomination of a major party—if even for one week. The front covers of the most widely read political magazines, *TIME*, and *Newsweek*, would both feature a pic-ture of Jesse Jackson with strikingly similar headlines and articles. The May 7, 1988, *Newsweek* cover ran a Headline "Power Broker caption beneath the photo that claimed to answer the proverbial question:

What Jesse Jackson Wants" [3] *TIME* Magazine's April 1, 1988, cover page was even more frank with its cover story caption, which read simply, in bold letters, *"JESSE?*"[4]

For years, millions of Black voters had only watched presidential elections from a distance. Now, as advertised, they actually saw their votes make history. It was a feeling of political empowerment that had never been witnessed in African American history. Suddenly, the prospect of a Black "protest candidate" being nominated as a major party candidate sent shock waves through the political structure of the Democratic Party apparatus. Despite their great dependency on Black votes for their general election victories throughout the country, the idea of Jackson as the nominee against Vice President Bush seemed, to many party leaders, to be a national disaster waiting to happen.

On the heels of its groundbreaking work during Super Tuesday, CEF moved its project north to Wisconsin, where it was headquartered in the city of Milwaukee. We took advantage of the same-day voter registration law there. Our voter registration and GOTV drive was centered on churches, college campuses, community groups, and several low-income projects and community centers. Our best organizers from Super Tuesday were dispatched to other states. Lilly Coney, Reggie Holt, Steve Miller, Dean Tinnin, Barry Sanders, Andrew Locket, Keith Jennings, Ron Charity, and Cynthia Downs were all dispatched to Ohio, New Jersey, Maryland, Pennsylvania, New York, and other states with large Black populations.

In mid-April, our MLK voter outreach program moved on to New York, where we again put together a comprehensive GOTV effort in conjunction with Countdown '88, a voter registration group led by a community activist named Selwin Carter. Our turnout drives were centered in three boroughs: Brooklyn, the Bronx, and Manhattan. Next to Super Tuesday, this would be our largest and most in-depth voter turnout effort among the nation's largest concentration of low-income and minority people. One hundred and fifty neighborhood canvassers were hired to help flush the vote throughout the targeted boroughs. One hundred and thirty of the 150 were teens and college students who had been recruited directly from our targeted neighborhoods in Harlem, the Bronx, and Bedford Stuyvesant in Brooklyn. Turnout in the Black community was high in each of the boroughs.

Jackson came into New York facing the opposition of longtime New York Mayor Ed Koch's powerful political machine, which had publicly expressed its

---

3 "The Power Broker: What Jesse Jackson Wants," *Newsweek Magazine*, March 21, 1988.
4 "JESSE?," *Time*, April 1, 1988.

strong support for Senator Al Gore early on. Koch and his forces controlled the entire political apparatus in most of the boroughs except for Manhattan, where Borough President David Dinkins supported Jackson and was seen as the biggest threat to Ed Koch's machine. Congressmen Charlie Rangel's and Ed Towns' support of Jackson, along with Dinkins' efforts, made Harlem and Brooklyn the strongest and largest base of support for the Jackson campaign in the State.

A massive turnout had Black voters lined up for blocks in many precincts leading to thousands of voters forced to stand in lines for hours, only to be told once they reached the booth, that their names had been purged from the list. To vote, they had to get a court order from a judge in downtown Manhattan. In some cases, the backlog of people at the courthouse seeking court orders was as long as the lines of people waiting to vote. All day long, the popular New York radio station WLIB had opened its telephone lines and urged voters to call in problems from polling stations. The problems were numerous: long lines, broken voting booths, polls closing early because they were short-staffed, lost ballots, polling places running out of ballots and shutting down for several hours. These widespread reports had the effect of intimidating and discouraging Hispanic, Black, and Afro-Caribbean voters throughout the day.

As we were in Manhattan, coordinating our citywide GOTV, I and several others made our way to Brooklyn to assist in the evening GOTV efforts. Among us was Peter Williams, an anti-racist activist involved in the Crown Heights and Bensonhurst Movements. As we traveled between boroughs in the car at 5:00 PM, we found major jams across the Brooklyn Bridge that had traffic backed up for hours. By the time we made it to our headquarters in Brooklyn, the polls had all but closed. Reports came in that people were growing impatient standing in line and were leaving in droves as the night wore on. Jackson himself took to the streets of Harlem, Brooklyn, and the Bronx late in the afternoon in an open-top car with a bull horn and sound trucks, urging his supporters with the repeated cry to *"Keep hope alive!* Stay in line!" *"Keep hope alive*, don't give up! You are somebody!" It would be one of the first times that he used the reference. *Keep Hope Alive* that would later become his motto.

Early news accounts had Jackson winning 76% of the vote in New York City, causing premature jubilation in many campaign headquarters and throughout the airwaves. Callers and some analysts began to predict that if Jackson won New York, he could easily lock himself in as the "frontrunner" and likely Democratic nominee. History would prove them wrong after the heavily voting precincts from upstate New York poured in. The national media declared Dukakis the winner at 9:01 PM, one minute after the polls closed. Less than 38% of the vote statewide had been counted. As the announcement was made, thousands of people were still in line all across New York, waiting to vote. It would take several weeks to finish counting the final results. As late as May 18 tens of thousands of votes had still not been counted. Dukakis had won the state with 51% of the vote with Jackson a close second at 37% and Al Gore a distant third place with only 10%.[5] With his third-place finish, Gore dropped out of the race.

By late spring, with most of the other candidates having dropped out of the race, only two candidates remained in the race for the Democratic nomination: Governor Dukakis and Rev. Jackson. Dukakis won most of the remaining head-to-head primaries with Jackson and went on to win the plurality of delegates toward his ultimately winning the Democratic nomination. The Jackson campaign had proven that Black voters could be effectively mobilized despite the voter purges. In state after state, the campaign had revealed that while many barriers to voting still existed, historic numbers of African Americans had been registered and turned out in response to the Jackson campaign.[6] However, the institutional barriers would remain and there could be no real victory on this issue until the matter of reforming our nation's election laws was dealt with at the national level by the U.S. Congress.

The period between the primaries and the general election would be even more challenging with regard to keeping this issue alive. CEF returned its focus to building public awareness of pending legislation in the U.S. Congress that would establish universal registration for all citizens of the U.S. Jackson had raised the issue of Same-Day Voter Registration several times on the campaign trail and placed the issue front and center for the first time in a Democratic presidential campaign. Although he rarely spoke to the issues of electoral reform in general, Election Day Registration was getting its first national debate.

After winning the delegates needed to secure the Democratic presidential nomination, Dukakis tried to streamline specific themes that the Democratic Party would ask for in its policy platform. Party leaders and the Dukakis campaign sought to keep "manifestos" out of the platform—a practice well established in past Democratic conventions. Many interest groups made up the Democratic Party and constantly sought to ensure that their issues were clearly embraced and highlighted in the Democratic platform. In 1988, Dukakis instead sought a

5 Taylor. Paul, "Dukaikis Wins N.Y. Primary," The Washington Post, (1988) accessed March 22, 2022, https://www.washingtonpost.com/archive/politics/1988/04/20/dukakis-wins-ny-primary/b6294ae1-f5fd-4f8c-8f1f-25ededc01946/.

6 Steve Kornacki, "1988: Jackson mounts a serious challenge, but a loss in one state ends the quest," nbc News, last modified July 29, 2019, https://www.nbcnews.com/politics/elections/1988-jackson-mounts-serious-challenge-loss-one-state-ends-quest-n1029601.

broad series of statements rather than any specifics, fearing they would be attacked as prisoners of the party's turbulent "liberal" past.

Jackson's demands flew in the face of this strategy. In July 1988, over 1,200 highly charged Jackson delegates converged on Atlanta in support of Rev. Jackson and his platform issues. It was a historic high for an insurgent Black candidacy. Atlanta, Georgia was the site of the 1988 convention, and the fired-up delegates, as well as tens of thousands of Jackson supporters, came into Atlanta from across the U.S. like a storm. They stood in stark contrast to the party regulars who supported Dukakis or other candidates who'd had delegates but dropped out earlier in the campaign.

Jackson dispatched a team of policy advisors to begin negotiating the Democratic platform with the party and the Dukakis campaign, led by Campaign Chairman Ron Brown and senior advisors Frank Watkins, Yolonda Carraway, Bob Bursage, Mark Steitz, and Steve Cobble. There were also advisors and close confidants Alexis Herman, Minyon Moore, Rev. Willie Barrow, Joe Gardner, and two up-and-coming and outspoken state senators, California's Maxine Waters and Michigan's Carolyn Kilpatrick. Negotiations with the platform committee took place in a remote setting on Mackinac Island, MI, while activists from all over the nation began to converge on Atlanta.

The delegates and party leaders were not the only supporters headed to Atlanta. Thousands of activists and supporters loaded buses, trains, and automobiles to be part of the Jackson challenge to the DNC Convention. Ron Daniels coordinated this mobilization of activists and non-delegate events outside of the convention. One week before the convention, Jackson mounted a bus and led a "Freedom Ride" caravan from Chicago to Atlanta. The multi-bus and car caravan made stops in many cities along the way, holding rallies, raising money, and registering voters for the upcoming general election. The caravan was over two hours late, but when it pulled into Atlanta, it was met by 40,000 supporters assembled in a large city park near the convention center. It would be one of the largest political rallies in the history of Georgia. Several thousand voters were registered on-site with the assistance of Ed Brown's Voter Education Project, the AFL-CIO, the Rainbow Coalition's Joe Beasley, and many other local activists. The campaign had proven that when an African American was on a statewide ticket, voter turnout doubled and even tripled in some cities and congressional districts. This would prove that a Black candidate could run and win in a number of congressional districts, city, and county Democratic primaries, particularly in the South.

The Jackson campaign marked the first time that the theory had been put to the test nationally and it inspired hundreds of local elected officials to consider, for the first time, their chances of being elected to local office. The case had now been proven by Jackson's victories. There were between 12 and 15 congressional seats in the South that African Americans could actually win. At this time, the only African American representatives in the South where Mike Espy (Mississippi), John Lewis (Atlanta), Harold Ford Sr. (Memphis), and Mickey Leland (the old Barbara Jordan seat in Houston). The 1988 election would be the last congressional election before the 1990 census and the redistricting of every congressional seat. The turnout of Black voters in the last presidential election under the lines drawn in 1981 would prove to be instrumental to the upcoming redistricting process that would redraw lines in 1991. As Jackson often noted, it was important for his campaign "wagon to be hitched" to the upcoming campaigns for state, congressional, and local elected offices.

For weeks, the media again ran stories about Jackson's growing influence in the Democratic Party and the American political system. The answer to the infamous question "What does Jesse want?" was a series of platform planks considered controversial: national health care for all Americans, a declaration that South Africa's apartheid government was a "terrorist state," and a call for peace talks in the Middle East on the Palestinian homeland. While many of these positions are considered mainstream by today's standards, in 1988 they were considered extremist by many political observers.

On issues of empowering African Americans and other disenfranchised citizens, Jackson called for 1) statehood for the District of Columbia, 2) the creation of a Democratic National Committee (DNC) Vice Chair for Voter Registration, 3) the creation of a DNC Office of Voter Registration and Participation (OVRP), and 4) support for Same-Day or Election Day Registration. Specifically, he called for the party to fully support the Universal Voter Registration Act, H.R. 3905, which had been introduced earlier in the year in the U.S. House of Representatives by Representative John Conyers,[7] and S. 2061, which had been introduced in the U.S. Senate on a bipartisan basis by Senator Alan Cranston (D-CA), with the support of Senator Ted Kennedy (D-MA), and Senator Arlen Specter (R-PA).[8]

The party platform adopted most of Jackson's language related to voting stating that "we believe that this country's democratic processes must be revitalized: by securing universal, same day and mail-in voter registration as well as registration on the premises of appropriate government agencies; by preventing the mis-

---

7 "H.R.3950–100th Congress (1987–1988): Universal Voter Registration Act of 1988," Congress.gov, (1988) accessed March 22, 2022, https://www.congress.gov/bill/100th-congress/house-bill/3950?s=1&r=55.

8 "US Congress S2061 Universal Voter Registration Act of 1988," Track Bill, (n.d.) accessed March 22, 2022, https://trackbill.com/bill/us-congress-senate-bill-2061-universal-voter-registration-act-of-1988/205425/.

use of at-large elections, the abuse of election day challenges and registration roll purges, any undercounting in the national census, and any dilution of the one-person, one-vote principle;"[9]

Thus, the call for universal registration seemed harmless compared to the other, more controversial issues that Jackson and his supporters had raised and became one of the first issues resolved by Ron Brown and the platform committee's negotiations team. Once this news of the settlement on support for universal registration reached Washington, we convened a call with Conyers' lead staff, Julian Epstein, and Ron Stroman. We discussed the possibility of taking the issue to the floor of the convention. However, we decided that even with the endorsement of the Democratic Party, the bill would go nowhere without more co-sponsors. There were already 65 co-sponsors—impressive for symbolic reasons, but not enough to get it a real hearing or for it to be scheduled for an actual vote before the entire Congress. Past attempts to pass the bill had usually ended with a "Died in Committee" designation in the Congressional Record. Since being introduced by President Carter in 1977, earlier versions of the bill had never received enough support to be passed out of committee.

The Democratic-controlled leadership in Congress had never really taken the bill seriously and the chance of anything happening was remote without more interest on the part of members of Congress themselves. The Democratic convention rules gave Congress members "superdelegate" status, allowing them to vote for the nominee and the platform. Knowing the convergence of so many key players in one place, I had pledge cards and sign-up sheets printed for circulation on the floor of the Democratic Convention. Our theory was that by signing the pledge card, members of Congress who were all superdelegates could pledge to support the Universal Voter Registration plank on the convention floor and simultaneously declare their support of the U.S. House of Representatives by signing on as co-sponsors.

The cards were distributed to Jackson's floor whips. However, Ron Brown and campaign operatives did not want the cards distributed while negotiations were ongoing in the suites with the Dukakis forces. Neither Jackson nor his supporters had yet to endorse the ticket. The decision by Dukakis to place the conservative Senator Lloyd Bentsen from Texas on the ticket had left Jackson delegates reeling with anger. Many felt that Jackson's strong second-place finish entitled him to serious consideration for the vice-presidential spot.

---

9 Gerhard Peters and John T. Woolley, "1988 Democratic Party Platform," The American Presidency Project – UC Santa Barbara, (1988) accessed March 22, 2022, https://www.presidency.ucsb.edu/documents/1988-democratic-party-platform.

Jackson himself was also unimpressed with Dukakis' promise to give him "serious consideration" and to consult with him on the VP selection. I was accompanying Rev. Jackson back from a voter registration rally in Atlanta when he heard the news of the selection on CBS Evening News from the television in his headquarters hotel suite. CBS lead anchor Dan Rather had declared that Lloyd Bentsen *would* be the convention's choice for Vice President. The Reverend froze in silence for several minutes, then declared in a defiant voice and the television screen that the final choice was up to the delegates, not Dan Rather, not the media, and not even Michael Dukakis. "The second choice of the delegates for president is standing right here!" he declared in a whisper as he stared at the TV newscast.

The Bentsen decision had put our plan for pledge cards on hold indefinitely. With one day left in the convention, the cards remained boxed and unopened in the Jackson trailer. Even after tacit agreement was reached on the entire platform, there was little interest among many of the Jackson floor managers to circulate the same-day registration pledge cards. It would require a considerable amount of interaction with and among people who had been at political war for most of the campaign season. Jackson had yet to speak, yet to make public peace with the nominee, and yet to concede that the historic campaign of 1988 had come to an end.

That moment instead came in a dramatic fashion with a speech that riveted the Omni Convention Center and touched the hearts of Americans all over the nation who watched on television. Before baring his soul about his childhood and his rise in politics, leaving many of us in tears, Jackson read off the key issues that were central to the campaign. He traced the many problems that continued to serve as barriers to voter registration. He also called for full enforcement of the Voting Rights Act, declaring in a loud, forceful voice, "If you want a change in this nation, you enforce that Voting Rights Act, we'll get 12 to 20 Black, female, Hispanic, and progressive Congresspersons from the south. We can save the cotton, but we've have to fight the boll weevils! We're got to have to make a judgment! We've got to make a judgment!" [10]

The "cotton" Jackson spoke of was the millions of unregistered voters who could spell victory for the Democratic Party in winning the White House. The boll weevils were the Southern conservative Democrats who had resisted any efforts to increase the strength of Jackson and the progressive forces within the

10 Michael E. Eidenmuller, "Jesse Jackson 1984 Democratic National Convention Address," American Rhetoric, last modified January 6, 2022, https://www.americanrhetoric.com/speeches/jessejackson1984dnc.htm.

Democratic Party. He had said these words in speeches before, but the loud roar of the crowd gave us the first real indication that party rank and file might actually be on our side.

When mention was made of "universal same-day on-site voter registration," the convention hall again erupted in applause and cheers. Upon hearing those cheers, I ran over and hurriedly dispatched a small team of volunteers to the trailer to help distribute the pledge cards. As the euphoria of the speech continued, we began passing out the cards to the Jackson floor whips who were in charge of his delegates on the floor. Finally, delegates—including hundreds of non-Jackson delegates—began to sign the cards in the afterglow of the speech.

By the end of the night, over 115 members of Congress had signed the cards pledging to be co-sponsors of the Conyers HB 3950 bill. A major victory and breakthrough had been achieved, not in Washington but outside DC among the family of Democratic activists from around the country. The cards were returned to Washington and turned over to Congressman Conyers' office for follow-up. By the November 1988 election, over 164 members had signed on as co-sponsors of the same-day voter registration bill. It was the strongest support shown since President Carter had introduced the idea in 1977. Congress, however, would recess before having a chance to pass the bill.

Dukakis would go on to lose the 1988 presidential election to Vice President George H.W. Bush, winning only 10 out of 50 states. Bush won decisively in the popular vote, 53.4% to 45.6% and with an Electoral Vote landslide 426–111. The 1988 election also saw one of the lowest voter turnouts in US history with only 50.2% of registered voters participating.[11] It was now crystal clear, at least to me, that one of the major contributing factors to the low voter turnout was the systematic and massive voter purging of Black, young, and low-income voters that had taken place in early 1988. While Dukakis lost the presidential election, the issue of voter registration reform would be carried forth into the next congress. The post cards pledging support from Democratic Members of Congress for universal registration would be used by our small group of voting rights advocates to help build support in the upcoming congress for even more comprehensive voter reform legislation.

---

11 "1988 United States presidential election," Wikipedia, last modified March 22, 2022, https://en.wikipedia.org/wiki/1988_United_States_presidential_election.

Chapter 4
Takin' It to the Hill: The Battle over H.R. 2190

On January 3, 1989, true to form, John Conyers introduced his Universal Voter Registration Act of 1989 (H.R. 17) in the first week of the 101st Congress, one week before the inauguration of George H.W. Bush as President. The bill specified that "Entitles any eligible individual to register for any Federal election by mail, in person, or at the appropriate polling place on the day of an election. Declared that such individual may register in person at: (1) a designated place for such individual's current address; (2) any Federal, State, county, or municipal agency that serves the public directly; or (3) any private agency that voluntarily agrees to register voters.[1] Conyers was able to recapture many of the members who had signed on during the Democratic Convention. He now had 116 co-sponsors, the most ever in his several years of advocating in support of universal registration and well over half of the 218 votes needed for passage. A loosely formed coalition of progressive organizations led by the group ACORN and Project Vote organized a letter to all members of Congress supporting the Conyers bill early in the legislative session and urging passage in the new Congress. With widespread grassroots support and a growing list of co-sponsors in Congress, the bill seemed to finally be on track for serious consideration.

At the same time, unbeknownst to Conyers, another major voter reform effort was being put together by the League of Women Voters and a small collection of good government groups that were advancing a more moderate approach to election reform. Washington State Representative Al Swift, a friend and colleague of the new House Speaker Tom Foley, also of Washington State, had introduced his own voter registration reform bill, H.R. 15, The National Voter Registration Act of 1989, later redesignated as HR. 2190[2] The centerpiece of the Swift legislation was not Election Day Registration, but a concept called "motor voter," a process that tied voter registration to the application for a driver's license. Motor voter had first been introduced to the nation in 1975 by Dick Austin, the first African Amer-

---

1 "Actions – H.R.17–101st Congress (1989–1990): Universal Voter Registration Act of 1989," Congress.gov, (1989) accessed March 22, 2022, https://www.congress.gov/bill/101st-congress/house-bill/17/actions?r=20&s=1.
2 "All Info – H.R.15–101st Congress (1989–1990): National Voter Registration Act of 1989," Congress.gov, (1989) accessed March 22, 2022, https://www.congress.gov/bill/101st-congress/house-bill/15/all-info?r=75&s=1.

https://doi.org/10.1515/9783110742473-007

ican Secretary of State of Michigan, which was Conyers' home state.[3] Washington State had been one of the first states to adopt motor voter, and its Republican Secretary of State Bill Monroe was one of the nation's leading advocates for making the practice national. Foley had appointed Swift to be chair of the House Administration's Subcommittee on Elections, the powerful committee that would have jurisdiction over the bill. Word went out from his staff that the new chairman planned to be an activist chair with the intention of moving—with the new Speaker's strong blessing—his own voter registration reform bill. Despite this high level of leadership support, Swift was only able to muster 51 co-sponsors, less than half of the Conyers' rival H.R. 17 universal registration bill.

Conyers was furious. By introducing his bill on the first days of the session, Conyers had signaled, to the Democratic leadership and members of Congress, his desire to take an early lead on the bill. While serving as the powerful full committee chairman of the Government Operations Committee, Conyers had over 20 years of seniority over Swift. However, with Swift at the helm of the sub-committee that had to report his bill out, he was at the whim of the subcommittee chairman. Conyers' sensitivity to this issue had been rooted in his prolonged battle to make Dr. King's birthday a national holiday. After first introducing the bill in the aftermath of Dr. King's assassination, and for 15 straight years afterward, he was the clear lead on the bill. Yet, in 1984, the Democratic party leadership embraced a compromise bill and had it introduced by a junior representative, Katie Hall. Hall, being only a two-term Congress member from Indiana, had no connection to the 15-year battle that Conyers, Stevie Wonder, Mrs. King, and other civil rights leaders had been waging.[4] Conyers had conveyed to his staff his desire to not have another major initiative seized from under him. He began to convey, to the outside civil rights community, his concerns about moving forward with this new "motor voter" version. Until now, the loosely knit coalition had been fairly united behind Conyers' effort. However, one of the bigger players, the League of Women Voters, began forming a new coalition of good government groups in support of the more moderate approach to election reform. The League itself had been working closely with Swift lead staff Karl Sandstorm and Herb Stone and in fact was the architect of the strategy of

---

3 "Richard Austin; Pioneered 'Motor Voter' Law," Los Angeles Times, last modified April 26, 2001, https://www.latimes.com/archives/la-xpm-2001-apr-26-me-55842-story.html.

4 Devetta Blount, "How former Indiana representative Katie Hall made the Martin Luther King Jr. holiday day happen," WHAS-TV, last modified January 20, 2020, https://www.whas11.com/article/news/history/king-holiday-katie-hall-indiana-ronald-reagan/417-f4cce98d-c6a9-4351-9d77-1ef7276e3a18.

moving away from the same-day registration concept and toward the much less controversial motor voter approach.

While criticizing the League for undermining Conyers, many of the groups supporting Conyers' H.R. 17 also supported Swift's H.R. 15. The race for co-sponsors was on. But Swift, with Speaker Foley's name following his on the bill, drew more co-sponsors (175) and soon began to appear as the engine that could move. As the co-sponsorships grew, so did the rift between Swift and Conyers. Swift moved ahead and scheduled a mid-March hearing on his bill—an action that would bring the issue to a head. Concerns now began to spread among the supporters of Swift's bill. Some supporters of the Conyers bill, which now had over 160 co-sponsors, began to talk of boycotting the hearing. However, with testifying remaining a coveted practice on the hill, this strategy went nowhere. Supporters did not want to lose a long-sought opportunity to have a national hearing that would generate some interest in the media and among the members of Congress. Swift called a meeting with the coalition members from the civil rights community to explain his plans to move forward. Concern grew that the Conyers-Swift impasse was escalating. The coalition asked me to appeal to Rev. Jackson to intervene and help break the impasse.

At the time, Jackson still lived and operated out of Chicago. His attention was focused on his home base, which was still reeling with political crisis following the sudden death of its legendary mayor, Harold Washington. In the upcoming late February mayor's race, Chicago's Acting Mayor Eugene Sawyer, who was filling out Washington's term, was being challenged by activist alderman Tim Evans and by Richard Daley, the son of the late machine boss Mayor Daley. Jackson had announced a major voter registration drive and had dispatched me and several other key supporters to Chicago to help with the GOTV effort. A historic special election with no incumbent made this safe territory for CEF. While in Chicago, I briefed the Reverend on the situation on Capitol Hill, urging him to break from the mayor's race and return to Washington to testify at the hearing on Swift's bill on March 21st. The hearing was on the same day as the general election. Getting the Reverend back to Washington on an Election Day in his hometown was no easy task. It was also unclear how his testimony would be received by the coalition or either of the two Congressmen.

At this point, Jackson was still a highly popular figure whose presence would be newsworthy even in Washington, D.C. and would ignite interest from the national media. Up to that point, the bill had received scant media coverage. As word of Jackson's desire to testify spread, forces within the coalition began to worry that his presence would draw attention to the rift between Swift and Conyers and among the coalition members who took different sides. Others looked at Jackson's presence as bringing his controversial campaign baggage to this bill.

They still had to contend with the Blue Dog Democrats in both the House and the Senate, who viewed Jackson as radical. Hints began to be dropped that the witness list was full, and that Jackson may want to testify at a later hearing in the spring.

As the February 28th date approached, Jackson himself began to have second thoughts about testifying. The Chicago registration drive had not gone well. Fierce infighting within the Black community and extremely cold February temperatures had kept this drive from being anything like the 1983 "Come Alive October 5!" voter registration drive. That drive, which Jackson helped spearhead, had registered over 250,000 new Black voters, catapulting Harold Washington into the mayor's office in 1983. It would also serve as a launching pad for Jackson's first run for President in 1984.

The mayor's race was heating up and his refusal to endorse either Evans or Sawyer until the very end had left Jackson boxed between both sides of the former Harold Washington coalition. Despite the late Jackson endorsement, Sawyer lost the primary election to Richard Daley, due in large part to the split in the Washington coalition between the two former allies. [5] Evans would go on to form the Harold Washington Party and run a losing independent campaign against Daley and the Republican nominee. Additionally, Chicago's practice of purging or cleaning its list every six months had left the voter rolls depleted of tens of thousands of Black voters. Jackson complained that the 30-day cutoff for registration had left only a few days for registering voters between the early February primary and the March 21st general election. With the election approaching and Daley leading in every poll, Jackson opted to leave the city on Election Day and testify at the hearing the following day. As he'd had no time to prepare for congressional testimony, Jackson asked me to prepare his remarks—the first time he had ever entrusted me with preparing a full speech that he would deliver.

Jackson now saw the hearing as a platform to reassert the need for same-day registration in light of the impending defeat of the Washington Coalition. The other major political development of 1989 was the election of Ron Brown, the Jackson campaign's convention manager, as the new Chairman of the Democratic National Committee.[6] We had calculated that testimony in Washington would remind the party and the nation of one of its many promises made in Atlanta.

---

5 "Harold Washington Party," Wikipedia, last modified February 23, 2022, https://en.wikipedia.org/wiki/Harold_Washington_Party.

6 Andrew Glass, "Ron Brown elected as head of DNC, Feb. 10, 1989," Politico, last modified February 10, 2017, https://www.politico.com/story/2017/02/ronald-brown-elected-as-head-of-dnc-feb-10-1989-234705.

Given that Ron Brown was the former Vice Chair for Voter Registration at the DNC, his appointment to that position had fulfilled the pledge made to Jackson. Brown's status as party chair was the best opportunity to keep its pledge in support of same-day voter registration that had been approved as part of the party's elections platform.

With all eyes and cameras in the overflow committee room fixed on him, Jackson began his testimony by paying tribute to John Conyers for his many years of advocacy, from the 1965 Voting Rights Act to the current voter registration reform effort. He then went on to endorse the Conyers Bill, H.R. 17, itemizing his support for each of its provisions. With strong prodding from me, as a strategic goodwill gesture he also supported the motor voter provisions of H.R. 15, but without ever mentioning Representative Swift's bill by name (i.e., my compromise with him for helping to calm the waters).

He criticized the frequent purging of voters in Chicago, the crippling effects of the purge with regard to non-voting in virtually every other state, and other administrative barriers to voting. Then, in typical Jacksonesque fashion, he delivered an impassioned appeal to both Republicans and Democrats on the committee to "make a moral judgment and rise above partisan politics and once and for all swing open the doors of political participation for all our citizens. *"Universal voter registration is neither pro-Democratic nor anti-Republican. It is neither liberal nor conservative, but rather represents the moral center. The moral center, which is so basic and central, that it reflects only the best in our American tradition."* [7] He broke from his prepared remarks and included a "calling of the roll," as he cited the names of the many martyrs in the fight for the right to vote: Medgar Evers, Jimmy Lee Jackson, James Chaney, Robert Goodman, and Mickey Schwerner, among others. He noted that the hearing was being held 24 years after the March from Selma to Montgomery—"the true people's lobby" demanding that Congress pass the Voting Rights Act of 1965.

"Just as the Constitution was incomplete without the Bill of Rights, so too is the Voting Rights Act incomplete without the Universal Voter Registration Act." It was the key phrase that made the necessary link between the two movements. He concluded by appealing to the "morality" of the committee members, challenging them to settle once and for all the question of full citizenship for African Americans first raised by the Founding Fathers.

"Like the Founding Fathers, you have a choice—that choice that over 200 years ago was whether to grant full citizenship to its African American people or whether to relegate

---

7 House Administration Sub Committee on Elections Hearing on HR 2190. March 21, 1989, Testimony of Rev. Jesse Jackson.

their status to a position that was higher than animals but lower than humans. They chose the latter option and proclaimed African Americans 'three-fifths of a person.' It would be a distinction that would be remembered as an immoral judgment. It was a decision that has had lasting social political and economic ramifications to this day."

"Today this committee and ultimately the Congress can settle once again for the three-fifths option and continue to disenfranchise two-thirds of the nation's unregistered citizens. Or the committee can take the moral high ground and empower all the people. I hope that you choose the higher ground."[8]

The Jackson testimony had moved both factions and the coalition to end the impasse and come together. Reps. Swift and Conyers, with some coaxing from me and Rep. Swift's staff, agreed to meet and be co-sponsors of a new bill that would combine both pieces of legislation. The new bill would be numbered H.R. 2190, the vehicle by which the next battle for registration reform would be launched and the first comprehensive National Voter Registration Act (NVRA) would be born in 1989. While the bill began in harmony, it would deeply divide the coalition and stall the enactment of the bill well into the next decade.

H.R. 2190

The NVRA bill had finally reached the stage of being "marked up," Capitol Hill jargon for voting a bill out of committee. The sub-committee hearing room for the House Subcommittee on Elections accommodated less than 15 seats for the audience. Upon my arrival, I saw a stretch of at least 30 people standing in line, waiting for a seat to open. The coalition had been provided with the final bill's provisions and language. A series of meetings with the congressional staff and members of the coalition had finally produced a united coalition with all sides and Congressmen Swift and Conyers, the Speaker, and the rest of the House Democratic leadership in agreement with all of the provisions.

For their part, Republicans on the committee were still opposed to the bill outright. They were expected to vote against the bill along party lines, as was routine. Swift's desire for a bipartisan bill was never taken seriously by the coalition. Democrats had control of the committee and House floor. Voting the bill out was considered a routine step. The inability to get into the hearing was no big deal since everything was a foregone conclusion. I waited outside the hearing room with the handful of reporters and spectators who also had not made it into the committee hearing room.

---

8 Ibid.

Toward the end of the hearing, members of the coalition who had been able to get in began to file out, some in a rushed urgency, others with arms raised, waving in the air. Something had gone wrong, terribly wrong. Without the knowledge of the coalition or Conyers, Representative Swift had gone behind the scenes to negotiate with the Ranking Republican Member Bill Thomas, Minority Whip Newt Gingrich, and Republicans on the committee for their support of the bill. They subsequently promised their co-sponsorship and that of the Minority Whip Newt Gingrich in exchange for adding major new controversial sections of the bill. That section would impose a "federally mandated" two-year mandatory list cleaning purge of all voter registration rolls nationwide. Such a provision was the first-ever proposed at the national level since the days of post-reconstruction. While some states have an array of list cleaning mechanisms, none had been *mandated* by the federal government. Republicans knew that such a provision in the bill would be fiercely opposed by the civil rights community and would, in effect, kill the bill. It would also provide a back door approach to remove many of the new voters who would be registered through welfare and other public agencies.

The NAACP and NAACP Legal Defense Fund were the first to declare that the change would *remove* more minorities and disadvantaged voters from the voter rolls than would be *added* by all the reforms being enacted. The amendment was extensive, six pages in length. Without the benefit of much discussion and no hearings on its impact, Swift accepted the new controversial provisions in the committee mark-up and voted with the Republicans to pass the Thomas-Gingrich and now Swift version of the bill out of committee as amended. The act would so outrage members of the civil rights community and other motor voter coalition partners that Swift was never fully trusted again after the mark-up. After months, and in some cases years, of very deliberate and delicate negotiations and discussion over simple word changes, something this significant—six pages of substantive changes and modifications—was passed with no notice or discussion with the coalition or most Democratic Congressmembers who had supported the bill.

Many questioned Swift's actions as well as his motives. His rationale was that he was seeking bipartisan cooperation early in the session. Being from Washington State, he was a close friend of the new speaker, Tom Foley, also from Washington State. He wanted to help produce a major bipartisan effort showing that the new leadership team was committed to "ending gridlock" in Washington and "getting something done." For months, Congress had been tied in knots following the fierce partisan battle, led by Newt Gingrich, to remove the former Speaker Jim Wright and strengthen the power of the GOP in the democratic controlled house.[9] Having Minority Whip Gingrich's and Speaker Foley's names on the bill as chief co-sponsors, he argued, would send a powerful signal.

An emergency meeting was held with the coalition to discuss the impact of the changes. By the end of the meeting, the NAACP, the National Urban League, and the Mexican American Legal Defense Fund (MALDEF) had joined with the NAACP LDF and announced their immediate opposition to the committee's marked-up bill. They urged other members of the motor voter coalition to join with them in their outright opposition. The League of Women Voters and the ACLU argued for a meeting with Swift before the coalition took a stand. There was a sense of urgency because the bill now had bipartisan support and was quickly making its way to a full committee mark-up.

After the flurry of accusations following the hearing, it was clear that there was also little trust between Swift's election sub-committee staff and coalition members. I went to Swift's committee staff and, for the first time, requested to meet with them one on one. I had not been in the room when the vote was taken and felt a need to get my own account of what had gone down, and more importantly, why. I was able to meet with Herb Stone, a committee staff member who had been working quietly with the coalition and was sympathetic to the issues that the civil rights groups were raising. I searched for answers to the question of "why": Why throw all the work we had done into chaos with this move? Herb, as was often the case, said that the decision was far above his pay grade and suggested that I talk with the lead counsel and close Swift confidant, Carl Sandstrom. A request was made for an immediate call to Swift's office to set up the meeting. In many ways, Sandstrom was the mastermind behind the Swift strategy to get the bill passed. Sandstrom took the meeting with me and tried, rather unsuccessfully, to explain the rationale for the congressman agreeing to this strategy. The question came down to this, he said: If the groups wanted to move the bill on to the Senate and the next stages toward passage, they had to get on board with the bipartisan package. Period!

I suggested that it was not period, and that Swift would have to explain himself to the coalition and convince them—both the good government groups and the civil rights organizations—that this was the best strategy and vehicle for achieving that. He agreed to chase down the congressman and get a commitment from him to meet with the groups within 48 hours. A decision was made to hold off on a final decision on the bill until after the meeting.

---

9 Philip A. Wallach, "The Fall of Jim Wright—and the House of Representatives," The American Interest, last modified January 3, 2019, https://www.the-american-interest.com/2019/01/03/the-fall-of-jim-wright-and-the-house-of-representatives/.

I was able to brief Rev. Jackson on the developments. I had publicly advocated withholding our decision until the meeting and reiterated this to the Reverend during the briefing. Much work had gone into merging the key elements of the Conyers bill into the Thomas-Gingrich bill, H.R. 2190. We had not seen the language nor had time to analyze it. Unlike the other groups, we (CEF and Jackson's camp) had held off on saying what we would do until I had time to see where things were headed and if something could be worked out. After hearing the dynamics of the case, Rev. Jackson agreed to oppose the bill if the Swift-Gingrich provisions were part of the final bill and vowed to return to Washington to ensure its defeat if necessary. Privately, I thought what, if anything, we could provide as a counteroffer.

On the other side of the aisle, to rank-and-file Republicans, the list cleaning provisions were a huge concession. Most had opposed the bill in general or advocated for making the bill voluntary or contingent on the availability of federal funding. Both were considered killer amendments. Swift and Democrats on the committee were well aware of past efforts to hold up legislative initiatives by making them "contingent on funding." With the approaching budget talks, motor voter—a new federally mandated initiative—could easily be flagged and negotiated out during any committee mark-up.

As the minority party in Congress for over 35 years, Republicans had become proficient in using budgetary maneuvers to dismantle or prevent the enforcement of laws that they opposed. It soon became folklore on Capitol Hill that if a budget item was added to any new federal mandates on states, the act of passing it would be only a partial victory. Hundreds of new laws were being held up by budget maneuvers that would tie up funding as a backdoor way of ensuring that the law would never be implemented. This was always in the back of the minds of NVRA advocates as they very carefully removed any direct funding streams that would place the NVRA in that situation. While seemingly counterintuitive, it was one of the protective measures of passing Democratic expansive legislation of this nature. In many cases, removing the funding stream was the only guard against a bill's backdoor defeat by a thousand budget cuts during its implementation. At a private meeting with only the civil rights groups the following day, Swift tried to rationalize his move by saying that he wanted a bipartisan bill going to the floor and ultimately to the *Republican* President Bush's desk for signature. He argued that a bill that was not bipartisan would have no chance of being signed into law and would not be worth the effort to pursue.

Round robins of impassioned pleas regarding the detrimental impact of the provisions on African Americans were given by coalition members. After an extensive back and forth of charges and prognostications, Swift, with great hesitation, agreed to work on modifying some of the bill's sections that were the greatest concerns. The full coalition soon joined with the civil rights community and agreed to not support the bill without the new changes being made in full committee mark-up. This represented a major step in keeping the coalition united. Swift asked for time to raise the concerns with Gingrich and Thomas and asked to meet with the full coalition by the end of the day. I met with the Conyers staff and warned them of the possibility that the bill could be dead if Swift was not able to make any progress. Conyers was somewhat irritated by the coalition putting any further trust in Al Swift and responded that the bill was already a non-starter for him. He announced he would introduce an updated version of his universal registration bill the following day and pursue a completely separate legislative path.

After meeting with the Republicans, Swift returned to the coalition late that afternoon and announced that he was able to make concessions on three of the six major concerns that were raised. One was that the mandatory public agency provisions requiring registration at welfare agencies, unemployment offices, and vocational rehabilitation centers would be preserved. The second was that language would be added to the bill stating that mandatory list cleanings (purges) must be conducted by states in a "uniform and non-discriminatory" manner. The third was that Mandatory Election Day Registration would be removed from the bill, but states that had adopted Election Day Registration would be exempt from the bill entirely. He was not able to make any progress on the remaining three issues that the coalition had raised. We were also informed that Gingrich rejected:

1. The removal of the entire amendment requiring a mandatory list cleaning requirement for states every two years.
2. Requiring language stipulating that the bill would not supersede the Voting Rights Act.
3. Maintaining the repeal of the purge for non-voting

At the full committee mark-up, the following Tuesday, Swift introduced and was able to pass the three changes that had been agreed upon, on behalf of the coalition. With each vote, the Republicans provided two votes needed to make the adjustments. After the third vote, Republicans kept threatening the loss of Gingrich's co-sponsorship if any further changes were made. Swift vowed that he could do no more and moved for the bill's mark-up to the floor. After Democratic members raised many concerns, the bill passed out of committee "on a bipartisan basis" with Swift joining with Republicans to ensure its passage. With that vote, the bill was now on its way to the full House for passage.

Chapter 5
The Enemy of the Good: Stuck in the Middle

There was now a clear-cut divide in the coalition. Civil rights groups, led by the NAACP, hoped for changes but clearly opposed the compromise bill. The "good government groups," led by the League of Women Voters, supported the new amended bill, while also supporting the concerns of the civil rights groups. While several whites in the group stood firmly with the civil rights community, few African Americans still strongly advocated for passage of the bill. The result produced a racial split in the coalition that was never acknowledged publicly.

I stood squarely in the middle of the two sides. H.R. 2190, if passed in its current state, would indeed be a setback for efforts to end voter purges. At the same time, this was probably the last opportunity to pass a major voting rights bill that could be signed by a Republican President. I advocated for the coalition to bring its concerns up to the full House leadership before killing the bill. Foley was the lead sponsor of the bill and, as Speaker, had the clout to control what came to a vote, with or without the coalition's support.

Each of the leading groups within the coalition was asked where it stood on the bill going forward. When pressed for a "yes" or "no" on moving ahead to passage, I decided to choose neither until we were able to appeal these concerns to the House leadership. I had checked Rev. Jackson's schedule and discovered that he had a pre-arranged breakfast meeting with the House speaker and the congressional leadership team. I vowed to ask Rev. Jackson to add it to his agenda of issues to raise with the Speaker during his meeting, and he agreed.

The original meeting was intended for Majority Leader Dick Gephardt, Bill Gray, David Bonior, Stenny Hoyer, and John Lewis. Jackson invited me and Congressman Conyers to attend the meeting with him, without first telling the host. In addition to voter registration reform, the issues of an urban policy, D.C. statehood, and the pending childcare legislation were raised. All had been part of the Democratic Party platform that they had agreed to at the 1988 convention in Atlanta with the staunch support of Jackson and his supporters. Jackson chastised the leadership for allowing a voting rights bill of such importance to the civil rights community to be brought to the floor in its present form. He again called for the passage of Conyers' universal registration bill. Foley promised that the same-day registration bill would be voted on as a separate amendment to the motor voter bill. He also reminded Jackson that he had appointed House Majority Whip Bill Gray (D) from Philadelphia as the leadership's point person in negotiating with Newt Gingrich and Bill Thomas.

https://doi.org/10.1515/9783110742473-008

Bill Gray had just been elected the House Majority Whip and was the highest-ranking African American in Congress. The civil rights coalition welcomed the intervention of the leadership and particularly the roll assigned Bill Gray to help mediate the bill. In the meantime, Ralph Neas convened a special meeting of the Leadership Conference on Civil Rights to discuss the bill and its prospects in more detail. The rules of the Leadership Conference stipulated that if any one member of the conference vehemently opposed a bill, the conference had to withdraw its support of the legislation.

Althea Simmons of the NAACP and Elaine Jones of the NAACP Legal Defense Fund were the two leading opponents of allowing the bill to advance any further. They stood firm that their organizations could never support a bill that would give a federal mandate to the practice of list cleaning (voter roll purges). Similar purges had long been used to remove millions of African American voters from the rolls every year, and they would not be party to mandating this procedure that had been used by states as a *new federal requirement*. At the LCCHR meeting, the Civil Rights Community brought its leading legal team. The NAACP Legal Defense and Education Fund brought in its director, Julius Chambers, and its top senior counselors: Elaine Jones, Lani Guinier, Dana Cunningham, Judith Brown-Dianis, and Penda Hair. They brought with them legal briefs showing, in case after case, the detrimental effects of list cleaning on the Black vote.

Lani Guinier warned that the passage of such a bill with a mandatory national voter purge system could lead to a dramatic decrease in Black voters while increasing registration among white voters, who accounted for a higher percentage of driver's license holders than Blacks in almost every state. On the other side, Richard Cloward of Human Serve, Mort Halprin of the ACLU, and Frank Parker of the Lawyers Committee for Civil Rights argued the general benefits of passing a major voter registration reform bill. Even Bill Taylor, a noted civil rights attorney with the Leadership Conference staff expressed to me privately that there was great benefit in passing even the weakened version of the bill, but the consensus rules of the Leadership Conference prevented him from saying so publicly. They argued that national postcard registration, agency-based registration, and abolishment of the purge for non-voting would lead to the most dramatic increase in voter registration rates in U.S. history. However, they went a step further and even argued that a mandatory list cleaning—with some major modifications—would be a step forward from the current state-by-state arbitrary registration laws. They argued the legislative route was the only way to develop a *national standard* for list cleaning that would be uniform and non-discriminatory.

Throughout the process, I supported the concerns of the civil rights community, but also expressed my belief that passage of this bill out of the House—even in its present form—would keep the bill options alive while still giving us time to get rid of the bad provisions in the Senate. I also argued that new standards could prevent state or county governments from enacting even more restrictive purging schemes, as I had witnessed in Cook County, Illinois and parishes in Louisiana that had notorious records for purging voters even more frequently.

Ralph Neas reminded the coalition that there were several options we could move forward and still address the controversial provisions. It could be done through a House-Senate conference or through a series of amendments from the floor, as Democrats still had a firm majority in the House. The counterargument was that there were no guarantees in the legislative process; Al Swift could not be trusted in conference to not sell us out again. Lani Guinier again argued more forcefully that the bill would lead to the most dramatic increase in white voter registration while at the same time mandating the largest purge and decrease of African American voters since Reconstruction. She argued that the coalition was taking a big chance with millions of Black voters, who would remain disenfranchised for generations if the current Swift version of the bill was passed. There was no more middle ground. You either believed that the changes could be made in the bill, and it was worth the gamble, or you believed that H.R. 2190 was a Republican plot to undermine the Black vote and set voting rights back 20 years.

I personally agreed with the arguments of the civil rights lawyers who made the most compelling and impassioned arguments. However, by now I had also concluded that if I were to oppose the bill with the rest of the civil rights coalition, it would very well kill the bill for good. Support for the bill had split along racial lines—with a few exceptions, including me. I argued that killing the bill now would be the end of our three-year effort to pass it. To those new to the discussion and growing coalition, it would simply be water under the bridge. But for those of us who had been with this effort for a while, it meant a lot of hard work over two years would go down the drain.

The arguments had been driving inside conversations for several weeks. To me, this was also a question of how this could be a vote not just for or against the bill but, rather, for or against the faith that we were placing in Bill Gray, now the highest-ranking African American in the U.S. government. The legislative power of Bill Gray as the majority whip was, in effect, being questioned and challenged from both outside and within his party and allied groups. As the House *majority* whip, he would be conceding defeat to the *minority* whip, Newt Gingrich, without even a floor fight. The same man who brought down Speaker Jim Wright would now have his next victory over the first African American majority whip. The least we could do, I argued, was meet with Bill Gray and lay out what was about to transpire. Soon after the extensive debate ended at the

LCCHR meeting, Ralph Neas again put off the final vote to withdraw all support for the bill until a meeting was arranged with Bill Gray.

Congressman Gray and his staff, led by Steve Champlin, who was driving much of the discussion, had expressed frustration and growing skepticism that this was still a fight worth fighting. There were a lot of other pressing issues on the majority whip's plate, he argued. Nonetheless, they agreed to convene a meeting of a small delegation from the coalition with Representative Gray. It would be the first in a series of meetings to negotiate the bill away from the Republican provisions and to keep the hope of passing a bill alive. The process would take weeks, or even months, to pull off. While the bill was not "dead," it was in a "comatose" stage.

What Exactly Were We Fighting For?

As I went home that night, I thought about a statement that Al Swift had made at the last meeting: "When all else fails, read the bill." When I got home, I pulled out my entire notebook of bill drafts and handouts. I reviewed not only the bill but all the background statistical data that we had developed as a rationale for why we needed the voter reform bill. Three central statistics were used as a rationale for why a voter registration reform bill was needed. Through much of the debate, the civil rights leaders and even leaders in the progressive community had questioned the impact that such a reform would have. Other issues before Congress were higher priorities. However, the evidence from the U.S. Census was clear and straightforward. In 1984, 68% of whites reported registering compared to 63% of African Americans. By 1988, those numbers had declined, with only 57% of African Americans registered compared to 66% for whites. [1] The rate for 18- to 21-year-olds, the last group granted the right to vote with the 26th Amendment, was only 51% registered in 1988, with 40% actually voting. In 1984, only 48% had registered and only 32% had actually turned out. The trend of democratic participation for African Americans and young people was dramatically going in the opposite direction less than 25 years after the passage of the VRA. [2]

---

1 "Table 2. Reported Voting and Registration, by Race, Hispanic Origin, Sex and Age, for the United States and Regions," U.S. Bureau of the Census, (1988) accessed March 22, 2022, https://www2.census.gov/programs-surveys/cps/tables/p20/440/tab02.pdf.
2 Ibid.

The numbers for participation by income also showed measurable disparities. In 1988, looking at the income levels of citizens who earned below
$5,000 per year, 49% were registered and only 37% actually voted. Those
with incomes over $35,000 per year were registered at 80% with 74% voting.
While whites were registered at the rate of 69%, blacks were registered at the
rate of 66%; among those who voted, the rates were 61% of whites compared
to 55% of African Americans. Thus, disparities existed by race, age, and income.[3]

Even with these glaring statistics, voter registration reform was secondary to
many of the other, more pressing issues on the civil rights and Black agenda:
Clarence Thomas' nomination to the Supreme Court, the Civil Rights (Restoration) Act of 1991 (a response to the U.S. Supreme Court decision on Grove
City),[4] and redistricting-related litigation surrounding the Shaw v. Reno case
pending before the Supreme Court.[5] To both the Democratic Party and the civil
rights groups, increasing majority minority districts for the first time since the
1982 Voting Rights Act Amendments took precedence over a new and potentially
weak voter registration reform bill. The historic increases in registration and
turnout of African Americans and young people on the heels of the 1984 and
1988 Jackson campaigns had given the impression of a growing and thriving
Black electorate. However, the 1988 U.S. Census statistics showed that the percentage of Black registration and turnout was beginning to decline again and
trailed white voter turnout totals.

If the merits of the bill were all that had to be considered, the groups' decision would be simple. However, other issues occupied the time and attention of
several non-electoral groups. The push for childcare legislation led by the Children's Defense Fund was in full swing. Several bills that were pending and still
being deliberated called for increases in funding for Head Start and home day-
care programs, increasing the minimum wage, and stopping the imposition of a
Republican push for a national sub-minimum wage. All were being actively advocated by the Republican leadership, and the FY 1990 Budget Act was establishing the "budget firewalls" that would soon determine what federal programs
were or were not entitlement programs.

---

3 Ibid.
4 "S.2104 – 101st Congress (1989 – 1990): Civil Rights Act of 1990," Congress.gov, (1990) accessed
March 22, 2022, https://www.congress.gov/bill/101st-congress/senate-bill/2104.
5 "Shaw v. Reno," Find Law, (n.d.) accessed March 22, 2022, https://caselaw.findlaw.com/us-
supreme-court/509/630.html.

The Gingrich-Gray Challenge

In his role as House Majority Whip, Representative Bill Gray, a prominent Democrat from Philadelphia, became the highest-ranking African American ever in the U.S. Congress.[6] His name would also become synonymous with the H.R. 2190 legislative struggle. As part of the House Democratic leadership and an active member of the Congressional Black Caucus, Gray understood support for the bill within the civil rights community was very low and diminishing. He also knew that the bill was a high priority for House Speaker Foley and his close friend from Washington State, Representative Al Swift. Holding the bill's bipartisan support was also important and necessary if there was any chance of getting it to the new President Bush's desk.

Gray's counterpart was House Minority Whip Newt Gingrich, an archconservative from Georgia. Grey knew that as a new whip himself, Gingrich would milk the bill for whatever political capital he could. Gingrich had just led a successful effort to depose the former Democratic Speaker Jim Wright, causing a long era of partisan gridlock that took hold of Congress. It was also important for the new Democratic leadership team to show that it was capable of breaking the "gridlock" that had engulfed Congress since the politically charged Gingrich-Jim Wright political battles.

Representative Bill Thomas (R-CA) was the Republican ranking member on Swift's Committee on Elections.[7] He and his staff had been meeting behind the scenes, privately negotiating his support for a compromise bill with Al Swift for several weeks. To the surprise of everyone on both sides of the aisle, he had persuaded House Minority Whip Newt Gingrich to sign on with him as an early co-sponsor of H.B. 2190. Why Gingrich, a hard-right archconservative, was on the bill at all was a mystery to everyone. It raised even more skepticism among supporters of the original voter reform bill. With sparks and accusations again flying in every direction, Gray called a meeting with key players in the coalition and the Democratic leadership to discuss strategies going forward. For the next 10 days, Gray bargained back and forth between the Gingrich-Thomas forces, the coalition members, Conyers' and Swift's offices, and the Speaker's Office. A key player throughout the deliberation was the staff of Speaker Foley, including Lorraine Miller. Speaker Foley and other House leaders including Majority Leader Dick Gephardt and Representatives Nancy Pelosi and Steny Hoyer

---

6 "GRAY, William Herbert, III," History, Art & Archives, U.S. House of Representatives, (n.d.) accessed March 22, 2022, https://history.house.gov/People/Detail/14072.
7 "Bill Thomas," Wikipedia, last modified January 1, 2022, https://en.wikipedia.org/wiki/Bill_Thomas.

from the Democratic leadership would also be among those who were briefed regularly.

I was able to participate in a number of those meetings in the speaker's office, which always included Foley and his trusted dog, who sat loyally and quietly by his side during all the discussions. While most meetings about the various dynamics of the bill could get hot and contentious, meetings with Speaker Foley and his trusted companion canine were always calm and free of rancor. Lorraine Miller was the key point person on the speaker's staff who kept the issue front and center in the speaker's office. She was always willing to meet with me privately after each meeting to give me her best reading on where things were headed. This proved to be invaluable as we walked through several political landmines surrounding the bill.

While Republicans in Congress claimed to be in favor of voter registration reform, there were four key elements of the bill where the disagreement was centered.

1. *Motor Voter:* Republicans claimed the federal bill was an intrusion on "states' rights" to control their departments of motor vehicles. It was similar to the claim that Southern segregationist governors often made in the 1960s against civil rights laws.
2. *Agency-Based Registration:* Republicans continued to assert that allowing agency-based registration in welfare offices and unemployment centers would give Democrats an unfair advantage because most poor and unemployed people would be more likely to register Democratic.
3. *Voting Rights Act:* Republicans rejected language demanded by the civil rights groups that nothing in the act could supersede or violate the Voting Rights Act. Republican leaders were well aware that many of the purges taking place across the U.S. were diluting the Black voting population and were being challenged in courts as a violation of the Voting Rights Act. They feared that the NVRA could be used as a tool to further strengthen the Voting Rights Act of 1965. They were correct in that assessment.
4. *Voter Purges:* Outlawing the purge for non-voting could reverse the trend of removing millions of minorities and Democratic voters that was taking place in state and county election offices all over the U.S. African Americans, while traditionally voting over 85% Democratic, had erratic voting behavior, voting higher in federal elections for President or Congress but showing exceptionally low turnouts for state and local races.[8] This low turnout between pres-

---

8 Aaron O'Neill, "Voter turnout in U.S. midterm elections by ethnicity 1966–2018," Statista, last

idential elections and "off-year" midterm elections was where many of the purges were triggered. Republican members insisted that the mandatory list cleaning mechanism that under their version of the bill would take place every two years, was the only way to "balance" the bill.

After the 10 days of deliberation, Gray was able to return to the coalition with a compromise framework for agreement that consisted of the following:

1. The bill would apply only to federal elections, meaning states would have the right to set up dual registration requirements for state and local elections.
2. Motor voter would be implemented by state-run departments of motor vehicles and not coordinated by the federal government.
3. A national registration postcard would be developed for registration for federal elections only. States could adopt the form as a "model" but were free to use their own forms for state and local elections.
4. Registration at welfare offices, food stamp offices, and vocational rehabilitation and unemployment centers would be optional, not mandatory.
5. States that had Election Day Registration (EDR) would be completely exempt from the new law as well as those states that adopted it in the future.
6. On the sixth and most controversial point, Gray was able to get Republican leaders to compromise on the mandatory list cleaning purge. Instead of the list being purged every two years as originally proposed, the list cleaning would take place every four years. Furthermore, voters would be allowed to stay registered on an "inactive list" through the next federal election. This would allow for a minimum of six years of inactivity before a voter was removed.

Gray's final argument was that the bill was not perfect but would allow the process to move forward to the Senate. In the Senate, Wendell Ford from Kentucky was preparing to introduce a companion bill that had none of the Republican changes that had caused all the controversy in the House. The Senate version, S. 250, mirrored the original version of the NVRA supported by the coalition but without the provisions that Gingrich and Thomas had added. To many in the motor voter coalition, this was the only bill still worth supporting. Quick passage in the Senate would send the bill to a joint House-Senate conference where

---

modified July 30, 2020, https://www.statista.com/statistics/1096123/voter-turnout-midterms-by-ethnicity-historical/.

the difference between the two bills would be worked out. It was the only hope, he argued, for keeping the bill alive.

With much debate and some dissent, the coalition supported the "framework" worked out by Congressman Gray. For the next few weeks, litigators and staff worked out language. As differences over interpretation of language mounted, the NAACP Legal Defense Fund began to move away from the Gray framework, deciding that it could not sign on to the bill unless its Voting Rights Act language was included verbatim. Gingrich refused and very vociferously removed his name from the bill as one of its co-sponsors. Even after winning the standoff, the Legal Defense Fund withdrew its support and, at the urging of several members of the coalition, agreed to a position of non-endorsement. Privately, I had concluded" that the NAACP LDF could not officially support a piece of legislation that it could very well challenge in court if the final version ended up being a violation of the VRA.

Nonetheless with momentum building in support of the bill, Speaker Foley scheduled the Gray Substitute for a vote in late March of 1990. It would be the first voter registration reform bill to reach the House floor in two decades. Throughout the floor debate, opponents of the bill argued that the Gray bill was being railroaded through Congress. Republicans offered all the amendments that the coalition and Gray had already rejected: 1) Making the whole bill voluntary, 2) Making it contingent on annual funding, and 3) Deleting language stressing that nothing in the bill would supersede the Voting Rights Act.

The majority of Republicans, led by Gingrich, went to the House floor, and declared that they would not support what they now considered a *democratically biased* bill unless it excluded the welfare and unemployment offices as registration sites. Despite Gingrich's opposition, Thomas and a number of moderate Republicans continued their lukewarm support of the Gray Framework. Proponents, led by Bill Gray, Swift, and Conyers, argued that less than 90% of the eligible US population had a driver's license. The purpose behind social service agency registration was to register those people who were unlikely to be registered under the motor voter program—the elderly, people with disabilities, and the poor.

The Republican leadership argued that the original Gray bill also required the states to allow mail registration while simultaneously limiting the ability of the states to verify the applicant's identity and eligibility. In 1990, only 27 states had a successful mail-in registration program. The Gray bill would set a national standard based on the same model to be implemented in all 50 states through the use of the first federal voter registration form. S. 250 specifically gave states the power to require in-person voting for new mail registrants in a jurisdiction. The only people exempt from that requirement would be those protected under federal statutes, like the Voting Accessibility for the Elderly and Handicapped Act of 1984 which required accessible polling places in federal elections for the elderly and people with disabilities.[9] In-person voting would be the anti-fraud device Republicans claimed was not present in the bill. As the discussion became more heated, Bill Thomas rose to his feet to support the bill, claiming it would not increase fraud. To the surprise of many Republicans and Democrats, he chastised his fellow Republican members who stood opposed to the bill.

The most common argument against the bill on the floor was that it was an "unfunded mandate," defined as a bill that imposes an undue burden on the states without providing the resources to carry out the bill. Republicans made outrageous claims that the bill would cost each state hundreds of millions of dollars to implement. However, the bipartisan Congressional Budget Office (CBO), whose sole responsibility is to estimate the cost of pending congressional bills, negated these claims and drew a far different conclusion. Its analysis of the National Voter Registration Act estimated an annual total cost below $20 million per year for all local and state governments to implement the new law.[10] Moreover, states like Michigan had designed and implemented their own state mandated motor voter programs at nominal costs.

Ironically, the coalition opposed tying the bill to any federal funding out of fear that Republicans would attempt to block funding for the measure year after year. This would leave Democrats vulnerable to the charges of expanding big government with another unfunded mandate. Supporters came back with the argument that many states had already taken the initiative in devising motor voter and agency registration programs.

The bill went to the floor with only lukewarm support from both sides of the coalition and the political aisle. All sides agreed that the bill in its present state was not acceptable. Many in the coalition urged the members of Congress to support passage of the compromise bill to allow the fight to move to the Senate rather than vote for the merits of the bill itself. The bill needed 218 votes to pass. However, the real target was to pass a bill with strong bipartisan support from both Republicans and Democrats.

Supporters were able to hold onto the support of over 224 Democrats and 65 Republicans. H.R. 2190 passed the House on a bipartisan basis, winning 289 to

---

9 "The Americans with Disabilities Act and Other Federal Laws Protecting the Rights of Voters with Disabilities," U.S. Department of Justice – Civil Rights Division Disability Rights Section, last modified September, 2014, https://www.ada.gov/ada_voting/ada_voting_ta.htm.
10 "Letter Honorable Paul D. Coverdell United States Senate," Congressional Budget Office US Congress, (1995) accessed March 22, 2022, https://www.cbo.gov/system/files/104th-congress-1995–1996/costestimate/53745-motor-voter-act.pdf.

132.[11] The most comprehensive voter registration reform bill had finally passed the House of Representatives for the first time in American history. It was a little-noted or celebrated fact given the various factions that had grown within the coalition and Congress due to the changes in the bill. The passage of H.R. 2190 in the House of Representatives allowed Senator Wendell Ford, chairman of the powerful Senate Rules Committee, to introduce the Senate version of the National Voter Registration Act, S. 250. It would become the new vehicle for which the coalition would now advocate. The bill was considered much more favorable to the civil rights community. It contained no mandatory list cleaning purges and made the public welfare agencies all mandatory registration agencies, not voluntary, like H.R. 2190 did. The Senate bill had a new set of much more prominent opponents. They were Senator Ted Stevens from Alaska, the ranking Republican on the Rules Committee; Mitch McConnell, Ford's Republican archrival colleague from Kentucky; Senator Alan Simpson, recognized as the man with the sharpest tongue in Congress; and Minority Leader Bob Dole, considered a moderate Republican veteran legislator who had nonetheless built his career on blocking major Democratic initiatives.

Democrats controlled 57 out of 100 seats—enough to pass any bill. However, the real hurdle that was effectively used by Republicans was the cloture vote, a senate rule requiring 60 voters to break a filibuster. Filibusters allowed any one Senator to stop any piece of legislation by simply refusing to relinquish the floor or stop talking in opposition to a bill. The very threat of the filibuster could prevent the bill sponsors from gaining the full 60 votes needed for the bill to get a hearing on the floor. Failure to identify the extra three votes needed would suspend any movement on the bill for several months. Interest on the part of many coalition members begin to wane as the chances of passing the bill began to lessen.

Dramatic increases in political participation were breaking out all over the world, it seemed—except in the United States, the self-proclaimed cradle of democracy! While it seemed less dramatic and earth-shattering, I began to feel that the fight we were waging to break down the remaining barriers to participation in our democracy was just as critical to the struggle for human rights, even if most of the nation or the world was not paying attention to this struggle. In my mind, we were leading a courageous battle to expand our democracy to millions of disenfranchised Americans. But in reality, we were a movement that did

---

11 "Actions – H.R.2190 – 101st Congress (1989 – 1990): National Voter Registration Act of 1989," Congress.gov, (1990) accessed March 22, 2022, https://www.congress.gov/bill/101st-congress/house-bill/2190/all-actions?q=%7B%22roll-call-vote%22%3A%22all%22%7D.

not have a large following. There were no major marches or rallies with thousands of people in support of the NVRA. There were no larger-than-life, charismatic leaders battling segregationist law enforcement. There were no billy clubs, no mass arrests, and no hard push even from the civil rights community saying, "We need to pass this bill now." It was a period when most of the attention of the nation was on what was happening to the democratic movements around the world, in Europe and Africa, and not on the systemic problems that had been keeping our American democracy from being fully realized.

There had, however, been a number of historic gains for African Americans at the ballot box during this era. In November 1989, Doug Wilder, the Lt. Governor of Virginia, was elected (by a razor-thin margin) as the first African American governor since Reconstruction. In New York, Manhattan Borough President Dave Dinkins was elected the first African American mayor of the nation's largest city. Norm Rice was elected Mayor of Seattle, Washington, and Kirk Schmoke the first Black mayor of Baltimore, Maryland. Back in Cleveland, State Senator Mike White became the first Black elected mayor since Carl Stokes was elected in 1967.[12] Because of these recent gains, even some voting rights advocates and observers saw the new NVRA bill as a potential threat to the 1965 Voting Rights Act. Long-time opponents of voter reforms were now using these key victories as arguments against the need for a voter registration reform bill. It proved, they argued, that the Voting Rights Act was working well "without the help" of the NVRA. The act was cherished, having been passed as a result of the historic march from Selma to Montgomery. The carefully prescribed amendments to the VRA in 1970, 1975, and 1982 had been a steady stream of bipartisan congressional bills that had opened the doors to many African Americans, Latinos, and low-income people throughout the South and across the nation—people who had been locked out of the political process.

The National Voter Registration Act (NVRA), on the other hand, was being advocated most heavily by predominantly white-led "good government" groups that were more middle of the road on the political spectrum. Most of the groups had not been involved in the legislative or legal process of passing those VRA amendments as were the NAACP, the NAACP LDF, and others. Many were nonchalant when it came to concerns about "adding to" the already heavily amended act. It was an odd mix of unlikely allies who lived and worked in different political and cultural worlds, with different experiences and different perspec-

---

12 R. W. Apple Jr., "The 1989 Elections; Black Success With Measured Approach," The New York Times, (1989) accessed March 22, 2022, https://www.nytimes.com/1989/11/08/us/the-1989-elec tions-black-success-with-measured-approach.html.

tives on what needed to be done to fix our broken democracy. The flawed legislative effort that had passed the U.S. House in 1990 after a lot of behind-the-scenes maneuvering had gone bad and it was far from certain that a bill would ever be enacted into law.

* * *

Representative John Conyers, now chairman of the powerful House Government Operations Committee, was still characteristically upset, stating that he should never have trusted Al Swift to take the lead on the bill. He placed a rare personal call to me at the CEF office, saying that he was going to introduce a revised version of his Same-Day Voter Registration bill and oppose the Swift/Thomas bill as part of any potential House-Senate conference compromise bill. He knew this move would essentially kill the NVRA's prospects in the House, but he doubted that the House would pass a Swift-Ford compromise bill anyway. Throughout this process, scores of Congress members in both the Democratic and Republican Parties would otherwise have been supporters of a voting rights-related bill. However, like millions of Americans, they believed that the battle for voting rights had already been won with the passage of the Voting Rights Act. They argued that groups like Project Vote, ACORN, the NAACP, and the League of Women Voters were continuing their efforts to conduct on-site registration. Combined with Rev. Jackson's two campaigns, which had him crisscrossing the country, over two million disenfranchised voters had been registered since 1984 *without* the help of additional legislation. Blacks were once again being elected to key positions in state and local governments. Their conclusion was in essence that maybe we didn't need the NVRA since the VRA "seems to be working just fine."

Nonetheless, a growing and disproportional pool of unregistered African American, low-income, and young voters was being added to the list of disenfranchised Americans every year. Two to three million high school graduates who turned 18 each year were not being registered. This was despite the fact that for over 15 years, Rev. Jackson had traveled to literally hundreds of inner-city high schools, urging young people to walk across the graduation stage with a diploma in one hand and a voter registration card in the other. Another pool of the unregistered was the 20% of the population who moved every year. Again, this group was overly represented by renters, those with low incomes, and racial minorities—non-property owners whose addresses could change more than once during an election cycle. Again, young people were over-represented in this grouping. Students who moved from one dormitory to another were summarily removed from the list, as were college graduates whose main focus was on finishing their degrees and finding employment wherever it took them. Maintaining a stable address was not a priority, and certainly not voting or political involvement. However, a current and stable address was *the* deciding factor in whether they could be systematically purged from the voter rolls and lose their right to vote.

With the NVRA bill in complete limbo, I met one-on-one with members of the motor voter coalition that I had privately called "the unofficial coalition of the willing." It began with a meeting in New York between me, JoAnne Chasnow, Richard Cloward, Francis Fox Piven, and Hubert James of Human Serve. The effort continued in Washington with one-on-one meetings I held between Melanne Verveer and Marsha Adler of People for the American Way, Mary Brooks and Lloyd Leonard of the League of Women Voters, Sonia Jarvis and Gracia Hillman of the National Coalition of Black Voter Participation, and Eddie Williams of the Joint Center for Political Studies and Steve Carbo with the Mexico American Legal Defense Fund.

In speaking multiple times with the Joint Center and National Coalition, I began to more clearly see that the dividing lines within the motor voter coalition were established based not so much on race than on one's belief in Congress's ability to pass a good bill. Along with Sonia Jarvis, a lawyer and expert in voter mobilization, I spent an extraordinary amount of time in meetings plotting out legislative and language scenarios that could help break the impasse, but neither of us was a leader of the big civil rights groups that carried the weight of the civil rights community within the coalition. Even the NAACP's legal counsel, Eddie Hailes, was sympathetic to the potential impact of the new bill in terms of empowering African American communities, but his legal training also prevented him from agreeing that this bill's good components outweighed the bad provisions. As long as Swift's H.R. 2190 was the vehicle and centerpiece of the discussion, the bill would not move.

At the request of motor voter co-chairs Mary Brooks of the League of Women Voters and Eddie Hailes of the NAACP, a meeting was held with leaders of the motor voter coalition and Majority Leader George Mitchell. While sympathetic to the concerns of the coalition, Mitchell refused to schedule a vote on the Wendell Ford Senate version of the bill until there was an assurance of 61 votes for cloture. Although only 60 votes were needed, he specified that he always required an extra vote to avoid being held hostage by any one Senator at the end of the vote.

On the day of the scheduled Senate vote on S. 250, the most votes that the pro-bill forces could muster were 54, from almost all the Democrats and only two Republicans: Mark Hatfield of Oregon and Jim Jeffords of Vermont. There were also some Democratic holdouts including Ernest Hollings of South Carolina, and David Pryor of Arkansas. There was simply not enough support in Congress for the bill to even be considered for a vote on the floor of the Senate. The final push to pass a law would have to come from outside Congress.

* * *

In September of 1990 one of the staunch members of the Civil Rights Coalition, Althea Simmons, the legendary 25-year director of the NAACP Washington Bureau, died after a prolonged illness.[13] It was a sad day for the civil rights community. Her funeral was held at the Ashbury United Methodist Church on K Street in downtown Washington. The church was packed with political leaders from around the nation. Her life had seen the passage of every civil rights and voting rights law since the 1950s. Her last two battles for the passage of the Civil Rights Act of 1991 and NVRA would be left unresolved for the next generation of leaders.

The funeral drew a huge gathering of civil rights lawyers and leaders. Outside the church after the funeral, I saw Elaine Jones and Lani Guinier from LDF for the first time in many months. We had not spoken since the coalition meetings on whether H.R. 2190 should have been advanced to the Senate. We had never really acknowledged it, but I believed that my determination to reach some accommodation on the controversial H.R. 2190 and its subsequent passage in the U.S. House had strained our friendship. Elaine Jones had been one of the closing eulogists. She had worked shoulder to shoulder with Althea for many years and gave a fiery and moving speech with rich stories about the many legislative battles waged and won by the legendary Althea Simmons. During the service, many of us were moved by her remarks as we realized that we all had an obligation to continue building upon Althea's legacy.

After the service, Elaine and I shared a long heartfelt embrace following the procession outside the church. "Althea is gone, Greg," she said, wiping back tears. "But we got to carry on. She left so much work undone. The civil rights bill, Clarence Thomas, motor voter..." Her voice trailed as she turned and walked away, still grieving.

"Elaine," I asked before she drifted away. "I know Althea was against the motor voter bill, but don't you think that she would want us to keep fighting for voter reform?"

"Althea was a fighter," she said, her voice growing stern as she waved her index finger. "She would fight to her grave against a bill that was going to set

---

13 "Althea Simmo NAACP Official Dies," The Washington Post, (n.d.) accessed March 22, 2022, https://www.washingtonpost.com/archive/local/1990/09/15/althea-simmons-naacp-official-dies/4356515f-16ba-4fde-9ecb-04fb3bc3c7b8/.

Black folks back! That would be like signing on to Bush's version of the civil rights bill. Remember what she said: "No bill is better than a bad bill."

"We can't let that happen, Elaine," I answered. "We can't give up."

"No, we can't," she agreed. "Althea would never give up the fight until the battle was won. We can't, either. We can't do that to Althea's legacy." We embraced again and went our separate ways. For me, it was a clear signal from Elaine and maybe, I hoped, Althea to "keep on keeping on."

After the service, I walked back downtown with Frank Parker, head of the Voting Rights Project of the Lawyers Committee for Civil Rights. He had privately been somewhat at odds with Althea over the merits of the motor voter bill. He also expressed regret that she did not live to finish the fight and that they had not resolved their differences on the bill before she died. He then made a confession over lunch: Despite his support for the weaker bill 2190, "Althea was right about everything that was wrong with the bill." The question was deciding how much of what she demanded be removed from the bill could we actually get taken out of the final version.

"The question is," he concluded, "will a Republican president ever sign a bill that turned every welfare office into a voter registration center?" In the political world where Althea had lived and died, the answer was no. It was clear that the political landscape would have to change if there was any chance of Althea Simmons' unfinished work being fulfilled.

Chapter 6
Back to Selma: Taking It to the Streets

The defeat of the NVRA made newspaper headlines all across the country. Articles and some editorial boards chastised the Senate for its failure to pass such a simple "electoral reform" bill. It would be one of the symbols of the "gridlock" that characterized a host of other issues. Increased public awareness of the issue created a new opportunity to build grassroots support for the bill.

The 25th anniversary of the voting rights march from Selma to Montgomery was being planned by the Southern Christian Leadership Conference and voting rights activists Rose and State Senator Hank Sanders. The Southern Rainbow Education Project, a progressive Southern independent affiliate of the National Rainbow Coalition, led by Montgomery's Dr. Gwen Patton, was angered over Senator Richard Shelby's opposition to the motor voter bill. Patton urged Rev. Jackson and the coalition to attend the march and make passage of the motor voter bill one of its central issues. Senator Shelby had been one of only three Southern Democrats to oppose the bill. The others, as mentioned, were Ernest Hollings of South Carolina and David Pryor of Arkansas. Rainbow activists in Alabama and South Carolina made plans to support the re-enactment of the Selma to Montgomery march as part of its voter outreach efforts, which had been dormant since the 1988 campaign. We were eventually able to get the National Voter Registration Act incorporated as one of the issues of the march.

A *Coalition of Conscience* meeting had been planned in Selma by Rev. Dr. Joe Lowery and Coretta Scott King. The last time the group met was at the conclusion of the 25th Anniversary March in August 1988. At the urging of Rev. Jackson, the group planned to conduct voter registration drives throughout the march. CEF designed and printed 1500 posters for marchers to carry. The poster had both Dr. King's and Rev. Jackson's images with the slogan: *"Commemorate the 25th Anniversary of the Voting Rights Act of '65: Pass the National Voter Registration Act of 1990, S. 250. Call or write your U.S. Senator."*

Over 6,000 marchers gathered in the Brown Chapel in Selma, Alabama on March 8, 1990. There were many other signs, printed by supportive labor unions, that greatly overshadowed ours. The predominant theme was simply "Pass the Civil Rights Bill," which was also being held up in Congress by a Republican filibuster led by Senate Minority Leader Robert Dole. While we were not necessarily competing with the civil rights bill, the motor voter supporters in Washington clearly wanted the NVRA bill to be the dominant theme. Other signs called for "Peace and Freedom," "Keep the Dream Alive," and "Keep Hope Alive."

https://doi.org/10.1515/9783110742473-009

I flew down to Selma with Rev. Jackson. On the way, we talked about the developments with the bill and how the Republicans and even some Democrats were pulling out all the stops to defeat it. The Reverend reminded me that the Voting Rights Bill, before it was the Act, was opposed by a majority of the *Democrats* in Congress in 1965 until the violent events surrounding the march from Selma to Montgomery. He argued that the impetus for these bills did not come from Washington but, instead, from the streets of Selma and Montgomery, Alabama. "That's where that bill was written!" he exclaimed. "Not in those halls of Congress where you hang out!" I was startled until I saw the smile that spread across his face. He said that he was proud of the work that I was doing on "that Hill" but, "They're never going to pass that bill until there is a President elected who's going to sign it." He was right.

During the march, I made my way up to Dr. Joseph Lowery, then President of the Southern Christian Leadership Conference (SCLC), and quickly briefed him while we marched. He echoed Rev. Jackson's feeling. "That bill didn't get signed because of the Congress or Lyndon Johnson," he told me as he quickened the pace of his marching. "That bill was won with the blood and broken bones of the people who had marched." He added, "They're never going to sign that bill until there is a demand by the people. Nobody knows what motor voter or NVRA is. They can't fight for something they don't know nothin' about!"

The men were a generation apart in age but remarkably similar in their experience and observations about the NVRA bill. Neither was surprised that some Democrats joined Republicans in opposing the bill. Both had marched with Dr. King and John Lewis on this same route 30 years ago, urging Congress to pass the 1965 Voting Rights Act. The march had raised awareness of the bill and was widely credited with turning the tide in Washington in support of it. Dr. Lowery resumed his march pace and I waded back into the crowd of marchers, absorbing both his and Rev. Jackson's messages to me. They had both marched with Dr. King here and I could feel and hear his echoes of agreement.

At the climax of our march in Montgomery, at the state capitol, several speakers called for passage of the NVRA, including Congressman John Lewis, who compared it to the fight for the VRA 25 years ago. SCLC President Joe Lowery referenced the bill in his remarks as well, although he repeatedly and mistakenly kept referring to it as the "Voters Rights Bill." As is often the case, Rev. Jackson was the last speaker and electrified the audience. Most of his focus was on President Bush's opposition to the civil rights bill and his accommodation of apartheid in South Africa. He blasted the Supreme Court and the Democratic Congress for not focusing its resources at home upon the end of the Cold War. He again advocated for passage of "Same Day On-Site Voter Registration," calling it the only solution to the disenfranchisement of the seven million unregistered African Americans. He referred to the defeat of the NVRA and chastised Alabama Senator Shelby for "voting against the voter registration bill."

The Selma to Montgomery march was not the only time we would interject the posters and information cards into events. The posters were distributed to several voting rights, civil rights, and registration groups. They were used in the "Save our Cities" march held in Washington on June 12, 1990. They were most heavily used at voter registration rallies that Rev. Jackson held on college campuses and in churches where most of our voter registration work was concentrated. Slowly, word about the new NVRA bill was spreading to public discussions in states across the U.S.

* * *

With the failure of Congress to pass national legislation, many state legislatures began to adopt their own voter registration reform bills. Over 23 states had some version of motor voter and registration reform bills. From 1988 to 1993, five more states adopted their own versions of motor voter before it had become national law. One of the few states in the Deep South considering reforms was Georgia, which had one of the highest levels of unregistered Black voters in the south. Passage of a reform bill there would be a major development in Southern voting rights history. There were over 150 counties in Georgia that were free to shape their own election procedures. Few state mandates existed to set reasonable standards for what election procedures counties would undertake. Passage of the NVRA was, to Georgia in 1990, what the Voting Rights Act was to Alabama in 1965. There was much resistance to changing any of Georgia's restrictive registration laws.

There would be no marches in Georgia for the NVRA. The passive resistance on the part of elected and election officials to any real changes to the system was strong. Therefore, a hearing of the Government Operations Committee of the Georgia legislature to discuss the marking up of such a bill was a controversial event. This rare hearing on a state voting rights bill was convened by Democratic State Representative Robert Holmes, a well-respected African American legislator and friend of the civil rights community, and Republican Senator Culvert Kidd. The hearing had been pushed heavily by Ed Brown, the executive director of the Voter Education Project. (VEP), the legendary Southern registration group.

Brown was a hard working yet quiet soldier in the field of voter registration. For years he lived and worked in the shadow of his brother, the legendary Black Panther leader Rap Brown and other past and more well-known VEP Directors John Lewis and Vernon Jordan. VEP had been established with the help of U.S. Attorney General Robert Kennedy in 1962 and a consortium of civil rights groups to assist in voter registration efforts in states covered under the Voting

Rights Act. [1] In its 30-year history throughout the 1970s and 80s, under the leadership of John Lewis, and Vernon Jordan, VEP was registering hundreds of thousands of voters throughout the south each year.

The Georgia hearing would be one of the last projects before VEP's demise a few years later in 1992. In the final years of the organization Ed was always struggling for funds. Throughout the planning for the hearing, Ed talked endlessly about how the foundations, civil rights groups, and liberals had allowed VEP to die a slow death. The continued existence of millions of unregistered black voters throughout the south, he argued, was testament that the work of empowering Black voters in the south was far from over.

I made the trip to Atlanta realizing that this was a rare opportunity to build grassroots support for the NVRA outside of Washington, DC. Many members of the Georgia Democratic Congressional delegation were still cool to the idea of a new Federal bill. The Georgia legislature was hardly a place to stir up a grassroots movement; but it was closer to the people than Washington D.C. It was also a place where the reform—even a statewide version of motor voter—would be a controversial political move in the hard conservative state house. By pushing for support of new federal legislation in front of the Joint House-Senate Georgia State Legislature hearing, I thought it might spur more Georgia legislators to support their own state reform bill instead. This was a rare bi-partisan joint committee hearing of both the Georgia House and Senate and I saw it as an opportunity to demonstrate that states were ready and willing to move forward with reform, even if the U.S. Congress was not.

To my surprise, no more than a handful of people were there to observe the hearing. The audience was made up primarily of the witnesses, including many who had flown in to testify. There was also a "victim's panel," that Ed Brown had helped to organize to testify about their struggles attempting to register voters. The panel was made up of Black residents from a tiny town in southeast Georgia. Black residents had been facing some of the worst economic and environmental conditions but had little political influence among the town commissioners. Nearly two thirds of the residents lived below the poverty line with only a small percentage of the population registered to vote.

Like many of the people there, I was moved by the testimonies. When my turn to testify arrived, there was no time to do anything but summarize. This time, I breathed a sigh of relief. I wanted to challenge them while they were still moved by the struggles in Keysville. It was clear from the questions asked

1 "Voter Education Project (VEP)," King Institute Stanford University, (n.d.) accessed March 22, 2022, https://kinginstitute.stanford.edu/encyclopedia/voter-education-project-vep.

by both Republican and Democratic committee members that there was a lot of skepticism about taking any steps to reform Georgia's voting systems that were controlled by each county. The people of Keysville raised such ire that one legislature remarked that he wasn't even sure where to start. I answered by giving him a simple answer: to start by registering every member of the Black community in Keysville Georgia to vote!

For most of my testimony, I talked about the federal legislation and the many legislative hurdles that we were facing in Washington. The NVRA's continued failure to pass a filibuster vote meant that we would have to look to the state legislatures across the country to pass their own state bills and soon. "The basic change being proposed," I testified, "is not so much a greater role on the part of the federal government in mandating new regulations to the states. It is rather the federal government establishing new procedures which will require greater cooperation (and uniformity) between federal, state, county, and local jurisdictions."

* * *

My Georgia legislature testimony was the same testimony and message that I would carry into other state capitols and political conventions. From 1990 to 1992, I traveled to Jackson, Mississippi; Raleigh, North Carolina; Richmond, Virginia; Harrisburg, Pennsylvania; Montgomery, Alabama; Trenton, New Jersey; Lansing, Michigan; Springfield, Illinois; Austin, Texas; and Sacramento, California. These travels consisted of meetings with key elected officials, legislative strategy sessions and workshops with local organizers, voter registration rallies, and occasional appearances on local TV news or talk radio programs. Most often, the supporters of local voter reform coalitions were the state and local affiliates of our national coalition partners, especially the League of Women Voters, the NAACP, Rainbow activists, labor leaders, clergy, and educators.

We concentrated on the states where we had the best chance of picking up the support of the 60th Senator. The states that would be our first line of offense were Georgia, targeting Senator Sam Nunn; Alabama, targeting Richard Shelby; and Pennsylvania, targeting Arlen Specter. Three states were already considering going to Election Day Registration and, as a result, could be exempted from many portions of the bill. Michigan, New Jersey, and Connecticut were the states considering that move, as was the District of Columbia. Three states were in litigation over existing registration procedures including Arkansas, and New York, who were considering converting to Election Day legislation.

Although speaking filibusters rarely take place in modern times, the threat of one was the real challenge. If a bill did not have 60 votes, it could not even be brought up for debate on the floor. Minority Leader Bob Dole had used this provision over and over again to block the Civil Rights Act of 1991, anti-apartheid legislation, jobs and training bills, and an array of other Democratic initiatives. Upon the passage of H.R. 2190 in the House, Minority Leader Dole had immediately announced his intention to invoke cloture and prevent the vote in the U.S. Senate.

Despite Dole's announcement, the coalition, and Senator Ford's Rules Committee staff, led by Jack Sousa, was much more successful in keeping alive the Senate version of the bill with strong voting rights protections that the coalition could embrace as a whole. It also remained silent on the issue of a mandatory list cleaning mechanism—a move that pleased the civil rights community. Senate Majority Leader George Mitchell held a series of meetings with coalition leaders and made it clear that unless the bill had 61 votes in hand, he would never schedule a vote. Coalition members were well aware that the 60 votes were not there, but still convinced Mitchell to schedule a vote to get "a real measure of support." On the first attempt, the bill passed 55 – 45, but five votes short of what was needed for cloture. Senator Mark Hatfield, a moderate Republican from Oregon, was the sole Republican co-sponsor of the bill. Mitchell gave the coalition "two weeks and nothing more" (according to his staff) to pick up the support of the opposing Democrats and moderate Republicans. The Democrat targets were Ernest Hollings of South Carolina and Richard Shelby of Alabama, both of whom had voted no on cloture. Other Republican targets included Robert Packwood of Oregon, Jim Jeffords of Vermont, and Arlen Spector of Pennsylvania.

In two weeks, a second vote was taken, and two holdout votes were picked up: Hollings and Jeffords. The second attempt was better, 57 to 41, but still short of the 60 needed for the cloture vote.[2] However, Senate Democratic Leaders were now unsuccessful in picking up votes after two different attempts in one legislative session—a rare occurrence. Under the Senate rules a bill dies a de facto death if it fails to win the 60 votes needed for cloture. After extensive lobbying by the coalition over several months, the 59th and 60th votes appeared: Republican Senator Dave Durenberger from Missouri announced his support without conditions, while Republican Senator Bob Packwood of Oregon expressed his support for the bill after meeting with League of Women Voters and NAACP leaders in Oregon. His home state Republican colleague, Mark Hatfield, was co-sponsor and had repeatedly lobbied him for support.

---

2 "On the Cloture Motion S. 250," GovTrack, (1991) accessed March 22, 2022, https://www.govtrack.us/congress/votes/102-1991/s140.

Pennsylvania's Arlen Spector was up for re-election and had received endorsements in the past from labor and civil rights groups. He prided himself on being an independent Republican who would never announce his intention to vote on an issue until he actually cast his vote. However, after being lobbied heavily by the local chapters of the Urban League, the NAACP, and the AFL-CIO, he expressed his "intentions" to support the bill—under one condition. Spector's condition was that he would vote for cloture only if the coalition had the 60 votes it needed for cloture in hand. "I will be the 61st vote," he declared in a private meeting with the Democratic leadership. 'What great courage!' I thought sarcastically. I always believed he must have calculated: 'Nothing to lose (by failing to vote yes with his other Republican leadership to meet cloture if it failed) and everything to gain (by being credited as a bipartisan leader on the bill if it happened to pass).

As always, the coalition was gathered at the entrance to the Senate floor on the day of the vote. As members filed in to cast their votes, the coalition made a final appeal for support for the bill. One by one, the 59 supporters came in to cast their "yes" votes. Senator Packwood was late arriving for the vote and, like the other 59 supporters, carried out his pledge and voted "yes" on the bill. Immediately after casting his vote, Packwood was surrounded on the floor by Robert Dole, Mitch McConnell, Alan Simpson, and several other Republican senators. From the Senate gallery stands, I could see hands flying in the air and finger-pointing. In the moments that followed, Packwood broke from the pack surrounding him and approached the Senate clerk who was recording the vote. The clerk then whispered into the microphone that Senator Packwood had changed his vote to NO. The vote count now reverted to 59 votes for the NVRA. Moments later, Senator Spector arrived from his office en route to cast his vote and filed past the coalition. "Thank you for your support, Senator Spector!" Mary Brooks from the League called out in a loud voice to him as he walked by. Spector simply waved and kept walking.

We held our breath as he walked through the sea of Republican senators. He was now our only hope of getting the 60 votes needed. Spector quickly assessed the situation, cast his vote, and walked back toward the door. Before he reached the entrance, the clerk announced, in a definitive vote, "Senator Spector votes NO!" Instead of the 61 votes we thought we had in hand when the day started, the bill received only 59 votes.[3] Despite winning a majority of the vote in the Senate, the bill once again failed to invoke cloture and break the filibuster. Upon exiting the Senate chamber, Spector zoomed past the devastated coalition mem-

---

3 Ibid.

bers without saying anything. As he walked away, I blurted out, "Senator Spector, what happened?" Spector stopped his stride and motioned us over. "You guys never had the votes!" he remarked in a surprisingly harsh tone. "People have a lot of problems with this bill. It could lead to a lot of fraud." Ironically, this was the same Spector who was one of the original sponsors of the Universal (Same Day voter registration bill just a few years earlier.

As Senator Packwood walked out of the chamber, the coalition members rushed over to him. He held up his hands as we approached and walked backward into the elevator. He had been a "yes" vote who'd actually kept his word and voted "yes" on the floor, then changed his vote after being visibly pressured to do so by his Republican leadership. He said softly that he had nothing to say. Although everyone was talking at once, the central question was heard above the clamor: "Why, Senator?" With a shrug and the look of a guilty child, he simply said, "I just changed my mind" as the elevator doors closed.

After three attempts, we had failed again. This time, reality sank in. The fight for the bill was really over. As we stood in the Senate reception area, literally kicking ourselves, the senators began to file back in. The very next vote scheduled on the floor was for a pay raise for members of the Senate. As the bells rang, the same senators filed back into the chambers. While we stood there consoling ourselves about the loss, the bill for the congressional pay raise passed by a simple majority vote. Ironically, *there was no cloture vote! No filibuster! no challenge on either side of the aisle, and no need for 60 votes.* There was precious little debate or rancor. In fact, there was an eerie silence about the whole vote. That bill would be headed for President Bush's desk for his signature. Our bill, meanwhile, was headed for the congressional archives' graveyard with thousands of other bills that had been introduced but failed due to a lack of significant votes needed for passage.

Though there was much discussion of whether the bill deserved a full debate on its merits, the failure of cloture meant that it could not even be debated on the floor of the U.S. Senate. Winning 59 votes out of 100 (59%) was a landslide by traditional democratic standards. Yet in the U.S. Congress, there was no room in the Senate to even discuss a bill to expand our nation's democracy. Meanwhile, a bill to raise the pay of U.S. Senators was not even debated and passed with only token opposition and no legislative maneuvers.

I stood in silence and watched them file back out, smiling, and jovial after passing their pay raise—*on a bipartisan basis.* The movement to pass the NVRA bill in the 102nd Congress was over. These were the guardians of our democracy—refusing to even allow a vote on a bipartisan bill to expand the right to vote to all its citizens. But there were no maneuvers, no floor fights when it came to voting themselves a pay raise in the midst of budget deficits. Like generations of senators before them, they'd had an opportunity to fulfill the broken promise of our democracy, but once again failed.

Suddenly, I had the same feeling I had at the Cleveland Public Library when I first registered to vote. It was an eerie feeling that this was really "their government" and not our business. In fact, as the senators and their staff made their way around my frame in the narrow hallway, the guard reminded me that I was in the way of the senators and needed to move on. I took his advice literally and did move on—to other issues. The political atmosphere was not ripe for the passage of this bill. I thought a lot about how Rev. Jackson had said that the fight for the VRA took place on the streets, "not in the Suites" or halls of Congress. I could now see firsthand what he and Rev. Lowery had been trying to tell me during the march to Montgomery.

The upcoming 1992 would be an election year. While the politics would be thicker, this would force the Republicans to oppose a bill to make it easier to vote in the middle of an election year. However, it would not happen here on Capitol Hill and not with a Republican president. The fight for the bill would have to come from the cities and towns where these Congress members and senators actually got elected: Pennsylvania, Alabama, Georgia, New York, and Ohio, as well as on the presidential campaign trail of 1992.

* * *

Later that fall, months after work on motor voter had been suspended, I thought it time to regroup and bring together all our forces from outside Washington, D.C. and around the country. We needed to rethink our strategy and approach to the issues of voter registration reform in the context of "electoral reform" that the coalition had decided upon earlier in the year. We had to convene a conference of all our allies on voter registration and electoral reform—the first since the 1985 mobilization when I stood with them as president of the United States Student Association.

Many of the 67 organizations supporting the bill seldom attended regular coalition meetings. This would be a chance for all the organizations that had supported the bill to regroup, meet in a room, and re-evaluate the strengths and weaknesses of the NVRA strategy. Most importantly, we needed to meet to develop a new strategy that would allow us to pass a strong civil rights version of the bill—even in an election year. A public education and mobilization campaign in support of the bill would need to be undertaken and carried out across the country at the state and local levels—and not in Washington, D.C.

The Citizenship Education Fund sponsored the gathering under the banner "National Conference on Electoral Reform," which was held September 13, 1991, at the Quality Inn Hotel on Capitol Hill. The theme of the conference was "Meeting the Challenge to Expand Our Democracy." Over 44 national and regional organizations answered our call and participated in the conference. The gathering was made up of the nation's top voting rights, civil rights, labor, student, and human service organizations. At this gathering, we invited and introduced a new organization to the coalition and to Washington: a Los Angeles-based student organization called Rock the Vote. They had developed a public relations/media campaign in support of motor voter in Los Angeles in conjunction with MTV and the entertainment industry, which also supported passage of the bill. Their plans included a campaign to attach cards in support of the bill to the CD releases of recording artists, among them R.E.M., one of the most popular rock groups in the nation at the time. They would also register students to vote on campuses against a growing move toward what they perceived as censorship. Their registration was centered on the issues of free speech and censorship. Many rap groups including the gangster rap group 2 Live Crew had been arrested for their questionable lyrics. Rap music in general was under attack by many religious and parent-based community organizations.

While Rock the Vote was a good slogan among the white student community, it was not catching on in the African American community—a central component of the entertainment industry. In Coalition with Rock the Vote, CEF developed a sister campaign, Rap the Vote, based on the same concept but with a focus on rap music instead of rock. Rock the Vote's founder and president, Patrick Lippert, was not able to attend but sent Steve Barr, a prematurely graying former student activist from Los Angeles. Dressed in blue jeans, a t-shirt, a baseball cap, shoestring-less Converse tennis shoes, and a plaid blazer, Steve gave a captivating presentation that focused on putting together a "winning" public relations campaign. He also advocated a buttonhole approach by pinning down wavering senators on radio and TV call-in shows. He would prove the effectiveness of this strategy weeks later by doing just that on a radio program with Nebraska Democratic Senator Bob Kerry, who had expressed great reservations about the bill.

Motor voter was an issue that the entertainment industry could easily embrace. This was evident by the taped public service announcements that Rock the Vote had produced featuring some of the industry's hottest artists. Entertainers like Queen Latifah, Ice Cube, R.E.M., and others produced their own unique messages asking young people to register to vote and support the motor voter bill. They were also instrumental in getting R.E.M. to wear "support motor voter" hats during their performance on *Saturday Night Live*. This one act alone helped raise awareness of the bill more than any actions we had ever undertaken in Washington, DC.

Professor Richard Cloward of Human Serve had attended the entire conference but remained relatively silent for most of the day. He seemed somewhat skeptical, believing that these sorts of PR efforts would drive people away from the serious issues at stake with voter disenfranchisement. Toward the end of the gathering, Cloward broke his long silence to make a statement that would create rifts among members of the traditional coalition. Richard was an aging social activist from the 1960s. He and his wife, Francis Fox Piven, had been the pioneers of agency-based voter registration. They lived and operated their national network of human service agencies out of New York City. He was also a professor at Columbia University. Cloward had argued that the bill would reach 92% registration by the year 2000 and would register more people faster than any legislation since the Voting Rights Act. He went on to suggest that the bill would be a vast improvement over the current law, *"even without many of the changes that had been demanded by the civil rights groups."* Others in the coalition had made similar claims privately but had never spoken those words in any public forum. Cloward's statement was read by the civil rights groups as a repudiation of their stolid position that a bill without the changes would actually be a step back from current law. They saw motor voter as an electoral reform bill that would register primarily non-African Americans and would impose a new national mandatory list cleaning mechanism that threatened to remove more African Americans from the rolls than it would add. Cloward's public stance made the rationale for declaring the NVRA an electoral reform and not civil rights bill even more clear. Some members of the coalition would never get over Cloward's remarks, which reignited the divide within the coalition. However, it also strengthened the resolve of other members to move ahead with the work of building support, knowing that it was worth the effort to advance electoral reform as an issue in the upcoming 1992 elections.

The Citizenship Education Fund's National Conference on Election Reform provided that clear opportunity to move motor voter from civil rights to electoral reform and helped to keep the coalition together. It would become one of a series of initiatives being developed to reform the laws that had ruled our election procedures and, ultimately, our democracy.

Chapter 7
The NVRA Filibuster Breakthrough and 1992 Elections

More than any other election year, 1992 marked one of the first years that African Americans and young voters exerted the most decisive political power in the nation's history. It was also the first election since the 1991 redistricting and reapportionment that reflected the impact of the 1982 amendments to the Voting Rights Act. Under the new VRA provisions that required the drawing of majority-minority districts, the number of Black Majority and Influence districts increased from 17 in 1982 to 38 in 1992. Likewise the number of Hispanic districts increased from 10 to 19.[1] Twelve of those new districts would be drawn from Southern states where the Black vote was concentrated.

It was also the election in which a record number of congressional seats were open due to unprecedented resignations and defeats of incumbents in the primaries. Moreover, there would be an array of African American candidates on the ballot for offices at every level including president, through the independent campaign of former Jackson advisor Ron Daniels. Two African American women launched campaigns for the U.S. Senate: Carol Mosley Braun ran for an open seat in Illinois, while Rainbow activist Gwen Patton challenged Senator Richard Shelby in Alabama.

Like in 1968, the 1992 elections took place against the backdrop of an emerging social and political upheaval that engulfed the nation. This time, instead of Alabama, Los Angeles was the center of the conflict. The high-profile trial of four Los Angeles policemen in the beating of motorist Rodney King had been widely publicized around the nation and world for months. In Simi Valley, California, where the trial had been moved, a nearly all-white jury acquitted the four officers involved in the beatings. The verdict led to the most widespread rioting in Los Angeles and around the nation since the 1968 riots that followed Dr. King's assassination.[2] The clash of Black protesters and the LA Police Department had captured the attention of the nation, and race relations were once again a major issue across the country. For over three days, law enforcement and polit-

---

1 "1992 United States House of Representatives elections," Wikipedia, last modified March 21, 2022, https://en.wikipedia.org/wiki/1992_United_States_House_of_Representatives_elections.
2 "Riots erupt in Los Angeles after police officers are acquitted in Rodney King trial," History, last modified April 27, 2021, https://www.history.com/this-day-in-history/riots-erupt-in-los-angeles.

https://doi.org/10.1515/9783110742473-010

ical authorities from around the state had been unable to control the fires and looting that had spread from South Central to Riverside, Beverly Hills, and Hollywood. Los Angeles was up in flames with over a thousand fires set across the city. Republican Governor Pete Wilson deployed 4,000 National Guard troops to assist the LA police already on hand.[3]

President George H.W. Bush was fresh off a decisive victory in the Gulf War. As he had done so many times before, Bush addressed the nation in language reminiscent of his speeches during the Persian Gulf War. In a primetime address to the nation on May 1, 1992, President Bush announced that he was sending 3,000 troops from the 7th Infantry and 1,500 Marines from El Toro Air Force Base to "help restore order" to Los Angeles. "These troops were in addition to the 4,000 regional police officers and 3,000 national guard troops that had already been deployed by California Governor Pete Wilson and LA Mayor Tom Bradley. Bush denounced the "brutality of a mob" and vowed "I will use whatever force is necessary to restore order."[4] After three days of rioting and looting, there were 63 dead, 2,383 injured, and over 12,000 people arrested and jailed. Property damage was estimated at over $200 million.[5]

The riots and youth disturbances began to spread across the country including San Francisco, Atlanta, Seattle, and Madison, Wisconsin, as well as hundreds of campuses around the country. President Bush's initial reaction to the verdict, despite his own misgivings, was that the judicial process had to be respected. He called on the Department of Justice to look into possible civil rights violations against motorist Rodney King by the acquitted police officers. In the meantime, he called for the restoration of law and order in LA and across the US. His harsh law and order statements were criticized by civil rights leaders and by Governor Bill Clinton, who was running for president and was the most likely Democratic nominee at the time. The presidential election would be a referendum on what kind of leadership was needed to end many of the conditions that had led to the Rodney King verdict and its aftermath.

The verdict would also remind many African Americans just how little influence they held in the judicial system. Juries, like the one that acquitted the police officers in the Rodney King case, were chosen from among the list of REGISTERED VOTERS. According to the US Census, in 1992 only 64% of African Amer-

---

3 "1992 Los Angeles riots," Wikipedia, last modified March 21, 2022, https://en.wikipedia.org/wiki/1992_Los_Angeles_riots.
4 20C History Project, "L.A. Riots: President Bush's reaction," Youtube, last modified October 19, 2015, https://www.youtube.com/watch?v=KD_3NOIEk-0.
5 "1992 Los Angeles riots," Wikipedia, last modified March 21, 2022, https://en.wikipedia.org/wiki/1992_Los_Angeles_riots.

icans were registered to vote vs 70 % of white voters. Among young people aged 18 – 24 the registration rate was worse at 52.5 %. Among Hispanics the rates were even lower at 35 %.[6] *This underrepresentation in the political process—was now graphically spilling over into underrepresentation in the judicial process.* This point was made over and over by community leaders in Los Angeles and around the country. The message: There will be more "Rodney King" verdicts until the full strength of African Americans, young people, and people of color is exercised and maximized at the ballot box.

The year 1992 would go down as a historic landmark election and the defining moment for the political course of the 1990s. It was the second to last presidential election of the 20th century. The race between President George Bush and Democratic challenger Bill Clinton became a generational battle not seen since the 1960 election between John F. Kennedy and Richard Nixon. President Kennedy was the *first* president born in the 20th century, and now, ironically, Democratic Nominee Governor Bill Clinton could become the *last* president of the 20th century. Additionally, if the nominee were to be re-elected in 1996, (as Clinton was), he became the first president of the 21st century. Given the gravity of this electoral decision, much was at stake in the 1992 elections.

In the 1960s, Kennedy and Johnson faced violence and riots in Alabama and Mississippi, as well as throughout the South. In 1992, both candidates were forced to deal with the aftermath of the L.A. riots and strife in other urban centers throughout the country. The next administration would be challenged to develop plans to provide long-term relief for staggering unemployment, particularly among black youth, the economic and structural decay of our urban centers, the growing health care crisis, and the escalating crime wave. *What distinguished this year from others was the emerging social and political upheaval that had engulfed the nation.* The riots in LA had captured the nation's attention. The presidential election would be a referendum on what leadership was needed to reform the criminal justice system and end many of the conditions that had led to the Rodney King verdict and its aftermath.

The election also centered on the need for policies and solutions to address lingering economic and social inequities. U.S.expenditures in the 1980s were centered on S&L bailouts, large military defense buildups in Europe and the Persian Gulf, and massive tax breaks for the rich. The election of 1992 was a referendum on whether those resources, the so-called "Peace Dividend," which was

---

6 Jerry T. Jennings, "Voting and Registration in the Election of November 1992," U.S. Bureau of the Census, (1992) accessed March 22, 2022, https://www.census.gov/content/dam/Census/library/publications/1993/demo/p20-466.pdf.

the estimated billions of tax dollars that would now be saved once the Soviet Union collapsed in 1991. The election would define whether these funds would be shifted to rebuilding America's infrastructure, re-investing in neglected inner cities, and providing the necessary training and retraining to put over 10 million unemployed Americans back to work.

The race between President George Bush and Democratic challenger Bill Clinton would become a generational battle not seen since the 1960 election between Richard Nixon and John F. Kennedy. In the 1960s, presidential candidates were seeing the beginning of major civil rights marches and violent resistance throughout the South and urban disturbances in the North. In 1992, the upheaval was over police brutality and the need to reform the criminal justice system were issues that all three major candidates for president—Bush, Clinton, and Independent candidate Ross Perot—were forced to deal with the aftermath of the riots in L.A. and other urban centers throughout the country. The next administration would be challenged to develop plans to provide long-term relief for staggering unemployment, particularly among Black youth, the economic and structural decay of urban centers, the growing health care crisis, and the escalating high school dropout rates. Despite the gravity of these prominent issues, I would always come back to the NVRA and (at least in my mind) the vital necessity of electing a President who would sign the bill into law.

Stuck in the Middle Again

Senate Majority Leader George Mitchell had sat here before. Some of the members of the motor voter coalition he now knew by name. Once again, the request would be for Mitchell to "prioritize," i.e., schedule the NVRA bill for a vote. His key staff had made it clear that there would be no vote and that there was no point in even scheduling a meeting with the Senate Majority Leader. He was a busy man with all the pressing issues pending in Congress. This bill had been voted on twice already and had failed to gain the necessary votes needed to be signed into law. The case, for all intents and purposes, was closed. The NVRA would not become the law of the land and there was no need to exhume what was already a dead issue.

The civil rights coalition, which had a less personal relationship with him, saw Mitchell's refusal to even meet with the coalition to talk about the bill as an affront to the African American community. Many of the civil rights groups were still reeling from the contentious Clarence Thomas nomination hearings, which had been a disaster. Thomas was now a Supreme Court Justice and they blamed Mitchell, the Democratic leadership, and Senate Judiciary Committee

Chairman Joe Biden for not waging a more aggressive fight to stop the nomination. Additionally, compromises on other civil rights legislation proved that the Democratic majority was vulnerable to the Republican Senate powerhouses who still wielded much power, particularly Senators Jesse Helms, Alan Simpson, Mitch McConnell, and Bob Dole.

Mitchell's staff saw a meeting with the Majority Leader as nothing more than window dressing—at best, a chance to say "no" face to face, but to what end? After a series of meetings with the chief of staff that got them nowhere, Mitchell's staff finally gave in to the coalition's demands for a face-to-face meeting with Mitchell. The exacerbated staffer concluded the last meeting by saying, "If it's that more important for you to hear a 'no' from the leader rather than me, fine." The meeting was scheduled for a small representation of the coalition.

Mitchell was in a jovial mood this time, talking about everything from the weather to George Bush's seemingly insurmountable lead in the polls for re-election. For this meeting, he removed his jacket and sat at a large wooden and very polished rectangular conference table in his office, with neither notes nor briefing papers. He argued that it was hard to pass anything in an election year that would be nothing more than a political football. Everyone would be looking to score for some rhetorical points, to blast the Senate once again for passing bills that would never become law; laws that were unfunded mandates and would lead to massive voter fraud; and, by the way, it would all be a waste of the Senate's limited time to pass legislation.

In my mind, I read it as they were busy and there were other things to do. The fundraising demands would be tremendous in 1992 and time spent on endless hearings, mark-ups, and amendments would take them away from their real number one priority: raising money and getting re-elected. Mitchell further argued that the bill would quickly become an early "Christmas tree" in the spring. "Christmas tree" was the term used on Capitol Hill for bills that would be loaded with endless amendments made up of the senators' pet causes—none of which would have a chance of being enacted into law on their own. This had happened to most bills of this nature throughout the past eight years, he argued.

"Why does your coalition think this instance would be any different? Tell me why," he challenged the group with a stern look and a tap of his finger on the table. After a long pause, he folded his arms, leaned back in his chair, and sat silently. The League of Women Voters Chief Lobbyist Mary Brooks, true to form, argued that it was still possible to pass a bipartisan bill, but not without some concessions on both sides. Elaine Jones of the NAACP LDF snapped back that they had already made their concessions by allowing Bill 2190 to be passed out of the House. The only vote that would be acceptable would be the same language that had been carefully crafted by the civil rights groups and agreed upon by the full motor voter coalition.

Mitchell weighed in: "Oh, I can get you a bill, but I'm not sure you're going to like the end result. You folks are going to have to choose between the bill you want and the bill that you can realistically politically get. That's a decision that you're going to have to make, not me".

"We have already made that decision, Mr. Majority Leader," Elaine declared, "and it's a good bill or no bill. What we need you to do is guarantee us that you will use your position to make sure it's a good bill. We can't have any more 2190-type bills—not here in the Senate".

"I can't guarantee what the final version of any bill will look like. That's why I say without 61 votes, you're wasting everyone's time. I can pass anything with a majority, I control 57 votes, but I do not control a single Republican vote. Even if we got the 61 votes, it would be next to impossible to override a veto from a Republican President. That would take 67 votes. Having said that, you find me those four Republican votes, and you'll get your bill."

"But how do we KNOW that Bush will veto the bill?" I blurted out. "When did he say, 'I will veto the 'motor voter' bill?'" Nobody answered. "We've heard him say he would veto the civil rights bill week after week. We heard him say he would veto the crime bill because of the assault weapons ban. But can anyone say for sure they had ever heard Bush, or any administrative official, say they would veto the NVRA bill?"

Mitchell motioned to his aide to get him the background material on the Bush presidential statements on NVRA from earlier February. "We'll get on it right away."

"We've already checked with the White House," Mary Brooks said. "There has been no veto threat issued." The League explained that their contacts in the White House still thought that H.R. 2190 was the same bill being debated in the Senate, which it was not. "They won't issue a veto threat to a bill with Republican co-sponsors."

"That's the other bill," Elaine Jones stated emphatically. "What about this bill? What about S. 250?" The League volunteered to "put in a call to the White House to find out."

"Not to beg the question," I stated, "but how could Bush veto a voting rights bill in the middle of a democratic revolution in the Soviet Union? How could the Republicans face voters at the polls in November after denying them a chance to make it easier for them to vote?"

Mitchell looked over at me and chuckled. "It's a good thought, son," he said almost apologetically. "But you are talking about a man who won the Gulf War with a 90% approval rating. Besides, there are no people in the streets of the capital demanding that this bill be passed. You mentioned the democratic revolution in Russia. Now, if it were President Gorbachev we were negotiating with, I think we would do better."

The comment brought a laugh from everyone.

"Don't waste your time waiting for Bush or any of these Republicans to take a stand for democracy," Mitchell went on. "They have no interest in making it easy for people who are unregistered to vote. It doesn't bother me! I'm from Maine, where we have Election Day Registration. But it bothers them."

I reminded him that the delegates at the 1988 Democratic Convention had passed, as part of their very "mainstream" platform, support for the original bill that called for Election Day Registration. But in this bill, instead of exempting only the four states that already had Election Day Registration, we could exempt all states that chose the option of converting to this type of measure. That argument did not get any traction as the meeting began to wind down. However, we did leave with a commitment to schedule another vote on the bill if we could produce 61 votes or more.

An important distinction of the bill was that the vote for cloture did not bind any Senator to vote for the bill itself. It simply allowed the Senate to debate the issue on the floor. Senators were no longer being asked to support the bill on its merits. They were being asked only to allow the bill to be discussed so that they could express their concerns or even offer amendments to change it. For their part, the senators knew that to vote for cloture would mean voting against their powerful Minority Leader, Bob Dole.

Senator Dole staunchly opposed the bill. He had made declarations that the bill was a ploy by Democrats to embarrass Republicans and President George Bush, who was running for re-election. Dole was joined by Senator Alan Simpson from Wyoming who was the most vocal opponent, making declarations on the floor that ridiculed both the bill and its coalition.

"There is no great movement to pass this bill," Simpson had declared during the last cloture vote debate on the floor of the Senate. "There are no protesters in the streets tearing down the walls of Congress begging us to pass this bill. The only people in the whole country who want this bill are that small band of people standing outside the door there with their buttons on saying 'support motor voter. He had motioned toward the Senate gallery and there we all stood outside the doors of the Senate, looking in. Only seven or eight of us out of a coalition of 67 groups had come up to Capitol Hill for the big vote. Senator Simpson called the bill a "violation" of states' rights and quoted the 10th Amendment to the Constitution from the floor: "The powers not delegated to the United States by the Constitution, nor prohibited by it to the States, are reserved to the States respectively, or to the people "[7] He vowed that the law would never be implemented in Wyoming and urged his colleagues to vote against the bill to prevent it from ever becoming law.

There was not much hope that the Senate would break a filibuster. The meetings of the motor voter coalition, once again, grew sparse. The work now centered on finding Republicans willing to switch their vote. There were a few senators who would even bother to meet in addition to Senators Hatfield, Jeffords, and Specter; there were other moderate Republicans who remained undecided and actually met with the coalition for more deliberations. They were Dave Durenberger (R) and John Danforth (R), both from Missouri, Bill Cohen (R) from Maine, and John McCain (R) from Arizona. The magic number of Republicans needed was four. If we could convince only two more Republicans to support cloture, it would give us the 60 votes needed to break the filibuster.

Each Senator spouted the party line about fraud and unfunded mandates imposed on states. Then each followed with his own reasons for opposition. Danforth and Durenberger shared in their opposition to the agencies. McCain wanted the military recruitment centers added as mandatory agencies. Cohen wanted the bill to be voluntary so states could adopt the federal guidelines but use their own standards for compliance. Specter primarily wanted an easy way out. He had indicated his support in meetings with the AFL-CIO and other civil rights groups in Philadelphia. However, he needed the Republican Party's support in his tough race against his strongest political challenge ever, Democratic Lynn Yeakel. As a result, he could never bring himself to say that he supported the measure and would vote yes for it on the floor.

The break finally came when Senator Durenberger announced that he was retiring from the Senate. Relieved of the pressures of the re-election campaign, he became freer to vote his conscience. He became the 60th vote, with Spector keeping his commitment to be the 61st vote. It was now early May and with time running out, Mitchell set a deadline of bringing the bill up for a vote before the summer recess. He had committed the fall session to working on the federal budget and appropriations. This bill, he declared, would not be allowed to "tie up the Senate" any further. The coalition assured him, through the League, that the 60 votes would be there "with one to spare," as Mary Brooks promised.

True to his word, Mitchell scheduled the bill for a vote in the last week of the session before the Memorial Day recess. After losing an unprecedented four votes

---

7 "10th Amendment: Rights Reserved to States or People," Constitution Center, (n.d.) accessed March 22, 2022, https://constitutioncenter.org/interactive-constitution/amendment/amendment-x.

over five years, it would be "the last shot" at passing the bill. On May 20, 1992, three years after first being introduced, the National Voter Registration Act of 1992 was passed by the Senate on a vote of 61 to 38.[8] The bill then moved to the House of Representatives where Minority Whip Gingrich and Rep. Thomas both opposed the bill after the failure to attach a Republican amendment. On June 16, 1992, after several weeks of legislative procedures and actions, The US House of Representatives voted to support the NVRA Senate Bill 268 to 153 on a bipartisan basis with 28 Republicans joining 239 Democrats in supporting the bill.[9] It was a major milestone bi-partisan vote that had confounded all the critics over the years.

Senators Ford, Mitchell, Hatfield, and others held a press conference on the lawn of the Senate and urged President Bush to "give the country a birthday present" by signing the bipartisan bill. The coalition's adulation over passing the bill was tempered by the threat that Bush would veto it. U.S. Attorney General Bill Barr had also made statements earlier that the bill would lead to fraud and abuse. As head of the government agency primarily responsible for enforcing the bill, Barr's vocal opposition was a bad sign and a potential setback after the bill had finally passed Congress. The Bush White House had expressed its opposition to an earlier version of the bill in February, saying it would open the door to election fraud and impose heavy administrative cost on states.[10]

With the bill now officially on President George Bush's desk, sources close to the White House confirmed that Bush was being heavily pressured to veto the bill by the Republican leadership of the House and Senate. Despite the support of over 60 civil rights, religious, disabled, veteran, labor, and student organizations from around the nation, the voice of this Republican leadership was strong. There was also vocal opposition from the National Association of Counties, which argued that the bill took away too much county control over their elections. Although charges were made that the bill was partisan for Democrats, it had received significant bipartisan support in the House (268 – 167) and captured 61 votes in the Senate, one more than needed to break the filibuster.

Rock the Vote developed an aggressive and cutting-edge campaign urging top recording artists and radio disc jockeys to encourage their fans and listeners

---

8 "Actions – S.250 – 102nd Congress (1991– 1992): National Voter Registration Act of 1992," Congress.gov, (1992) accessed March 22, 2022, https://www.congress.gov/bill/102nd-congress/senate-bill/250/all-actions.
9 "Roll Call 194 | Bill Number: S. 250," Clerk – United State House of Representatives, (1992) accessed March 22, 2022, https://clerk.house.gov/Votes/1992194.
10 Congressional Quarterly Almanac 1992, *Bush Rejects 'Motor Voter' Legislation*, 48 ed, 75 – 77. (Washington, DC: Congressional Quarterly, 1993).

to sign a petition urging President Bush to sign the "motor voter" bill. The campaign utilized pledge cards that were collected at colleges, concerts, courtyards, and cafes across the county. Students suddenly were responding to the campaign, with MTV News, BET, and radio disc jockeys across the country participating. After only four weeks, over 50,000 signed postcards had been collected and were being transported to Washington, DC by Rock the Vote. It was a successful campaign with wide publicity and lots of energy. The arrival of the cards was a carefully planned event. To highlight the delivery, a rally was planned in front of the White House as a last-minute push to show support. But it was approaching a 4th of July holiday weekend. The July 2 rally did not draw many of the throngs that Rock the Vote or the motor voter coalition had anticipated, with less than 100 people in attendance. Many coalition members had already left for summer vacation.

At the rally, speaker after speaker called on the administration to come out and receive the cards as a good-faith gesture toward the youth's "getting involved" in the political process. However, the moral appeals fell on deaf ears. The small band of protesters was outraged and railed against the president and the administration for ignoring the authentic project of the student leaders to petition their government. Except for CNN, none of the mainstream media outlets covered the event. MTV News, however, reported it, as did a number of student newspapers upon their return in the fall. The headlines of the stories would read similarly throughout: The Bush Administration added insult to injury by again threatening to veto a pro-democracy bipartisan voting rights bill and rejecting pleas to simply receive the 50,000 cards that had been signed by youth and students from across the country.

As predicted, President George Bush bowed to the pressure of congressional opponents and vetoed the motor voter bill on July 3, 1992. In his veto message Bush said he vetoed the bill stating it would expose the election process to "an unacceptable risk of fraud and corruption without any reason to believe that it would increase electoral participation to any significant degree." [11] While millions of Americans were in their cars driving to celebrate the birth of our nation's democracy, President Bush was vetoing a national voting reform bill that would have registered an estimated 50 million eligible voters. Vetoing bipartisan legislation to expand the nation's democracy was the president's gift to the nation on the eve of its 216th birthday.

---

11 "The 1992 Campaign; President Vetoes the 'Motor-Voter' Measure," The New York Times, (1992) accessed March 22, 2022, https://www.nytimes.com/1992/07/03/us/the-1992-campaign-president-vetoes-the-motor-voter-measure.html.

Bush's veto fell in line with many other vetoes that had strong popular support. As was the case with his veto of critical environmental reforms, sensible gun control, through veto of the Brady Bill, and now the motor voter bill, President Bush once again proved that his administration was out of touch with the American people. And he had no intention of signing legislation that his administration knew would empower millions of young people, African Americans, and other disenfranchised citizens. With his veto he also broke his promise to take a serious look at the root causes of the LA riots and the racial tensions it sparked.

After getting a policy decision from the White House head office, White House guards were instructed to not accept the 50,000 cards addressed to President Bush at 1600 Pennsylvania Avenue NW. This action infuriated members of the coalition when the White House returned the cards that young voters from all 50 states had signed, urging him to sign the bill. One Rock the Vote volunteer, who left the protest in tears, had worked all spring gathering petitions only to have them rejected by the White House. Her comments echoed the feelings of others at the protest: "The President and the Republican leadership are saying to youth and the poor that 'your vote does not count.' We are going to prove them wrong!"

Bush citing "fraud and corruption" as the reason he vetoed the measure was in essence declaring his administration's opposition to new federal laws that made it easier to register to vote—even one passed on a bi-partisan basis. By asserting that the provisions of the bill would promote corruption fraud, the president leveraged a charge against election procedures in 27 states that had already adopted all or parts of the bill. His action only heightened a deeply held view growing across the country that the Republican leadership was resisting growing voter enchantment within the election system.

Soon the realization of what had just happened began to sink in. The bill was now officially dead. After all that work, over three years to get it past all the obstacles in Congress, the fight was over. We had gone the final mile urging a popular Republican president to sign a bipartisan voting rights bill. We had exhausted all of our tools. The fact that he had done it on the eve of the nation's Independence Day kept coming back to me. It was clear that the expansion of democracy and making registering to vote easier for all Americans was just too much to ask. It was time to go home.

Members of the coalition vowed to take the legislation back to Congress seeking to override the President's veto. With 67 votes needed to override a presidential veto, the odds of securing the necessary votes were slim. In the aftermath of the veto, NVRA Senate bill sponsor Wendall Ford angrily vowed to seek a vote to override the veto. After several weeks The Motor Voter Coalition was able to convince Senate Leader Mitchell to schedule an override vote in the Senate after the Labor Day recess. On September 22, 1992, the Senate voted 62–38 to override the veto, gaining 6 Republican votes, including an unexpected Yes vote from retiring Wisconsin Republican Senator Bob Kasten.[12] Despite the highest level of support for the NVRA, it failed to gain the 67 votes needed to override. The fight for the bill's passage was finally over. Congress and the president would go on their extended summer recess. In the fall, both parties would dedicate their efforts to electing the next President of the United States and the new Congress. Supporters of the bill now knew that without a Democratic president, the chances of ever passing the NVRA or any voter reform legislation would be over.

★ ★ ★

The 1992 elections were the first election since the 1982 VRA amendments had been adopted making the 1991 redistricting and reapportionment a historic first. New majority-minority districts helped create a wide expansion of African American candidates on the ballot for offices at every level. With no Jackson for President '92 campaign on the horizon, Rainbow Political Director and Black nationalist activist Ron Daniels tried to pick up the mantel. He declared his "independent" campaign for president with little fanfare. Daniels was a prominent name among Black political scientists but was a much lesser-known political figure to the general public. His campaign did not garner the energy or attention of the 1984 or 1988 Jackson campaigns for president. With little chance of winning the Democratic nomination, Daniels would bypass the Democratic presidential primaries and instead seek ballot access as an independent candidate for president on state ballots.

For the youth, African American, and low-income vote to be maximized to its full potential, these constituency groups would have to strive for drastically increased registration and turnout of voters on Election Day. The recruitment of candidates for offices at every level was also underway as Black candidates emerged across the country to run for city councils, county commissions, state assemblies, Congress, and even mayoral posts. In 1992, sleeping political giants with the potential to impact elections began to emerge. Simply by virtue of their geographic concentrations on college campuses, housing projects, and urban areas, political power began to be wielded more aggressively by young and

---

12 "Roll Call Vote 102nd Congress – 2nd Session," United State Senate, (n.d.) accessed March 22, 2022, https://www.senate.gov/legislative/LIS/roll_call_votes/vote1022/vote_102_2_00226.htm.

urban voters than ever before. If there was ever a time for the disenfranchised to speak in a loud and clear voice, it was now.

In 1992, a new generation of young African American leaders were emerging and assuming the responsibility of empowering their communities and expanding America's democracy. Throughout the nation, there was a dramatic increase in political involvement in the aftermath of the L.A. upheaval. The events would remind African Americans just how little influence they currently had over the judicial and legislative system. Civil rights leaders and criminal justice reform advocates warned that there would be more police misconduct and Rodney King verdicts until African Americans and all people of color maximized their political power at the ballot box to end the disparity.

These calls for greater voter participation resonated with Black voters and even more with young voters. The Black vote in November saw a dramatic increase over the 1988 presidential election with 54% voter turnout among both African Americans compared to 51.5% in 1988.[13] Among young voters the increase was even more dramatic with 18–24 year-olds turning out at a rate of 42.8% vs 36.2% in 1988.[14] While still less than half of the eligible voting population casting a ballot, it represented the largest turnout of young voters since the passage of the 26th amendment in 1972 granting 18–21-year-olds the right to vote.[15]

It was on the strength of the increase in these two voting blocks that Bill Clinton would go on to win the White House decisively over George Herbert Walker Bush. The strength of his support among African American and young voters across the U.S. was a decisive factor that finally broke the Republicans' 12-year hold on the White House. It also helped Democrats maintain their control of Congress. With the election of a Democratic House and Senate, it was now possible for many of the initiatives that had been vetoed or stalled to receive a second look. It was a landmark election and it breathed new life into our efforts to make one final push for the passage of the NVRA.

---

13 Jennings, "Voting and Registration in the Election of November 1992," U.S. Bureau of the Census, (1992) accessed March 22, 2022, https://www.census.gov/content/dam/Census/library/publications/1993/demo/p20-466.pdf.
14 Ibid.
15 Ibid.

Chapter 8
The Final Push for Passage of NVRA "Motor Voter" Bill

The 103rd Congress convened on January 3, 1993. It marked the first time in 12 years that the Democrats controlled both houses of Congress and the White House. Representative Al Swift and the Democratic leadership in the House of Representatives once again introduced the National Voter Registration Act (NVRA) of 1993, this time as bill H.R. 2.[1] However, instead of moving their legislation through the process, they waited for action from the Senate.

The chair of the Rules Committee Senator Wendell Ford indicated that he would take the lead again in the new Congress and introduce a revised version of his bill, S. 250. The Senate version of the NVRA of 1993 was now numbered S. 460. The bill included all the elements of his old Senate bill with a few additions. This time, however, he included a provision for a less onerous four-year mandatory purge and the voting rights protection language long sought by civil rights groups.

Never one to wait, Congressman Conyers introduced his own version of the NVRA on January 4, 1993. Conyers' bill was nearly identical to the Swift bill, which included all the key components that had been the centerpiece of the previous bills. However, Conyers' version had some modifications:

1. An *expanded agency program* that would increase the number of authorized voter registration locations to include unemployment bureaus and all public schools.
2. A provision that exempted states from NVRA if they enacted Election Day Registration, and
3. A *national mail-in registration card* that would create a uniform national voter registration form, making it possible for any citizen, including homeless people, to register and vote for the first time ever in all 50 states.

* * *

On January 25, 1993, I met with Representative John Conyers about the prospects for the bill in the 103rd Congress which had just begun. He mentioned that he wanted to take advantage of our victory in November and give the new president a voter registration reform bill to sign in the first 100 days. The motor voter co-

---

1 "H.R.2–103rd Congress (1993–1994): National Voter Registration Act of 1993," Congress.gov, (1993) accessed March 22, 2022, https://www.congress.gov/bill/103rd-congress/house-bill/2.

https://doi.org/10.1515/9783110742473-011

alition had been advancing the bill in the same timeframe. While ambitious, the first 100 days was a goal for us both to organize around.

Conyers was also looking for new staff and had an opening for a legislative director. He had his longtime trusted aide and director of the House Government Operations Committee, Julian Epstein, meet with me to explore the possibility of my becoming part of Conyers' staff. Both Julian and the congressman had observed my work within the motor voter coalition and had often relied on my advice and counsel during the multi-year legislative battles. However, taking on a full-time staff role would mean a lot more. Julian knew that I would have a hard time resisting the opportunity to be a key player in this phase of the work. When he and the congressman met with me for the interview, they offered me the job on the spot and sweetened it with the prospect that I would have primary responsibility to help steer the final passage of the NVRA on behalf of the congressman and the Congressional Black Caucus. Both were heavily invested in lining up new legislation for the new president whom they had all worked hard to elect. Having a steady government job with benefits on Capitol Hill and doing the work for which I had grown so passionate was an offer that was hard to resist. However, it would also mean leaving Rev. Jackson after over nine years together, since his first campaign began in late 1983. Still, as a new husband and father, I had a hard time refusing the offer.

On February 3, 1993, I began my new role as a Hill staffer. It would be the first time that I would work on the inside of the congressional structure. Soon, I discovered that the staff of the congressional office yield an enormous amount of influence. I eventually learned that the details of walking a bill through committees, legal counsel, and House rules was an entire process in and of itself—far beyond anything that I had imagined from the outside. Getting a bill passed would be a political maze without a clear-cut path. While I stayed in close contact with many of my friends and allies from the motor voter coalition, there was definitely a new character and heavier weight to my responsibilities. It was now my job to sit on the other side of the table and tell the coalition of Congress's limits in terms of passing the bill, even with a Democratic president. As a hill staffer I was no longer allowed to be part of the Motor Voter Coalition's legislative strategy meetings. This was by far the hardest adjustment for me to make given all the close friendships I had made over the years.

In introducing his new bill, Conyers cited statistics from the U.S. Census from 1986–1990, with dismal turnouts in off-year elections with no presidential race.[2]

---

2 Jerry T. Jennings, "Voting and Registration in the Election of November 1990," U.S. Bureau of

The percentage of voting African Americans dropped four points to below 40 % in the 1990 midterm elections. Only one-fifth of the Hispanic population participated in federal elections.[3] The worst voting rates belonged to youth. For every person below the age of 25 who voted in 1988, three others stayed home.[4]

There had been great fear that the 1992 turnout would dip below the 50.1 % who showed up in 1988, the last presidential election.[5] However, the dramatic increase in turnout of 55 % in the 1992 election revealed an important new trend: More Americans were showing an interest in voting and participating in the political process. The lack of registration was clearly the biggest obstacle to participation in the democratic process. It was time for Congress to act. The NVRA offered hope that the federal government would take that lead and open up the process to encourage greater participation. The momentum to pass the bill was greater than ever. America now had a president who was willing to sign the NVRA bill. It was just a matter of which version of the bill would end up on the president's desk for signature.

Republicans now saw the writing on the wall. Their outright opposition through the filibuster had failed in the last Congress. Now, they switched their strategy to weakening the bill through a series of amendments. On March 15, the U.S. Senate passed a series of Republican-led amendments to the NVRA that virtually gutted most of the more significant and empowering elements of the bill.[6] The new amended Republican version of H. R. 2 dramatically undermined the very intent of the legislation to expand our democracy and voting rights. The changes were imposed on the bill by the team of Minority Leader Bob Dole, Mitch McConnell, and Alan Simpson. The three tag-teamed the lead on the Senate floor and led a tirade against the bill, once again threatening to filibuster it unless dramatic changes were made.

Again, Senate Majority Leader Mitchell and Senator Ford found themselves short of the 60 votes needed to overcome the Republican filibuster. This time, three Democratic senators, Richard Shelby of Alabama, David Pryor of Arkansas, and Ernest Hollings of South Carolina, joined Republicans in expressing their

---

the Census, (1991) accessed March 22, 2022, https://www.census.gov/library/publications/1991/demo/p20-453.html.

3 Ibid.

4 Ibid.

5 Jennings, "Voting and Registration in the Election of November 1992," U.S. Bureau of the Census, (1992) accessed March 22, 2022, https://www.census.gov/content/dam/Census/library/publications/1993/demo/p20-466.pdf.

6 "H.R.2–103rd Congress (1993–1994): National Voter Registration Act of 1993," Congress.gov, (1993) accessed March 22, 2022, https://www.congress.gov/bill/103rd-congress/house-bill/2.

opposition to the bill. Now boxed in a political corner by Republicans and Democrats, Ford was forced to agree to the series of weakening Republican amendments to save the bill from an early death. The Senate Republicans stripped the public agencies from the bill that had allowed for voter registration at welfare offices and food stamp agencies, unemployment offices, and vocational rehabilitation centers servicing the disabled. They argued that people applying for benefits were naturally Democrats. To "balance the bill," they added military recruitment centers and hunting and fishing licensing stores as voter registration agencies. The presumption was that new military recruits and sportsmen were more likely to be Republicans. By mandating only motor voter and these three agencies, the bill was now biased against the chronically underrepresented. The poor, particularly low-income women and people of color would be denied this same level of government assistance in registering and political enfranchisement.

Another Republican provision amendment permitted states to erect systems for checking citizenship. The provision required states to set up extraordinary verification procedures targeting citizens with Hispanic surnames. Other people of color would also be vulnerable to intimidation by provisions allowing observers to challenge their citizenship simply based on their physical appearance. Even after all Republican amendments were added to the bill, every Republican voted against it except for the five moderate Republicans. The vote was 62–37, with 57 Democrats and five Republicans voting "yes" and 36 Republicans and one Democrat voting against the bill.[7] We now found ourselves in a situation in which the Senate had passed a bill that would not be an advance but, instead, a step backward from the current law. The bill would increase the existing disadvantages for African Americans and low-income people and create a wide gender bias. It eliminated registration for welfare recipients, who were predominantly low-income women, the disabled, and young people, while registration would be mandated in agencies servicing predominately able-bodied white men: hunting and fishing licensing outlets and military recruitment centers.

Another group vulnerable to the revised Senate bill was the nation's unemployed. The Republican amendment removed provisions that would have allowed registration at unemployment and job training centers. Many unemployed workers were in the process of being displaced and moving, making them prime candidates for purging. They, more than any other Americans, were experiencing instability with constantly changing addresses, which made them the most vul-

---

7 "Roll Call Vote 103rd Congress – 1st Session," United States Senate, (n.d.) accessed March 22, 2022, https://www.senate.gov/legislative/LIS/roll_call_votes/vote1031/vote_103_1_00117.htm.

nerable to the new federally mandated purges. The original Democratic bill would have protected those voters from purges by mandating registration when people applied for their unemployment claims.

Many disabled and veterans' groups spoke out loudly against the Republican bill because it also removed provisions allowing departments of vocational rehabilitation to register the disabled when they applied for benefits. Many of the affected disabled were veterans who had sacrificed their able bodies to preserve our democracy. Their lives were already littered with barriers to full physical and economic participation. It was a mystery to many why Republicans would construct additional barriers to their political participation. Instead of empowering the traditionally unregistered citizens, the amended Senate bill, as it now stood, further disenfranchised poor, working-class unemployed Americans and millions of disabled citizens. Additionally, Hispanic, Caribbean, Asian American, and other citizens of color could be subjected to renewed barriers based on their surnames or physical appearance.

The House version of the bill, H.R. 2, was a replica of S. 250, the original Democratic version of the bill. Republicans, led by Newt Gingrich and Bob Michel, the Minority Leader, launched a fierce attack on the bill when it was debated on the House floor. They levied what would become the largest assault against a voting bill since the battle over the 1965 Voting Rights Act. Many of the arguments against the NVRA were alarmingly similar to those made 28 years earlier. This time, "states' rights" was replaced with "unfunded mandate" as the battle cry. The old strategy of the "nullification" of federal laws at the state level was replaced with "non-compliance," with the new "unfunded federal mandates."

Representative Swift and the House Democratic leadership, led by Representative Steny Hoyer, joined Conyers and the coalition in supporting the original House bill. A House-Senate conference committee would be the last resort to eliminate the bill for its opponents. House and Senate conferences were formed when each house of Congress passed a different version of a bill. In this instance, many of the key legislative players were named to the conference committee. On March 2, 1993, Conyers released a press statement that the upcoming House and Senate conference "must restore the bill to one of fairness and genuine reform. As it stands now, the Senate bill is turning back the clock and reestablishes the practice of second-class citizenship." Conyers blasted the Republican bill, stating that the House "must object to what the Senate has done on moral and constitutional grounds of equal protection under the law."

As voices of opposition grew, the Clinton administration, to everyone's surprise, announced its support of the Senate Republican bill. White House spokesperson Dee Dee Meyers was quoted in a news release as saying that the president, while wanting a better bill, would sign the Senate-passed version of motor voter. Republicans immediately jumped on the statement, claiming that their bill was now bipartisan. This statement was made immediately after the Senate vote before the bill reached the House floor and before the first phase of the negotiations with Republicans on the conference committee. If a Democratic president supported the Republican bill, it would receive enough support to win passage with no compromises. The White House endorsement greatly undermined our leverage in passing a better bill in conference. The result would be a major setback for voting rights.

Representative Conyers' response was to announce his opposition to the whole bill and urge the Congressional Black Caucus to join with Republicans in urging its defeat in the House. He threatened that he would reintroduce a new bill calling for Election Day Registration, abandon the motor voter concept altogether, and start over. I shared the congressman's frustration but counseled him that the move, while our last option, would be the end of the five-year effort to pass a comprehensive registration reform bill. Conyers reluctantly opted to request a seat on the conference committee as an alternative to completely opposing the bill and abandoning the effort. The committee was reserved for members of the two committees in the House and Senate: The House Administration Committee and the Rules Committee. He was a member of neither. Conyers appealed for a seat, noting his longstanding involvement with the bill and that the composition of the committee would be enhanced by a member of the Congressional Black Caucus being represented throughout the deliberations.

While waiting for a decision from Speaker Foley, I talked to Lorraine Miller, who was now in the White House Office of Legislative Affairs. She had been Speaker Foley's top staff on the bill and was now with the Clinton administration. She was familiar with the issues and had fought all the battles surrounding the motor voter bill. After a day of discussions with White House officials, Dee Dee Meyers issued a new statement that her comments were an off the cuff response to a question by a reporter. She clarified that yesterday's comments were only to convey that the president would sign the bill *if* a compromise could not be negotiated.

After days of trying to seek further clarification, we were finally able to speak with Tracy Thornton and Lorraine Miller from the White House Senate legislative office. They clarified the president's position on the Senate bill and made it clear that he believed that the bill was "insufficient" as passed by the Senate and should be improved in conference. To calm matters, President Clinton placed a call to Senator Ford, the Senate's bill manager, and expressed his "optimism" that the legislation would be improved in conference. Those actions lessened the damage caused by the original announcement, but time was running out.

We used the following days to marshal our forces in support of the House version before the conference began. After a meeting to brief members of the Congressional Black Caucus, we quickly gained the support of CBC Chairman Representative Kweisi Mfume and the entire Congressional Black Caucus. We also began negotiations with three targeted Republican staff from Senators Durenberger, Specter, and Packwood's offices. Once again, we were in search of the 60 votes needed to break the Republican filibuster in the Senate. These developments made our role and firmness in our position all the more critical to the bill's outcome.

Keeping Faith

Conyers had a disdain for the conference committee and the whole negotiations process. Like most congressional members, he attended only the first meeting, arriving late, and complaining the entire way over that the conference was a complete waste of time. He had little faith that the leadership of either party would come to an agreement on the bill. He was not going to aid and abet anything producing a bill that "set back voting rights 20 years." This was the cliché that many in the coalition and the Black Caucus used to describe the legislation's worst-case scenario.

When Conyers and I arrived at the conference committee meeting, the contrast of our presence was stark. There was a large oak table with thick binders for the congressional members of the conference. Overall, with staff, about 25 congressional staffers—over 20 men and only four women, all white—were crammed into the small conference room. Here we were, debating the issues of voting rights and civil rights, and we stood as the only two representatives of the African American community. Conyers sat in the meeting for less than 20 minutes, then grabbed his briefing book and headed toward the door. The committee chair, Al Swift, called out for Conyers and asked if he had any comments.

"Not particularly. You guys all know what the issues are," he said with thick sarcasm. "It's all there in your thick black notebooks. Let me know what you guys come up with." He grabbed the doorknob. "My guy's here." Conyers walked out and, on impulse, I got up and followed him out. We walked in silence for a minute when, suddenly, he stopped and turned around to me. "Where are you going?" he exclaimed as he handed me the big briefing book. "Get back in there!"

The dynamics of our situation now rested in the hands of 12 people who met as the bipartisan conference committee staff. There was little give on either side. The uncontested parts of the bill were motor voter, postcard registration, and a growing acceptance of the now four-year mandatory list cleaning requirement which was a generally agreed-upon change from the two-year provision that had originated in the House. However, suddenly, the narrative on the Republican side changed. Now the disagreements came out against the agency registration provisions, the purge for non-voting, and provisions that allowed the states to opt out of Election Day Registration.

Some members of the coalition were ready to concede the EDR. It had never been their thing to begin with and it had already been overshadowed by the other components. Besides, it was supported by only a handful of groups, mainly the Rainbow Coalition, CEF, ACORN, the Congressional Black Caucus, and USSA. Ironically, these were the groups that represented African American, low-income, and young voters, who all could benefit from the provision, as they had unstable addresses. Election Day Registration was the only immediate remedy for their transient addresses.

In the second round of talks, the EDR was withdrawn from the bill by agreement between Republicans and Democrats. Instead, the conference accepted the Simpson amendment, shutting the door to any other states that would want to take similar actions to convert to Same-Day Registration. In colorful language from his Wyoming roots, Simpson was rumored to have said that he did not want a "run of the farm," so he had to "shut the barn door" before there was a stampede of states running off to get out of the NVRA provisions by enacting Election Day Registration.

Through negotiations with both sides, the conference committee agreed to divide the language of the agency provisions into three or more parts so they would have to be voted on one by one separately rather than approved as a whole. It was a ploy to get one or more of the federally funded agencies that serviced unemployment centers, welfare offices, and social service agencies removed. Instead, they still insisted on adding hunting and fishing license and military recruitment centers—i.e., agencies that did not cater to minorities—to the list, to bring "more balance" to the bill. Both sides agreed to restore vocational rehabilitation centers that serviced the disabled as a mandatory agency. An agreement was made to accept one Republican agency and reject one Democratic agency. Military recruitment centers were added as a mandatory agency and unemployment centers were eliminated. Several more minor amendments were agreed upon. In the end, the final disagreements were over the elimination of welfare and public assistance agencies from the bill. In exchange for this elimination, the Republicans would allegedly agree to end their filibuster and support the bill as a whole.

We now faced a dilemma that was do or die. We needed an answer by a "last day" established by the committee to make a final decision. After that deadline, the bill would be "laid on the table" along with hundreds of other bills on which Congress had never been able to agree. The bill would essentially be dead and placed in the graveyard of good, intended conference committee bills that could not be reconciled between the two chambers—a common practice on Capitol Hill in the 102nd Congress. An informal staff whip count revealed that there were not enough votes in the Senate to pass the bill, even with the new agreements.

Members of the civil rights community added their voices of opposition to the passage of a bill without public assistance agencies. In addition, members of the CBC and a handful of liberal Democrats in the House and Senate threatened to vote against the bill if the agencies were not included in the final version. The conference staff negotiations took place during the recess, while the members were back in their respective districts. By phone, I briefed Congressman Conyers on where everything stood. I tried my best to remain optimistic even while other senior staff, including Julian Epstein, raised serious doubts that it would still be worth supporting the conference bill. Conyers argued that the bill had been weakened to a point where he questioned if it would benefit those it was designed to help the most. Both Julian and Conyers had all but given up hope of coming to any resolution.

"They get rid of Election Day Registration; they get rid of unemployment agencies, and they want *me* to support the bill?" Conyers railed over the phone, then signed off, never answering his own question. We were at a crossroads, and it was time for a reality check. After over five years of struggle, the question came down to this: Were we willing to accept a bill that had virtually everything we had asked for with two or three albeit major exceptions? Were we willing to forgo a chance to register an additional 7 to 10 million people who were on public assistance in exchange for the most comprehensive reform of voter registration laws in US history? What if Lani Guinier had been right years ago when she asserted that the bill could proportionally register more upperclass whites with driver's licenses than the low-income African Americans and Hispanics who would be less likely to own cars and have licenses?

We discussed all these issues to death and decided, as Conyers' staff, that we would have to choose one of the two options: have Conyers lead the floor fight against the watered-down Republican version of the bill or concede on the agencies and allow the bill to become law in a severely weakened version. The collective recommendation from the Judiciary Committee staff to Conyers was that the benefits of the bill were greater than the lingering demands on our side. It was decided that we should give up on the welfare offices in conference and, if necessary, all of the registration at public agencies to ensure we got the votes to get the remainder of the reforms through to final passage.

We divided responsibilities. Julian Epstein, Conyers' longtime staff director for the House Oversight Committee, who made the final call on most major staff decisions, informed the congressman and the House Democratic leadership of our recommendation. While I had argued for preserving the bill, I was distraught over the way we had to end the fight: by throwing in the towel on a provision that I thought was one of the most essential elements of the bill's benefits, allowing the registration of low-income voters of all colors, who had among the lowest voter registration rates.

"What's wrong now?" said committee counsel Perry Applebaum, who had read my sour mood at the meeting. Perry had argued for opposing the bill and having Conyers wage a full-scale floor fight against it. "This is what you wanted, isn't it?" I really didn't have a conclusive answer. I wanted to keep fighting to save the agency provisions, but I knew it might kill the whole effort. There were no good options in the end, and it was a hard call. Before I left the staff meeting, Julian pulled me aside and reminded me (again) that I was no longer a member of "one of those outside advocacy groups." "You are a lead congressional staffer of a key member of the House-Senate Conference Committee," he said. "This is the kind of decision that staff have to buck up and make." It was the only way to get things done in a divided government. I was instructed to inform the conference staff of our final concession to drop all the agencies from the bill and to report back to the committee and Conyers on their response.

I walked slowly to the conference meeting in the Capitol building. In all my years of working on the bill, I had never felt so depressed or defeated. We had worked hard and given it everything we had. It was a long way to travel to give up what I personally thought was one of the core principles of the bill. Removing this opportunity to register low-income people meant that Blacks, Hispanics, and even poor whites were also being disenfranchised—again. Low-income white women actually made up the majority of people on public assistance and would be the most affected by this change. They, like minority voters, would be disproportionately left out of the great promises of this bill to "expand our democracy." Instead of breaking down barriers, we were erecting new ones by removing all the agencies from the bill.

Suddenly, that old feeling came back: that feeling I'd had at the Cleveland Public Library when I turned 18 and first registered to vote. It was that feeling of the long, cold stare from the registrar when I asked for a voter registration card; the exact feeling I'd had at Ohio University at the office of the Athens County registrar, who told me that I was only a student and not a tax-paying citizen who was eligible to vote on campus. It was the same feeling I had after we had won one of the cloture votes by winning 60 votes, then losing after a Republican senator was pressured into changing his vote on the floor. It was the same feeling I'd had after President Bush vetoed the bill on July 3. All those experiences started the same way: with hard work and great optimism, only to end in great disappointment. The fundamental right to vote was once again being held back from millions of U.S. citizens—because of politics, the politics of exclusion. Here were members of Congress who should have been fighting for the right for inclusion in the political process. Instead, they were proving once again that in America, the right to vote was not a right but a privilege, *for the privileged.*

My walk over to the Capitol building began with sadness, which boiled over into anger and resentment the closer I got to the committee room. I did not want to be there. I wanted to be on the other side of the marble wall, to be one of the members of the motor voter coalition again, railing against Congress and its staff for not taking a stronger stand for democracy. That afternoon, I had gotten calls from Joanne Chasnow and Francis Fox Piven from Human Serve as well as members of the motor voter coalition. They had gotten wind that something was going wrong, and they wanted to weigh in. However, I could not bring myself to return their calls. I knew what we were about to do was wrong, and everybody on the conference committee staff knew it—on both sides. Instead of eliminating mandatory public agencies, we should have been *adding* mandatory agencies that served the public, like public schools, community colleges, universities, and homeless shelters, which served the most basic needs of the most disenfranchised of all.

Throughout American history, our government treated the right to vote like a prized possession of the U.S. Congress, granted and very selectively awarded to a limited number of Americans. For decades, other Congresses have clung to the status quo. They were fearful that any expansion of the electorate would be a quantum leap for them. On both sides, the instructions were clear: the smaller the electorate, the easier the path to re-election and maintaining control of the political levers of power in Washington and in state capitols across the U.S. NVRA was an actual threat to both political parties, I concluded, but more of a threat to Republicans, who were fearful of losing power with a new Democrat president and Congress.

Passing the full version of the bill we wanted would, in essence, mean that their congressional districts would become more representative of the actual population. Passage would dramatically expand the pool of eligible voters beyond the regular "likely voters" who currently made up their individual congressional districts. That was why they insisted on removing the provisions that would register more poor people, more young people, and more people of color. They demanded a mandatory list cleaning mechanism every two years so that they would be able to continue rotating people out of the system. If they were forced to make the voting system easier, they had to remove the provisions (the agencies) that would register the most disenfranchised. In essence, they coupled expanded voter registration reform with a more aggressive system to remove voters from the rolls. It was a major step forward and backward at the same time.

Suddenly, I began to see our entire effort in the most cynical light. This was the way the U.S. government had worked since its inception, to restrict the franchise and expand it only when forced to or during great moments of upheaval. Senator Simpson was right; there was no highly visible show of support for this bill. It was a miracle we had even gotten this far.

When I finally reached the committee room, I sat silently during most of the meeting. I knew that in the end, we had to give up, to concede and support the final agreement. I began to question in my mind: Is this what Congressman Conyers' 28-year legacy in Congress would come down to? Is this where Dr. King or Medgar Evers would have stopped and thrown in the towel? Wouldn't they have fought to the death? Didn't they, in fact, fight to the death? 1993 marked 25 years since the assassination of Martin Luther King, Jr., and 30 years since the assassination of Medgar Evers, who was gunned down in his front yard while trying to register Blacks in Jackson, Mississippi to vote. There could be no worse tribute to their legacy than to pass a weakened voter registration reform bill that did not empower the most unempowered people of our nation.

"I can't," I said faintly to myself as I sat at the table. I know there had to be another way out. My mumbling drew attention to me from the head of the negotiations. The staff were all veteran Capitol Hill staffers and here I was, with less than three months of Capitol Hill experience. "Who am I to even challenge them?" I asked myself.

"Where is Mr. Conyers?" they asked. I took their question literally.

"I don't know where he is. Somewhere in Detroit, I guess." My joke fell completely flat and was followed by some whispering among them.

"I mean, where is he on this bill?" the committee lead staffer clarified with impatience.

"I don't know," I said, trying to buy more time. "We're still waiting on his call back on our staff recommendations."

"Well, what's your staff recommendation?" they persisted.

There was dead silence in the room. I found myself at the edge of a table full of hard-nosed, seasoned staffers who were growing increasingly impatient with me and my stalling tactics. Before I could open my mouth to answer, two members of the Senate Conference Committee staff hurried in, nearly out of breath from the long walk over from the Senate. They had a message from Republican Senator Durenberger. He was willing to accept the agency language with a few minor language modifications. His request was a requirement that each agency application would have a series of questions that would ensure the applicant was not coerced into signing up for any parties as either Republican or Democrat. The changes were minor and preserved the integrity of the agency registration method, embracing all the Voting Rights Act protections built into the bill. Hard last-minute lobbying by Justin Dart, Jim Dixon, and the disability community had finally paid off after several months of lobbying the senator.

Another provision allowed states to opt out of the motor voter law by adopting Election Day Registration. Many smaller and Western states like Wyoming and New Hampshire chose to avoid the costs of implementing the provisions of the new law by establishing a weakened version of Election Day Registration and being waived out of the new NVRA federal obligations. Many of the same Republicans who had vehemently opposed Election Day Registration now claimed to support it as the only viable option releasing their states from the new federal mandates for the motor voter bill.

I quickly agreed to both provisions "in principle" without waiting for word from committee staff or Conyers on the original decision to give up the agencies. It was a better deal than we had ever imagined. No one on that committee knew at the time that we, at least as a staff, had been prepared to give up the entire agency provision to save the bill. Had Senator Durenberger's staff person not walked in at that precise moment, we would have lost those provisions or, even worse, failed to come up with an agreement and sent the NVRA once again to a sudden and final death. Instead, the breakthrough we had sought was here. In the end, it was the disability community who had saved the day with their extra push.

During this time, virtually all of the leading members of the motor voter coalition had been working on the members of the conference from behind the scenes. Eddie Hails, Mary Brooks, Lloyd Leonard, Sonia Jarvis, and Marsha Adler from People for the American Way, Ron Jackson from the Urban League, and Ralph Neas, Jim Dixon, and other leaders of the motor voter coalition had . been holding a round of non-stop meetings with key staff members in the House and Senate. Once news of the Durenberger breakthrough spread, coalition co-chairs Eddie Hailes and Mary Brooks convened the coalition for deliberations at the League of Women Voters office. After an intense exchange that included a firm "this is it, guys" reality check from longtime League of Women Voters lobbyist Lloyd Leonard, the coalition quickly signed off on the final version including the new Durenberger language. Even the civil rights groups, i.e., the NAACP, the Urban League, and the National Coalition on Black Voter Participation, signed off on the bill, as did Rev. Jackson (after some coaxing from me). The NAACP Legal Defense Fund (LDF) was the last holdout. As potential future litigators, they remained silent on the final version of the bill, but in essence withdrew their vocal opposition.

For his part, Conyers was frustrated with the entire process and was ready to move on. It was still the first 100 days of a new Democratic president and there were many other bills to get to. I knew deep down that he preferred to have his original bill H.R. 17 as the vehicle. The whole effort left a bad taste in his mouth. However, he was one of the principal sponsors of the Voting Rights Act in 1965 and now the NVRA over 30 years later. It was a milestone for him and for all of us who had worked for years to get to this point. He released a statement in support of the bill and verbally expressed his support at the Democratic Caucus and congressional leadership meetings—something he had never done throughout the entire process. This sent a signal to all his colleagues on the Judiciary Committee and the CBC that this conference committee version was now the final version and had his full support.

The compromise Conference Report was renamed the *National Voter Registration Act of 1993* and passed by the U.S. House of Representatives 259–164 on May 5, 1993. Ninety minutes later, the US Senate took up the newly passed conference report where it passed 62–36 on a bi-partisan basis.[8] The nearly six-year legislative battle since we first began advocating for reform in late 1986 had finally come to an end. That night, the supporters of the bill all went home late, after the vote, too fatigued to even celebrate. That night, I found myself alone in my office at the Rayburn Building on Capitol Hill. It was suddenly so quiet, with no one moving around except the clean-up crews and Capitol Police. No more meetings, no more bells ringing, and no more negotiations over various provisions of the bill. The long fight was over. That old feeling finally began to dissipate. It was now all over but the bill signing. A major promise of our democracy to ensure the right to vote for all its citizens was moving closer to being fulfilled.

The Clinton White House had decided to do a major bill signing in the Rose Garden on May 20, 1993, to mark one of the administration's first legislative accomplishments. Instead of a small gathering of legislators and the president, it would be a big event open to all the bill's major stakeholders, held under a big tent on the South Lawn, complete with color guards, the uniformed Navy band, and all the ruffles and flourishes. The invitation list included everyone who had anything to do with civil rights or voting rights—over 250 participants. The speak-

---

8 "Actions – H.R.2 – 103rd Congress (1993 – 1994): National Voter Registration Act of 1993," Congress.gov, (1993) accessed March 22, 2022, https://www.congress.gov/bill/103rd-congress/house-bill/2/all-actions?overview=closed#tabs.

ers included Conyers, Representative Al Swift, Senator Wendell Ford, Senator Mark Hatfield, Speaker Tom Foley, and Assistant Majority Whip Stenny Hoyer. It also included key members of the President's Cabinet including former DNC Chair and now Commerce Secretary Ron Brown, Labor Secretary Alexis Herman, and Patrick Lippert, the energetic leader from Rock the Vote, who had courageously fought for passage of the NVRA within the entertainment industry. He was able to make the trip from Los Angeles for the ceremony despite his ongoing health challenges and courageous battle against AIDS.

On our ride over from the Capitol to the White House for the ceremony, Conyers mentioned his trip to attend the signing of the Voting Rights Act in 1965. He spoke of being one of only five African American members of Congress back then. He recalled how he had been one of the young lawyers from Detroit whom President Kennedy had chosen to form the Lawyers Committee for Civil Rights Under Law. He would use this experience to run for Congress in 1964 as a young civil rights lawyer and activist. Twenty-nine years later, he was riding over to the White House again, this time as chair of the U.S. Congress' Government Operations Committee and co-sponsor of another historic voting rights bill.

The day was not without some major glitches. Logistical security issues turned into major protocol problems. Elaine Jones from the NAACP Legal Defense and Education Fund had not been cleared for entrance into the ceremony and was forced to stand outside the gates for several minutes before the signing. Rev. Jackson's name had been mysteriously left off, as had the names of Coretta Scott King and Medgar Evers' widow, Meryle Evers, who had come to Washington amid a major legal battle to convict the murderer of her slain husband. Conyers made note of their absence in his remarks. To know that they were somewhere hovering around the White House, on the other side of the fence, put a damper on what should have been a joyous occasion.

I wanted an opportunity to shake the new president's hand as he walked out of the ceremony but was constantly pushed back by the press of the crowd. As I watched the motor voter coalition members line up behind the president for an official photo, on impulse, I moved toward them to get in the photo. However, Conyers was ready to go, and I was driving my car, which was allowed to park in the big horseshoe driveway in front of the White House. Another committee staff member motioned for me to come on, as the congressman was waiting on me to leave. "Besides," he said, looking at me glaring at all my friends lining up for the photo, "you're not a member of the coalition anymore."

Like the absence of the three women civil rights legends, I left feeling that it was a glaring omission that I didn't get a chance to get in the picture or shake the president's hand at the event, or to spend time with the motor voter coalition on a day we had all worked so hard for years to see. But they deserved all the specials that they were receiving. After over six years of demanding work for many of them, they deserved it! We all did.

As fate would have it, I got another chance a few months later. I was in a reception line for an event during Louisiana Day at the White House as a guest of Minyon Moore, my old friend from the Rainbow Coalition and now DNC Chief of Staff. This time, I got in the reception line to greet the president and First Lady Hillary Clinton. When the time came to take our picture, I re-introduced myself, as this was the first time, I had seen him since our encounter at the Rainbow Conference in 1992, before he was president. After the quick pose for the official snapshot photo, I stole a quick conversation.

"Mr. President, I want to thank you for signing the motor voter bill. I worked on that bill with a lot of other people for almost six years."

"Six years?" he exclaimed with a laugh as he shook my hand. "That's great! You all who worked on it for six years did all the work. Hell, all I did was just sign the bill!"

"But Bush vetoed the bill," I reminded him. "If you weren't elected president, none of this would have ever become law."

"We need both," he said. He turned to shake the next hand, then turned back to me and paused for a moment. "Six years?" he said, shaking his head almost in disbelief. He then walked a step forward and raised his hand in the air for a high five. I immediately responded and slapped his hand. It was followed by a firm, full palm handshake in the air and a slap on my shoulders. "Good work, man!" he said, followed by "And congratulations!" from Hillary Clinton, who had a warm smile on her face. It was the congratulations that I hadn't heard on the day the bill was passed or signed at the Rose Garden. It was not customary for staff members to take too much credit for a bill passing in a congressional office. Therefore, the acknowledgment and congratulations from the president and first lady meant a lot to me, as it was one of the few times, I had heard the words in that difficult period. Much of the work I had done was behind the scenes and behind two well-known leaders—Jesse Jackson and Congressman Conyers—for whom I had worked over those five and a half years. We all played a significant role and the nexus of our commitment to voting rights came together as we did our part to push forward this important piece of legislation.

I again made my way to the reception area and was out the door in five minutes. With the signing of the bill, the fight to enact the NVRA was now complete. It was also the moment when I finally reconciled all my issues with Bill Clinton, the politician I had met and worked against a year ago on the campaign trail. To me, he had made up for my misgivings about him by signing the bill I had fought so hard to pass for years. He may not have understood what he was even saying, but by signing the bill, as President of the United States, he had become a critical component of our coalition's longtime effort to pass the bill into law after a veto by now-former President George H.W. Bush a year earlier.

Once again, I found myself walking alone, this time in front of the White House on Pennsylvania Avenue instead of the Capitol grounds, as I had done the night that Congress finally passed the bill. After seeing several empty cabs drive right past me a couple of blocks from the White House, I decided to take the long walk back up Pennsylvania Avenue to my congressional office in the Rayburn Building on Capitol Hill. I couldn't stop thinking about all the work that had gone into passing this bill—from my first meeting in the fall of 1987 while working with Jesse Jackson through the passage in the spring of 1993 while working with Congressman Conyers. I thought about how both these great, legendary, yet imperfect leaders had gone the extra mile to make the right to vote a centerpiece of their life work. I thought about Rev. Jackson from his work with Operation PUSH and with Dr. King and SCLC earlier and about Congressman Conyers, one of the original co-sponsors of the Voting Rights Act of 1965 and now a lead sponsor of the NVRA. Toward the end of that long walk back to the Capitol that night, I thought how blessed I was to be part of both these leaders' historic efforts. For a fleeting moment, I almost felt that fate had placed me in these key slots during the most critical times to help push this new landmark bill through the legislative process.

The new law was not designed to take effect until January 1, 1995, so I knew that it would be almost two years before the bill would be fully implemented. It seemed like a long time to wait. However, I was glad that we had made the extra push to give ourselves and the states the time they needed to get ready for the critical implementation. I knew there was still a lot of opposition to the new law in the states but didn't realize the extent to which the Republicans and opponents who fought it would find a way to continue resisting its effective implementation at the state level in the coming years. That would be the battle to come, but for those first few months of 1993, I felt like the country had taken a major step toward fulfilling one of the key promises of our democracy.

Most ironic of all was that an unassuming Black kid from Cleveland, Ohio, who had become a struggling student at Ohio University, had been part of making the effort a reality. Little did I know at the time that my work was far from over. Much was to be done to ensure that the NVRA was fully implemented at the state level. Also, even more work was to be done to develop mechanisms for utilizing the new provisions and thereby ensure that Black and disenfranchised voters were registered and mobilized to vote in the months and years to come. The phase of our work to reform voter laws was coming to an end, but the work to ensure proper implementation of the new law was far from over.

Many of these barriers have been deconstructed through the passage and enforcement of the Voting Rights Act of 1965. Even after amendments in 1975 and 1982, turnout levels continued to drop. By the 1990s, the struggle had continued moving from voting rights to voter registration reform and electoral reforms. When we looked at the statistics from 1992, we saw that the US had a 55% voter turnout according to the study by the Committee for the Study of the Electorate—a high-water mark since the initial passage of the Voting Rights Act.[9] Yet, The US rank 30 out of the 35 of the leading democracies in voter turnout, one of the lowest percentages among industrialized nations [10]

The numbers had been dropping precipitously since the expansion of the eligible pool of voters in 1972. In the first election since the passage of the 26th Amendment, granting 18-year-olds the right to vote, the turnout rate was 55.4%[11] In 1976, the overall turnout was slightly lower at 54% according to the US Census.[12] In 1980, it dropped even further down to 52.8%, and by the 1988 presidential elections, turnout just barely made it over the halfway point of 50.16%.[13] Were those trends of low voter participation allowed to continue, it would not be long before the US would no longer be considered the beacon of the greatest and most thriving democracy. With the declining trends in voter registration and turnout, it was conceivable that the US would drop below the 50% mark, meaning that less than half of the nation was participating. In fact, that *was* the case in 1996, when only 49% of US citizens voted, the lowest level of participation ever recorded in a presidential election since 1924.[14]

Had current trends continued without the intervention passage of the NVRA in 1993, by 2000 the United States would have been one of the most undemocrat-

---

9 Jerry T. Jennings, "Voting and Registration in the Election of November 1992," U.S. Bureau of the Census, (1993) accessed March 22, 2022, https://www.census.gov/library/publications/1993/demo/p20-466.html.

10 Drew Desilver, "In past elections, U.S. trailed most developed countries in voter turnout," Pew Research Center, last modified November 3, 2020, https://www.pewresearch.org/fact-tank/2020/11/03/in-past-elections-u-s-trailed-most-developed-countries-in-voter-turnout/.

11 Erin Duffin, "Youth voter turnout in presidential elections in the U.S. 1972–2020," statista, last modified March 19, 2021, https://www.statista.com/statistics/984745/youth-voter-turnout-presidential-elections-us/.

12 "Voting and Registration in the Election of November 1976," U.S. Bureau of the Census, (1978) accessed March 22, 2022, https://www.census.gov/content/dam/Census/library/publications/1978/demo/p20-322.pdf.

13 Richard L. Berke, "50.16% Voter Turnout Was Lowest Since 1924," The New York Times, (1988) accessed March 22, 2022, https://www.nytimes.com/1988/12/18/us/50.16-voter-turnout-was-lowest-since-1924.html.

14 "1996 United States presidential election," Wikipedia, last modified March 18, 2022, https://en.wikipedia.org/wiki/1996_United_States_presidential_election.

ic nations in the world in terms of voter participation. By 1996, after only one year, the NVRA barely had time to make an impact on registration rates. With less than half of the nation participating in elections, the United States could no longer lay claim on the international stage to the title of the world's leading democracy. In truth, the disenfranchisement of major portions of the US population throughout most of American history had made such a claim questionable from the very beginning.

The NVRA was not a magic bullet. It did not solve all the problems with voter registration and political empowerment. It's even fair to say that it might have created new ones. But the legislation's intent and direction can be compared to sledgehammers breaking against the Berlin Wall that took place in 1989, the same year the NVRA was first introduced. Beyond the Voting Rights Act, the NVRA cut through many centuries of oppression and political disenfranchisement. Even after its passage there would be many roadblocks related to full compliance with NVRA's various provisions that would continue throughout the early years following its passage.

Chapter 9
The States' Resistance and the Battle for Compliance

After passage of the NVRA bill in the late spring of 1993, the need to build and maintain the motor voter coalition began to diminish. It was no longer necessary to continue meeting and spending hours trying to hold things together. The movement to reform voter registration laws at the federal level had come to an end; now it was time to move on to other struggles and legislative battles. The implementation stage would now begin, and it became necessary to place more emphasis on how states would implement the law and comply with its provisions.

The cries of the NVRA being an unfunded mandate never subsided. More and more conservative state governors and legislatures began dragging their feet in enacting the major provisions of the new law. Departments of motor vehicles and boards of election were quite separate and distinct and very independent of each other. Many state and county election officials saw the motor voter law as intrusive and as the federal government's means of trampling on the rights of states to conduct their own elections—especially state and local elections. To many of them, the NVRA was a nuisance and should never have been enacted into law. Because it was an unfunded mandate without federal funding, they resisted efforts to implement it at several levels. I clearly understood why the coalition resisted efforts to include funding in the final version of the new law. One of the most utilized weapons that opponents used to kill the implementation of laws was simply not funding them. Opponents would continue to use this against the bill for years to come. In some states, like California, Illinois, Louisiana, Mississippi and South Carolina, there were strident rebukes of the law, with Republican governors like Pete Wilson of California, Mike Foster of Louisiana, and Kirk Fordice of Mississippi filing lawsuits in federal court to halt the NVRA's implementation in their states.[1]

Even the Clinton White House was reluctant to carry a big stick when it came to enforcement. The administration's White House domestic advisor, Bruce Reed, raised reservations toward any plan that would place pressure on the states to carry out the law. Clinton had run as a new Democrat who believed in "triangu-

---

1 "Young v. Fordice (95–2031), 520 U.S. 273 (1997)," Legal Information Institute – Cornell Law School, (n.d.) accessed March 22, 2022, https://www.law.cornell.edu/supct/html/95-2031.ZO.html.

https://doi.org/10.1515/9783110742473-012

lation," which required showing independence from traditional liberal Democratic orthodoxy. This passive resistance also seeped into the Clinton Justice Department, which was very slow to take evasive action against states that openly refused to enforce the new law at the state level. The last thing the Clinton White House wanted was for its administration to be seen actively suing governors and states that it might need in the 1996 re-election campaign.

As the midterm elections of 1994 took form, Clinton's popularity began to plummet among independent and moderate voters. After being a champion of some core Democratic issues like the motor voter bill, the Brady "handgun control" bill, and a national single-payer health care system, he began moving away from the more progressive issues and embraced more core blue collar issues like tough-on-crime measures ("three strikes and you're out") increased mandatory minimum sentences, the expansion of the death penalty, and scaling back affirmative action programs through "mend it, don't end it" proposals.[2] As a result of all the focus on the politics surrounding the upcoming 1994 elections, voting rights groups took the initiative to file litigation to exert pressure on state legislators to comply with all the provisions of the NVRA. Advocacy groups quietly raised concerns at the lack of aggressive action by the Department of Justice, (DOJ) in defending the new law against recalcitrant states during the most critical early periods after passage. Meanwhile opponents of the NVRA were also active in litigation, led by two major conservative groups, *Judicial Watch* and *True the Vote*. They were critical of the lack of action by the DOJ in pushing states to comply with the more controversial mandatory list cleaning provisions.[3]

Many members of the motor voter coalition worked hard with local affiliates to pass implementation legislation at the state level, with varying degrees of success. The leading voting rights groups initiating litigation included Project Vote/ACORN, the ACLU, the Lawyers Committee for Civil Rights Under Law, the NAACP Legal Defense Fund, and in later years, the Advancement Project, Common Cause, and a variety of disability groups. Most of these efforts were quiet legal and administrative battles that took place in half empty state legislative committee rooms or meetings of state and local election boards. Like the motor voter national effort these compliance efforts received little to no press or media cover-

---

2 Bruce F. Nesmith and Paul J. Quirk, "Triangulation: Positioning and Leadership in Clinton's Domestic Policy" in *42: Inside the Presidency of Bill Clinton*, ed. Michael Nelson, Barbara A. Perry, and Russell L. Riley (Ithaca: Cornell University Press, 201).
3 J. Christian Adams, "Legal Memorandum: A Primer on "Motor Voter": Corrupted Voter Rolls and the Justice Department's Selective Failure to Enforce Federal Mandates," The Heritage Foundation, last modified September 25, 2014, http://thf_media.s3.amazonaws.com/2014/pdf/LM139.pdf.

age either local or nationally in the early years of its implementation. The stories of ongoing Republican opposition or the courageous forward-moving democracy reform advocacy were largely hidden from public view despite the importance of these efforts to the early success of the new law.

As more lawsuits were filed, it became clear that this bill might suffer from some of the same problems that confronted the Voting Rights Act of 1965 in its early years. A young, ambitious lawyer and Director of Project Vote in Chicago, Barack Obama, was one of the many local attorneys who worked with allied groups to take legal action against Illinois Governor Jim Thompson after he vetoed the NVRA state implementation bill that the Illinois legislature had passed.[4] After long, drawn-out litigation with civil rights attorneys and voting rights advocates, Mississippi, Illinois and other opposing states began to lose their cases as the federal courts ruled in support of the constitutionality of the new motor voter law.[5] The success of the early implementation litigation was centered around ensuring states legislatures passed, and governors signed enabling legislation to bring state laws in compliance with the new federal mandates. Once this threshold had been met, it would open the floodgates of administrative and litigation battles across the US over various provisions of the new law. Most litigation centered around the intent and definition of the list cleaning and maintenance restrictions, compliance with the public agency components, the enforcement and timing of voter purges, photo ID requirements, and post card registration guidelines for non-profit groups undertaking voter registration efforts.[6]

The Republican cries of the NVRA being an unfunded mandate filtered down to the implementation plans at the local level. Departments of motor vehicles and boards of election were quite separate and distinct and very independent of each other. Many state and county election officials were repeatedly told by Republican lawmakers that the motor voter law was intrusive, a way for the federal government to trample on the rights of states to conduct their own elections —especially state and local elections. To many of them, the NVRA was a nuisance and should never have been passed into law, without federal funding. They resisted efforts to implement it at several levels. Even Moderate Republican Gover-

---

4 Stephanie Strom, "On Obama, Acorn and Voter Registration," The New York Times, last modified October 10, 2008, https://www.nytimes.com/2008/10/11/us/politics/11acorn.html.

5 "Young v. Fordice (95 – 2031), 520 U.S. 273 (1997)," Legal Information Institute – Cornell Law School, (n.d.) accessed March 22, 2022, https://www.law.cornell.edu/supct/html/95-2031.ZO.html.

6 "Case 3:11-cv-00470-JJB -DLD," Justice.gov, last modified July 12, 2011, http://www.justice.gov/crt/about/vot/nvra/la_nvra_comp.pdf.

nor 'Jim' Thompson of Illinois supported lawsuits in federal court to halt NVRA's implementatio. Strident rebukes of the law were led by conservative Republican Governors like Pete Wilson of California, Mike Foster of Louisiana and Kirk Fordice of Mississippi, all supporting lawsuits in federal court to halt the NVRA's implementation.[7]

With even some Democratic controlled federal agencies beginning to drag their feet on implementation planning, advocacy groups stepped up their calls for a more robust action by the administration to push NVRA implementation plans. With the NVRA January 1, 1995, effective date rapidly approaching, the DNC General Counsel's office led by Joe Sandler, and my DNC Office of Voter Registration and Participation weighed in and made repeated requests to the administration's political and legislative affairs offices to take some definitive executive action. Finally, on September 12, 1995, President Clinton convened voting rights advocates including members of the motor voter coalition to the Oval Office. To demonstrate the administration's determination to fully enforce the new law, he signed an Executive Order #12962 that directed *"departments, agencies and other entities under the executive branch of the Federal Government to cooperate with the states in carrying out the Act's requirements."*[8] This unprecedented executive order would direct all departments (including the Justice Department) to accelerate their efforts regarding the NVRA law. It was also a clear signal to Republican governors to end their resistance to the NVRA law and work with the federal government to pass enabling legislation to ensure its full implementation before the January 1, 1995, effective date.

In an act of open defiance of increased federal pressure, California Governor Pete Wilson categorically refused to enforce the law. He filed a countersuit against the federal government, claiming "states' rights" to resist federal government intrusion. His resistance took place during the gap between passage in May of 1993 and the implementation start date of January 1, 1995. Other Republican governors would follow with similar legal or administrative actions including Michigan Governor John Engler, after signing the motor voter bill passed by the General Assembly, signed an executive order virtually prohibiting state agencies from spending any resources on implementing the bill.[9] Governor Carroll Campbell of South Carolina, in a farewell gesture on his last day in office, vetoed

---

7 See Kurtis A. Kemper, Annotation, Validity, Construction and Application of National Voter Registration Act, 185 A.L.R.Fed. 155 (2003)

8 William Jefferson Clinton, "Statement on the Implementation of the National Voter Registration Act of 1993," Govinfo, (1994) accessed March 22, 2022, https://www.govinfo.gov/content/pkg/WCPD-1994-09-19/pdf/WCPD-1994-09-19-Pg1758-2.pdf.

9 DNC Office of Voter Registration and Participation Memo to DNC General Counsel

the motor voter state compliance bill. His successor, Governor David Beasley, followed Wilson's lead by filing a new lawsuit in state court challenging the statute[10].

Mississippi: Continuing a Legacy of Resistance

Although advocacy groups litigation was labor intensive and time consuming for litigators, they were ultimately successful in pushing back against the resistance in states that opposed implementation. One of the states which I traveled to support key leaders fighting the compliance battle was Mississippi. With the Mississippi State Assembly's failure to pass NVRA-enabling legislation in 1994, Democratic Secretary of State Dick Molpus courageously began to administratively implement a provisional implementation plan for the new motor voter provisions of the law, in defiance of the sitting governor and legislature. In just over 5 weeks, over 4,000 voters had been registered in the state's motor voter agencies alone.[11] Then, on February 10, 1995, Mississippi's Republican governor, Kirk Fordice, a vocal opponent of the 1965 Voting Rights Act, brought an abrupt halt to the five-week effort by ordering Department of Motor Vehicles and election officials to stop administrative implementation of the bill. As a result, the Republican chair of the Mississippi Senate Election Committee tabled a bill that would have made NVRA registrations valid for all elections in Mississippi. The House Committee followed suit and withdrew its enabling legislation pending the end result of federal litigation. Fordice's and the legislators' actions threw Mississippi back into the familiar role of the nation's leading defender of states' rights. Mississippi would become the last state to maintain a dual system of registration: one for state elections and a separate one for federal elections.[12] The question of whether Mississippi's new NVRA compliance provisions required VRA preclearance set off a volley of litigation between the Department of Justice and the state of Mississippi. After over two years of legal challenges in the federal courts, the issue was not finally resolved until March 31, 1997, when the US Supreme Court issued a ruling that confirmed that Mississippi's NVRA enabling legislation did indeed require VRA pre-clearance.[13]

---

10 Ibid.
11 "Young v. Fordice (95–2031), 520 U.S. 273 (1997)," Legal Information Institute – Cornell Law School, (n.d.) accessed March 22, 2022, https://www.law.cornell.edu/supct/html/95-2031.ZO.html.
12 Ibid.
13 Ibid.

In one other case, in Louisiana, the U.S. Justice Department had refused to pre-clear the NVRA implementation plan that the legislature had submitted. The provision in violation was a requirement for new voters to provide photo identification, a procedure that the NVRA prohibited. Implementation efforts were frozen pending action by the legislature to amend their plan. NVRA advocates in the legislature declared that they lacked the votes to pass the plan without this provision. A stalemate ensued for months while the legislature, governor, secretary of state, and Justice Department battled back and forth. Both Mississippi and Louisiana had statewide governors' races in 1995 which would be dramatically impacted by the success of the implementation efforts. Had the NVRA provision gone through and been implemented properly, tens of thousands of new voters would have been registered in both states within a matter of months.[14]

Much like the 1992 elections which were watershed, the 1994 midterm elections ushered in an even more dramatic seismic political shift. The 1992 elections had been the first year of implementation of the 1982 amendments to the Voting Rights Act. The new Redistricting lines had been drawn in 1991 that created scores of congressional districts that were much more favorable to Black and Brown communities. The 1994 elections were the first test to see if those electoral gains would last. Once again, the strength of the VRA would be tested to see whether the reforms of 1982 and the congressional gains of Majority Minority districts in the election of 1992 could be sustainable. For all we knew the gains could have been a one-time blimp on the screen that was tied to the turnout of the 1992 presidential elections.

The prospects for Democrats maintaining control of the Senate began to fall as the President's popularity continued to plummet along with the approval ratings of the Democratic controlled Congress. As chair of a major committee working on several major initiatives, John Conyers began to grow worried that much of what we were working on would be threatened by the loss of the House of Representatives to the Republicans. He and his committee had much on the line: 1) A major new initiative invoking environmental justice programs into the Environmental Protection Agency, EPA and other relevant agencies, 2) the continuation of "Re-inventing Government" programs being spearheaded by Vice President Al Gore that was pushing for a more advance expansion of the "world wide web" or what would come to be known as "the internet", and 3) enhanced major reforms to the telecommunications regulations in both government and private industry. The other major initiative was a long-negotiated minority set aside program for the Department of Defense that had been quietly

---

14 DNC Office of Voter Registration and Participation Memo to DNC General Counsel

negotiated for months behind the scenes with the Joint Chiefs of Staff, General Colin Powell. The program would serve as a model for a proposed government wide set aside of 10% for minority contracting. It was being quietly negotiated in light of recent controversies over Affirmative Action. With a federal budget of over One Trillion Dollars, it would have been the largest Minority set aside program ever.

As Conyers and I talked more and more about what was at stake he concluded that the Democratic Party, which was struggling to mobilize Black voters, needed my help in the elections more than he did on Capitol Hill. It was late in the cycle, but I agreed that at this point it was all hands-on deck. I took a leave from Conyers Staff and took up short term work for the Democratic Congressional Campaign Committee (DCCC) which was being run at the time by Executive Director David Pluff, and Political Director Cathy Duval. They recruited Donna Brazile who was D.C. Delegate Eleanor Holmes Norton's Chief of Staff. Donna and I worked together in a small office on the 2nd floor of the DNC, using all our past expertise to try and boost African American GOTV efforts in key battleground states.

I was assigned the key states of Ohio, Michigan, Virginia, North Carolina, and Georgia. In taking on these states, I was able to resurrect many of my skills and contacts from the Jackson Campaigns but found that it was a tough sell in a year without a major popular political figure leading the effort. Donna and I both stayed glued to our phones with multiple strategy meetings with Pluff and Deval in between. However, I did get a chance to go into Virginia for the last two weeks once the DCCC emptied out their offices in Washington to send staff out to all the most important battle ground states.

In Virginia, the very vulnerable US Senator Chuck Robb was facing a fierce challenge from former Lt. Cornel Oliver North who had garnered support from a wide array of evangelicals and even some conservative Democrats across the state. Only a massive turnout of Black Voters could prevent what many pundits viewed as a race that favored Oliver North. The key to that effort was Congressman Bobby Scott and his political operation. Scott had just been elected in a Southeastern VA Congressional District in 1992. Scott's efforts were led by his chief of Staff Joni Ivy and Cynthia Downs-Taylor, a Hampton Roads NAACP activist, and former field staffer during my days at the Citizenship Education Fund. With only meager resources they were able to mobilize African American Clergy, students at Hampton University, Virginia Union, and other campuses along with several local Black Elected Officials.

The effort also targeted Black Veterans in the highly concentrated Norfolk Navy Yards, led by Wallace Williams who was the national President of the Black Vets of America. We had both drove down together from DC to give it everything we had for the last few days before the election. Our efforts would prove successful with some of the best mobilization of the campaign. We were ecstatic on election night as the results from Richmond's election headquarters came in. The turnout from Rep. Scott's new Majority Minority district was overwhelming. Additionally, high numbers from "yellow dog democrats" in Northern and Southwest Virginia turned out and made a major difference in other VA counties across the state. In a race that was considered a tossup by political pundits, Senator Chuck Robb was re-elected to another term, defeating Oliver North 45.6 to 42. 8% in a political upset.[15]

Excited by our big victory in Virginia, Wallace and I started our trip back to DC. We tuned into National Public Radio (NPR) for news of what was happening in other states. To our shock Democrats were being blown away in a major Republican title wave that was taking place across the nation. State by state began to report their results with 10, 20, 30 and soon over 40 Democratic seats being reported as lost from the time we left Norfolk till we entered Washington, DC. By the time we got back to the DNC headquarters it was all but over.

We rushed into the DNC war room ready to report our victory in Virginia, only to find the faces of our DNC and DCCC colleagues' cake white with a look of fear that I had never seen before. They were all huddled in rooms staring at the Television monitors that were reporting that Democrats had already lost control of the US Senate and could even lose the House of Representatives that they had controlled for over 40 years. They were waiting on the results from California, Washington state, and Oregon on the west coast where polls were just closing. They were all hanging on to the hope that those three strong democratic states would pull them out of the nightmare with so many Democratic seats losses in every other region of the country. But when the results finally came in well past midnight, there was no west coast exemption from this red political tidal wave. Everyone knew it had all come to an end when even the sitting Speaker of the House of Representatives Tom Foley was defeated in what was considered a very safe Washington State democratic seat. After over 40 years, Republicans now controlled both houses of Congress for the first time since Reconstruction in the aftermath of the civil war. The reign of the Democratic Party in Congress was over, with Democrats losing a record 54 seats in one night![16]

---

15 "1994 United States Senate election in Virginia," Wikipedia, last modified October 13, 2021, https://en.wikipedia.org/wiki/1994_United_States_Senate_election_in_Virginia.
16 "1994 United States House of Representatives elections," Wikipedia, last modified February 16, 2022, https://en.wikipedia.org/wiki/1994_United_States_House_of_Representatives_elections.

The lower-than-expected Black turnout across the country was cited as one of the contributing factors in the Democratic party's massive loss. Ironically however, none of the newly established Majority-Minority seats were impacted.[17] They had withstood the Republican title wave and the VRA reforms of 1982 had proven to be sustainable. It was the only good news of the 1994 elections. Nonetheless, Democratic leaders at the DCCC blamed the loss in part on new Majority-Minority Black districts that concentrated Black voters into a number of districts particularly in the south.[18] They also cited a lower-than-expected Black voter turnout for the loss while at the same time failing to admit that their late and last-minute Black Voter mobilization effort may have been simply too little and too late. They also failed to factor in the issue focus of the party over the last two years: the 1994 Crime bill and the weakening of affirmative action and welfare reform. They also underestimated the impact of long-term economic inequities and the accelerated unemployment levels that continued to plague their communities. They were all issues that I believed contributed to the depressed Black voter turnout. The highly acclaimed Bill Clinton Political Operation that had claimed to appeal to moderate Democrats failed to pull their weight in mobilizing those voters in support of the President's new initiatives.

As I went home that night, I realized that the work that we had undertaken last year to pass the NVRA in 1993 in the first year of the administration was critical to the future of voting rights. Had we waited till after the 1994 elections as some had suggested, it would never have been passed into law. In fact, many of the initiatives that Conyers had declared were at stake were now all either legislatively dead or at risk of being stalled including the 10% Minority Set aside package that was ready to go to the floor for a vote the following January.

As I prepared to go back to my job on the hill, the party leaders begin to pick up the pieces and asked me to stay on to help the DNC restructure its political operation. They elevated former Jackson Operative and my good friend Minyon Moore to Political Director, the first African American to ever hold that job. Minyon asked me to be a part of her leadership team as Deputy Political Director along with a longtime DNC operative, Maureen Garde She also offered for me to become the Director of the recently established DNC Office of Voter Registration and Participation with Alison McLaurin who served as the deputy director. It was the same office that Rev. Jackson's campaign had helped create by making it one of their demands of the party following the 1988 campaign.

---

17 Steve A. Holmes, "The 1994 Election: Voters; Did Racial Redistriction Undermine Democrats," The New York Times, (1994) accessed March 22, 2022, https://www.nytimes.com/1994/11/13/us/the-1994-election-voters-did-racial-redistricting-undermine-democrats.html.
18 Ibid.

The party agreed that I could bring my strong commitment to voter registration to the new job and help the party develop a more cohesive voter outreach program in the aftermath of the 1994 election. I did not say yes automatically. January 1, 1995, would usher in the first year of NVRA's implementation and I was worried about not being back on the hill to help oversee these efforts. After some coaxing, Minyon and party leaders agreed that I could continue my work on the Motor Voter Implementation by helping to coordinate the Democratic Party's efforts in states where there was strong resistance from Republican Governors.

Conyers was at first closed to the idea of my staying at the DNC and extending my leave of absence to a full departure. But he had lost his chairmanship of the House Government Affairs (Oversite) Committee along with 22 other senior CBC members who lost the opportunity to be chairs or sub-committee chairs of key congressional committees. They had all lost confidence that the party had its act together. Congressional Black Caucus (CBC) members overall were equally worried that party leaders had poorly managed the 1994 midterm elections and may not have things in place in time for the upcoming presidential elections in 1996. To Conyers, my staying at the DNC and helping them pull things together was worth it to him. He said he believed I would add value to whatever efforts were being reconfigured at the national party and referenced our win in Virginia against the national trend.

Given what was at stake, I agreed to stay on at the DNC and shift my focus full time to the party's rebuilding efforts. However, I readily offered to come back to Capitol Hill if the need arose since it was not yet known what actions the Republican Congress under the new ultra-right wing speaker Newt Gingrich would take. His "Contract with America" plan had toppled the Democrats control over Congress for the first time in over 40 years. And there was a lot of uncertainty and apprehension in Washington on what this new political alignment would mean in the upcoming Congress and in the next presidential election in 1996.

As the new DNC Deputy Political Director and head of the Office of Voter Registration and Participation, I placed a strong emphasis on highlighting the NVRA bill as a major Clinton Administration accomplishment. Letters were also written to the White House from the DNC's general counsel and my office that extolled the virtues of the NVRA and the importance of its full enforcement by the Department of Justice. After some urging, we were able to convince the administration to support a *National Voter Registration and Empowerment Day* that would encourage boards of election and grassroots groups to conduct voter registration drives in public agencies, schools, churches, and other population centers. Our office worked alongside supportive Democratic Secretaries of State, elected officials, party activists and allied groups who were recruited to join the effort. We developed a national poster made up of a black and white photo of the front line of the 1993 20th anniversary of the March on Washington. Over 20,000 of these posters were distributed across the US and help set the tone for a campaign for early implementation of NVRA and full enforcement of the VRA.

By the 1998 midterm elections, there were signs that the registration rolls were beginning to swell. Hope began to grow that the transformation of the American electorate was underway. More African American, Latino, young, and low-income voters were getting registered in departments of motor vehicles and public service agencies.[19] These numbers increased even more through robust voter registration drives by voter registration groups that were able to take full advantage of postcard registration that was now legal in all 50 states.

---

19 "The Impact of the National Voter Registration Act of 1993 on the Administration of Federal Elections," Federal Election Commission, last modified June, 1997, https://www.fec.gov/about/reports-about-fec/agency-operations/impact-national-voter-registration-act-1993-administration-federal-elections-html/.

Chapter 10
The 2000 Florida Election Debacle

By the 2000 election cycle, the motor voter law kicked in earnest. In the first five years since its effective date of January 1, 1995, over 25 million people had registered to vote, with dramatic increases in states like Ohio, Pennsylvania, Virginia, North Carolina, Nevada, California, and Florida. [1] The political demographic landscape was beginning to change in many states as its provisions led to a historic number of new voters added to the rolls since the NVRA's 1995 enactment.[2] As the NVRA was being implemented, the nation was soon to witness new and unprecedented challenges that would accompany the dramatic increase in voter registration and turnout for the 2000 election.

The motor voter bill, which few political observers had paid any attention to, was now the driving force behind the massive turnout of voters that would transpire in the 2000 election between Al Gore, Clinton's Vice President, and Texas Governor George W. Bush, the son of the former Republican president who Clinton had defeated. The early impact of the NVRA would play a major role in the 2000 election that emerged as a watershed moment in the history of election administration. An unprecedented voter mobilization effort launched by the NAACP in Florida and 21 other states led to a massive increase in the number of voters who turned out, overwhelming election officials in several states. One of the most dramatic increases was in the state of Florida, which experienced a 70% turnout, significantly higher than the 49% turnout in the last presidential election.[3]

The counting of Florida voters who exercised their right to vote on Election Day proved to be overwhelming for election officials who were not prepared for the massive turnout. The lack of strong national standards for counting votes revealed some of the major flaws and weaknesses in the nation's election administration system. The Florida election debacle would usher in a new century with America facing one of its most challenging eras of democratic self-redefinition. It would be the election that redefined and challenged some of the most basic principles of our democracy: one person, one vote; majority rule; states' rights

---

1 Ibid.

2 Estelle H. Rogers, "The National Voter Registration Act: Fifteen Years On," American Constitution Society, last modified November 18, 2009, https://www.acslaw.org/issue_brief/briefs-2007-2011/the-national-voter-registration-act-fifteen-years-on/.

3 "2000 United States presidential election in Florida," Wikipedia, last modified March 3, 2022, https://en.wikipedia.org/wiki/2000_United_States_presidential_election_in_Florida.

https://doi.org/10.1515/9783110742473-013

(again); and the role of the federal government in protecting not only the right to vote but also the right for those votes to be counted.

In June 2000, the NAACP, the nation's oldest and largest civil rights organization, decided to dramatically expand its civil and political voter mobilization apparatus. For the first time in its 90-year history, it created a 501(C)(4) political arm called the NAACP National Voter Fund, (NVF). The effort was launched by the chairman of the NAACP's National Board of Directors, Julian Bond, the legendary SNCC leader and former Georgia State Senator. The 64-member board, well known for its fierce advocacy and adherence to tradition, broke with that tradition to form this new arm of the organization, which would be responsible for developing an unprecedented voter mobilization effort in 22 battleground states where the African American vote could play a crucial role in the 2000 elections.

An unprecedented amount totaling millions of dollars was invested in massive voter registration and mobilization efforts. Bond tapped longtime Midwest Academy co-founder and citizens' rights advocate Heather Booth as its first director. The president of the NAACP, former congressman, and former chair of the Congressional Black Caucus, Kweisi Mfume, would serve as its first president. The remainder of the founders included civil rights lawyer William Brackett, California-based civil rights attorney Peter Graham Cohn and Executive Director Heather Booth.The NAACP-NVF produced a hard-hitting, controversial television ad depicting the brutal death of James Byrd, a Black farmer from Tyler, Texas who was viciously chained to the back of a pickup truck and dragged for miles by white racists. The ad's message highlighted the harsh attack as a hate crime and criticized Texas Governor George W. Bush for his failure to sign a hate crimes bill into law in the state of Texas. The ad caused great controversy in the conservative media's talk radio and echo chamber. In addition to the radio and television ads, the theme was used in national posters, direct mail, handbills, and even billboards in key states. These ads featured the face of James Byrd's daughter, Renee Mullins, whose moving words about the death of her father inspired millions of Black people to register and vote in the 2000 elections.

As the summer wore on, Conyers asked me to take another leave to accompany him to Los Angeles for the 2000 Democratic Convention, where he was able to meet with the Democratic nominee, Al Gore, and his presidential campaign to develop strategies to maximize the African American vote. While in LA, Conyers and I visited several Black churches in Pasadena in support of a local prosecutor, Adam Schiff, who was running for Congress in a Republican district held by Congressman Jim Rogan, one of the Clinton impeachment managers on the House Judiciary Committee. Schiff went on to win that election and begin a distinguished congressional career. After all the excitement of the LA convention in the summer, it was hard to come back to Washington in the fall to simply work on mundane congressional administrative office duties when the presidency and control of the U.S. Congress were at stake.

At this point, NAACP NVF Director Heather Booth and Communications Director Andi Pringle (a former Jackson campaign aide) reached out to me to inquire if I could help with the five-city national GOTV bus tour that was being planned toward the end of their massive GOTV efforts. The bus tour was being led by one of the foremost event planners and logistical experts, James Day, and his wife, Michelle. The five cities were Philadelphia, Pittsburgh, Columbus, Cleveland, and Detroit. Conyers was more than happy to accommodate "loaning me" to the NAACP to help with the African American turnout effort. Conyers was a leading sponsor in the house of Senator Ted Kennedy's Hate Crimes Prevention Act of 1999, S. 622[4] and having a chance to lift the issue would help build support across the US for the bill that was stalled in Congress. Also, the tour was ending in his hometown of Detroit and would be a welcomed addition to African American GOTV efforts there.

The noted celebrities on the Bus tour included Renee Mullins, the daughter of James Byrd; Dule' Hill, the up-and-coming African American cast member of the number one show on television, "The West Wing," and a local D.C.-based rap group. Part of my job was to build community support for the bus tour in each town and help supplement the program with local entertainment talent and key community leaders. While the rallies we planned were not big, the large wrapped 55-seat mega-bus did garner lots of attention as it rolled through some of the lowest-income and lowest-performing voter turnout areas of the cities. The highly visible bus blasted loud rap and gospel music from loudspeakers from the lead car. We also ran repeated messages from celebrities and NAACP leaders, calling on people to get out and vote. The bus complemented the door-to-door canvassing that NAACP NVF staffers were coordinating in those same neighborhoods. The bus route would be the very last point of contact with the targeted voters, who, by Election Day, had received three pieces of mail, three knocks at the door, and three phone calls and had heard a barrage of radio ads in the weeks leading up to the election. In most cases, an unprecedented 11 voter contacts helped spur turnout to historic levels.

---

4 "Actions – S.622–106th Congress (1999–2000): Hate Crimes Prevention Act of 1999," Congress.gov, last modified March 24, 1999, https://www.congress.gov/bill/106th-congress/senate-bill/622/actions?r=4&s=1.

As the campaign was winding down, we were tasked with adding a component to the tour: setting up literal cookouts of hot dogs, burgers, snacks, and soft drinks at multiple major polling sites, where long lines of people were waiting to vote. The water and refreshments would be an incentive for people to stay in line during the lunch and dinner hours rather than having to leave before getting a chance to vote. The refreshments were especially important for the elderly and diabetic voters, who needed food to control their blood sugar levels while standing in the long lines.

By Election Day, the bus tour had been through Philadelphia, Pittsburgh, Columbus, and my hometown of Cleveland over the last seven days. It was now at the final stop in Detroit. On Election Day, the lines to vote were everywhere across the city. We had worked through the night to make sure there were enough food stations at as many polling stations as possible in Detroit. Late in the day, we took the large, branded, wrapped bus, and observed many polling places, witnessing first-hand the long lines that were evident at several polling sites across the city. All the lines seemed to have no end in sight, with long rows of people shivering in the cold Detroit wind. We stopped at one school and saw the line stretching well around the block. To get a closer look at the problem, we walked in with a team of election observers led by Simone Lightfoot, the NAACP's Detroit coordinator, and NVF's state director, Brook McCauley. We saw that the line was even longer than we thought and continued well into the school. It was wrapped around the entire hallway and up a stairwell to the second floor. Several hundred people were literally crammed in the narrow hallways and seemed to be growing increasingly impatient with the slow-moving line. Our presence as NAACP officials in full yellow and black jackets and hats gave some people hope that we had finally arrived and would be able to straighten out the problem. In some instances, light applause broke out as we made our way through the hallways.

After several minutes, we finally reached the gymnasium where the voting machines were set up. As we looked at the beginning of the lines, we could see a lineup of voting booths spread across the front of the room. What was striking was that only five or six machines were working, with lines behind them; over half of the machines had no lines and bore out-of-order signs. It was no wonder that the lines were so long, with over half of the voting machines not working. We called in the problem to the 866-OUR-VOTE hotline and went to the local election protection headquarters to confer with them. They informed us that they were already aware of the problems. It was not uncommon, as similar polling sites were reporting the same problem all over the city of Detroit. They said that a judge was considering a temporary restraining order to extend the hours of voting in Wayne County past the 7:00 PM deadline to accommodate the long lines. However, it was unlikely that new voting machines could reach polling sites in time to speed things up.

We left the building the way we came in, with many asking us what the hold-up was with the lines on our way out. This time, we could clearly see the faces of the hundreds of people who were standing and waiting. Many were growing increasingly agitated and disappointed that we were leaving without resolving the problem. We explained about the broken machines and how we had reported them but there was nothing more we could do—other than offer them the refreshments that we were already distributing. As we reached the end of the long line, having failed to bring any relief, one of the men in line stopped me.

"Ain't nothing y'all can do?" he pleaded. I told him no. The election judges might extend the hours for voting, but we did not know if or when any new machines would arrive to replace the broken ones. The look on his face and on others around him was one of great disappointment and disgust.

"I got to get back to work!" someone yelled out.

"I got to pick up my kids from school," another woman said.

As we walked away, the man who had asked the first question said something that haunted me for many years to come: "Y'all did a good job getting us out here, all excited to vote," he shouted out to me and the entire crowd. "But looks like y'all didn't do nothing to fix *this* problem!"

He was right. Gone was that sense of hope that had been raised when we first showed up. It was clear that the board of elections did not seem to have prepared for a turnout this massive. For several weeks leading up to the election, the crowd had heard non-stop ads running on Black radio; they had received at least three pieces of mail, three calls to their land lines, and three knocks at the door from the NAACP and the NAACP National Voter Fund canvassers: a total of 9 to 11 contacts. It was the formula that had been devised by the NAACP NVF's director, Heather Booth, and her national field directors, Bernard Craighead, and Marvin Randolph. Field tests early in the year had proven that this was the optimum number of contacts needed to produce a solid voter turnout. They were correct. The formula worked; the turnout was 58.2%, a dramatic increase over the 54.5% turnout in the 1996 elections.[5] We had control of the messaging around hate crimes and were able to provide large quantities of food and refreshments, a bus tour with celebrities and music, and the unprecedented, concentrated voter contact mobilization to get our voters out to vote. But what we had no control over was the election administration apparatus of Detroit and Michigan and

---

5 "General Election Voter Registration/Turnout Statistics," Michigan.gov, (n.d.) accessed March 22, 2022, https://www.michigan.gov/sos/0,4670,7-127-1633_8722-29616-,00.html.

perhaps other cities. They were simply not prepared to absorb the massive new influx of voters that the Black mobilization and newly implemented provisions that the NVRA had helped to produce.

For the first time, I could visually see how the NVRA that liberalized voter registration procedures helped lead to this massive turnout. Passing the NVRA into law was a great and historic accomplishment. However, its provisions did not prepare our system of election administration for the large influx of new voters. As pioneers of the NVRA, we had also not prepared ourselves for our own success in passing the historic legislation that dramatically increased the number of eligible voters nationwide. The effects of the NVRA were successful and an expansion of our democracy. Its provisions empowered millions of new voters across the US, with many voting for the first time. However, it also created a new category of policies and procedural problems that were left up to state, county, and local election administrators to figure out—with no additional federal funding. This was no longer a theoretical policy matter. The long lines and record voter turnouts formed the true picture of what our reforms had accomplished. It was also a graphic picture of our inability to sufficiently prepare the states for the results of that dramatic increase in voter registrations and or to provide them with the resources and machinery needed to ensure that all the new voters could be accommodated.

As the tour came to an end, the mood seemed to change due to all the lines and frustration at the polls. I placed a call to other organizers around the country and discovered that the problems we had witnessed in Detroit were similar in other cities. The largest and most widespread problems were being reported out of the state of Florida. On-the-ground organizers reported identical problems with long lines. Even more problematic was the issue of people being turned away by the thousands. Students at many HBCUs and other college campuses who thought they were registered to vote were not on the state's voter list. Thousands of voters across the state of Florida reported being turned away and even multiple cases of voters being falsely accused of being felons. The stories seemed surreal until we later learned that their being turned away at the polls were a major contributor to the election administration irregularities that were soon to be revealed.[6]

We were finally in the hotel to rest after the long non-stop bus tour stretch and were ready for the victory party. Detroit was obviously the best place for me

---

6 "Voting Irregularities in Florida During the 2000 Presidential Election: Chapter 9 Findings and Recommendations" U.S. Commission on Civil Rights, (n.d.) accessed March 22, 2022, https://www.usccr.gov/files/pubs/vote2000/report/ch9.htm.https://www.usccr.gov/files/pubs/vote2000/report/ch9.htm

to land after being on leave from my job as Representative Conyers' Chief of Staff since early September. I was able to reconnect with the Congressman's district Director Ray Plowden and other congressional district staff at the Congressman's election night reception. Conyers himself had just finished a whirlwind tour of churches and community centers in Michigan but had also traveled to other states, including Ohio and Illinois, pushing for the Gore/Liberman ticket. He ended his campaign in his home district and wanted to make sure there was a place for election workers to gather after a long election season. We all ended up at the Renaissance Hotel and awaited the returns.

Like most good Democrats I was elated when so many of the returns showed Al Gore on target to winning the White House. The Governor of Texas and son of the former president George Bush was simply no match for the near incumbent Al Gore. He had survived the impeachment of Bill Clinton and the Monica Lewinsky scandal, and attempts to paint Gore as a clone of Bill Clinton. Americans were not ready for a return to the Reagan/Bush years, I thought, and the 1.5 million popular votes spread between Gore and Bush proved it! I paid little attention to all the Election Day banter by the pundits. Nothing mattered now but the vote of the American people. They had spoken, and Gore was clearly beating Bush in the popular vote by well over a million votes. The Electoral College vote was a mere formality...or so we thought.

The NAACP and NAACP NVF's *Arrive with Five* and *Souls To the Polls* GOTV program in Florida was led by NAACP Florida State Conference President Adora Obi Nweze and Executive Director Beverly Neal. The program was credited with helping to swell the historic number of African Americans who turned out in 2000. The provisions of the NVRA were finally in full swing and the results were astounding! Citizens were being registered at record numbers at departments of motor vehicles and social service agencies and now, through a massive, expanded field postcard voter registration mobilization effort led by the NAACP, Black churches, fraternities, sororities, and several other allied organizations. Tom Joyner, the nation's top Black radio disc jockey at the time, had partnered with the NAACP to recruit over 1,400 volunteers to work on Election Day through his popular "Tom Joyner Morning Show." Matched with the NAACP NVF's James Byrd TV ad, the radio spots that ran on a constant basis, and the massive field operations, all combined produced one of the largest Black voter turnouts in Florida and U.S. history.[7] It was more than the election apparatus could handle.

---

7 Ari Berman, "How the 2000 Election in Florida Led to a New Wave of Voter Disenfranchisement," The Nation, last modified July 28, 2015, https://www.thenation.com/article/archive/how-the-2000-election-in-florida-led-to-a-new-wave-of-voter-disenfranchisement/.

The NAACP's biggest effort by far was in the Southern Region V, where the largest numbers of African American votes were concentrated. The mobilizations in Georgia, North Carolina, Virginia, Texas, and Florida were scoring historically unprecedented record turnouts of voters. Long lines characterized the efforts across the country but nowhere were they more prevalent than in the state of Florida. The NAACP, Black churches, Historically Black Colleges, and community activists helped swell voter rolls with tens of thousands of new postcard registrations—one of the new provisions of the NVRA. In addition to these campaigns, the political atmosphere was super-charged as Florida Governor Jeb Bush, the brother of the presidential candidate, was in a major battle with the civil rights community over the issue of education funding and affirmative action. This highly publicized issue helped produce a perfect storm of awareness and heightened political engagement of the African American community.

As election night wore on, the news anchors went quickly through state after state, calling them for either Bush or Gore. Most states were a clear-cut win or loss, with just a handful of battleground states being too close to call. By early evening, it was clear from the popular vote that Vice President Al Gore was still in the lead by over a million votes nationwide. It seemed evident that the only thing left was to call the last one or two states to make it official. At the time, most of us paid little attention to the Electoral College vote. In every presidential election since 1896, the winner of the popular vote had gone on to win the Electoral College. Therefore, there was little reason for news commentators or the public to question the outcome when the margin was close but decisive.

NBC News was one of the first networks to call Florida for Al Gore and declare him the winner of the Presidency of the United States, complete with graphics and dramatic music in the background. The crowds were jubilant in the Detroit hotel ballroom where I joined a number of local elected and community leaders and Election Day workers who had gathered after working tirelessly to produce the massive turnout in Michigan. The loud music and roar of the crowd drowned out the sound of the television news. It was over! Al Gore had won and our Black voter turnout operation, both in Michigan and across the country, had been successful. After a few more congratulatory hugs and high-fives, I was exhausted and decided to head back to the hotel early. There was still some wrap-up to do from the bus tour and we were scheduled to head back to Washington D.C. early the next morning.

When I returned to my hotel room, I watched in horror as the Fox News anchors frantically argued that the election in Florida should not have been called by the other networks for Gore. They argued that Governor Jeb Bush had let them know that the count in Florida was not conclusive, and his brother was not yet conceding the state or the election to Gore. Governor Jeb Bush cited voting irregularities related to the massive turnout. It was to be expected coming from Fox News, which everyone knew had a bias for Republicans. But to my and the nation's surprise, CBS pulled back the projection that it had made earlier in calling the race for Al Gore, citing questions about the vote count in key counties in Broward, Miami-Dade, and Duvall Counties, where the Black turnout in Jacksonville, Florida was the most concentrated and most overwhelming. As the night wore on, the other networks followed suit and either pulled back their projections on the winner or said it was too close to call. It soon became apparent that our celebration was premature. The final results took longer than we had imagined.

It was a long, quiet ride back to Washington, D.C. Most of the celebrities and Renee Mullins were given plane rides back to their homes with a large thank-you for helping us mobilize the historic turnout. The bus was mostly empty except for the small staff and local rap group from D.C. Gone was the excitement of the election. It had been replaced by an eerie feeling of uncertainty and disappointment that we had not achieved a clear-cut win that night.

The Florida Recount Debacle

As the days passed, closer analysis revealed that many of the problems of Election Day in Florida went well beyond the large number of voters who showed up at the polls. The massive turnout overwhelmed poll workers and the outdated election administration apparatus, which was ill-prepared for such a large turnout. In addition to the long lines, there were shortages of Election Day workers, polling places running out of ballots, dysfunctional voting machine breakdowns, and relatively innocuous features of the voting machine apparatus that would have a profound impact on the outcome of the election in Florida and the nation.

The punch card voting machine was a primitive device consisting of voting cards designed with small dots; voters would use a stylus to punch holes next to the candidate of their choice. The small pieces of paper that were punched out by the voter were called *chads* and the containers beneath the voting cards were called *chad boxes*. As the number of voters grew throughout the day, the chad boxes became full and had to be emptied more frequently by the election workers to ensure that the voting device functioned properly throughout the day. With a shortage of election workers, woefully inadequate to meet the demands of the overwhelming turnout, the chad boxes filled up by the hour and weren't emptied regularly in a number of polling places. As a result of the jammed packed chad boxes, tens of thousands of legally cast ballots contained chads that had not been punched all the way through. Thousands more were "hanging chads" that had been punched by voters but did not go all the way through enough to separate them from the voting card.[8]

These hanging chads would become the centerpiece of litigation brought by the Bush for President Campaign lawyers, who challenged whether those votes should be counted. Even further, they challenged what would become known as "pregnant chads" or chads that had markings that had pushed the dot out from the cards but did not break away from the card. This challenge would lead to tens of thousands more ballots being contested and not included in the initial count of Florida's vote canvassing boards in each county.[9] While mundane in its application, these election machine malfunctions threw the entire results of the presidential election of 2000 into complete chaos.

Now more than two weeks into the back and forth between the Bush and Gore lawyers, there was still no clear resolution to the issue of who had won the Florida election. The NAACP called for Congressional hearings to be held in Florida to get firsthand accounts of what had happened from Florida voters, election workers, and other election officials. When the Republican-led Congress refused to hold hearings, NAACP President Kweisi Mfume, the NAACP Florida State Conference and the newly formed Advancement Project conducted hearings themselves. Hundreds of Florida voters would recount their harrowing experience on election day. The response was so overwhelming that the US Commission on Civil Rights and its longtime member Mary Francis Berry led the charge to conduct official proceedings in the Florida state capitol in Tallahassee. The commission convened and voted to conduct official hearings on reported voting irregularities and possible violations of civil and voting rights related to the election.[10]

After three days and over 30 hours of testimony from 100 Florida voters, election officials, and election observers, the commission's findings were astounding! The election system had failed the voters of Florida in multiple areas and led to widespread voter disenfranchisement of thousands of African Americans, bi-lingual voters, seniors, disabled voters, and students. Their findings included:
1. Flawed voter purge procedures that denied thousands of Florida voters across the state their right to cast a regular ballot,

---

8 "Bush v. Gore," Encyclopedia Britannica, last modified December 5, 2021, https://www.bri tannica.com/event/Bush-v-Gore#ref1046312.
9 Ibid.
10 "Voting Irregularities in Florida During the 2000 Presidential Election: Executive Summary," U.S. Commission on Civil Rights, (n.d.) accessed March 22, 2022, https://www.usccr.gov/files/ pubs/vote2000/report/exesum.htm.

2. The lack of a uniform appeal process for voters who were not listed on voter rolls,
3. Polling places that were closed, closed early, or moved without proper notice,
4. The mishandling of the NVRA mandated motor voter registration forms by the Florida Department of Safety and Motor Vehicles leading to widespread inaccurate voter lists,
5. A Florida Secretary of State private vendor had erroneously identified tens of thousands of legally registered Florida voters as ex-felons and were denied the right to cast a vote,
6. The presence of unauthorized law enforcement vehicle check points near polling places,
7. Inadequate voter education on the mechanics of using voting machinery,
8. Inadequate and inconsistent poll worker training,
9. Voter Data transfer issues and chain of command concerns of election ballots,
10. Limited access to polling places for voters with disabilities, and
11. The failure of voting systems machinery including the outdated and poorly designed butterfly ballot" that led to a massive number of spoiled ballots and ballot confusion.[11]

The Florida Office of Secretary of State led by Katherine Harris and county election officials in several counties lack of preparation for the large turnout had created unprecedented long lines and chaos on election day across the state. Despite all the accounts of election irregularities, Secretary Harris failed to fully cooperate with the U.S. Commission on Civil Rights and voter integrity experts to address the many issues plaguing the election system. With the state of Florida's voting system on full display in the national media, Harris took several steps to defend the integrity of the election procedures in the face of clear evidence that the election process was fraught with many failures. Vice President Gore's campaign was able to win the legal battle at the Florida Supreme Court for a recount of contested ballots in 3 key counties where there were tens of thousands of uncounted ballots weeks after election day. As the state Supreme Court ordered hand recounts in contested counties, the process dragged on for several weeks after the election. Like Florida Governor Jeb Bush, Secretary Harris was a

---

11 "Voting Irregularities in Florida During the 2000 Presidential Election: Chapter 9 Findings and Recommendations," U.S. Commission on Civil Rights, (n.d.) accessed March 22, 2022, https://www.usccr.gov/files/pubs/vote2000/report/ch9.htm.

staunch supporter of candidate George Bush and appeared to be doing everything in her power to delay or undermine the recount of tens of thousands of uncounted ballots from contested counties. [12]

Back in Washington, I had returned to my job on Capitol Hill and began working with the House Judiciary Committee, the Congressional Black Caucus, the NAACP, and other civil rights groups on briefing books that were being prepared for a long-anticipated (and overdue) meeting with Attorney General Janet Reno. Two large binders were presented that detailed the hearing's findings on the voting rights infractions that had occurred in Florida. It consisted of the transcripts from the NAACP hearings and sworn affidavits from election workers from across the state—even beyond the three or four counties in question.[13] In case after case, there were clear voting irregularities and violations of the right to vote being denied to Black and Hispanic voters as well as seniors and students in several counties. At this point, we believed that the remedy was nothing short of a complete recount of all the ballots across the state to capture any other voting irregularities. Only then could we know how bad the problem was and its true impact on the election results.

On the night before the meeting, there was great expectation that the attorney general and her deputy, Eric Holder, would look favorably upon all the evidence that had been presented to them by the CBC members and the civil rights community. There were hours and hours of transcripts and news reports of broken machines, flawed ballot designs, long lines, and persons being denied the right to vote after being falsely accused of being felons. All were signs that the voting process in Florida had denied African Americans the right to vote in cities across the state. This included over 27,000 ballots that were disqualified from the city of Jacksonville, which observers believed to be overwhelmingly Black voters, due to ballot design issues.[14] In Miami Dade County there were cases of elderly Jewish people who had their votes registered as cast for the hard-right third-party candidate Pat Buchanan by mistake. The butterfly ballot produced many election administration errors, proving that election officials

12 "Florida Secretary of State Rejects Counties' Appeal For More Time," ABC News Internet Venture, last modified November 12, 2000, https://web.stanford.edu/class/polisci179/ABCNEWS_com%20%20Secretary%20of%20State%20Rejects%20Recount%20Appeal.htm.

13 "US may probe Gore, Bush Florida vote," New Vision, (n.d.) accessed March 22, 2022, https://www.newvision.co.ug/news/1018269/us-probe-gore-bush-florida-vote.

14 "Election Digest," Orlando Sentinel, last modified December 5, 2000, https://www.orlandosentinel.com/news/os-xpm-2000-12-06-0012060211-story.html.

and many counties were woefully inadequately prepared for the massive turnout of African Americans in the state.[15]

Also included were the initial findings from the US Civil Rights Commission which concluded that "many of the problems encountered were foreseeable and should have been prevented" and "the failure to do so resulted in an extraordinarily high and inexcusable level of disenfranchisement, with a significantly disproportionate impact on African American voters."[16] Additionally, the report cited the causes including: *(1) a general failure of leadership from those with responsibility for ensuring elections are properly planned and executed; (2) inadequate resources for voter education, training of poll workers, and for Election Day trouble-shooting and problem solving; (3) inferior voting equipment and/or ballot design; (4) failure to anticipate and account for the expected high volumes of voters, including inexperienced voters; (5) a poorly designed and even more poorly executed purge system; and (6) a resource allocation system that often left poorer counties, which often were counties with the highest percentage of black voters, adversely affected.*[17]

After reviewing the briefing notebooks and reports for well over a week, Attorney General Reno agreed to meet with the delegation of CBC members and civil rights groups. I accompanied Conyers to the Justice Department meeting and sat in great anticipation while we waited to hear the actions that Attorney General Reno would take. It was our hope that she would launch an official DOJ investigation and support our call for a full statewide recount. We were all shocked when she stated she did not find the evidence remarkable beyond routine election administration problems. As a Florida native, she said she understood the elections landscape very well, but did not feel she could intervene, and at this point there was nothing further she could do. She said it was up to the Florida Supreme Court, which had full jurisdiction at this point. The Florida Supreme Court had ordered a recount of the handful of counties in question, and she did not believe that the Justice Department could go any further than that.[18]

---

15 "Voting Irregularities in Florida During the 2000 Presidential Election: Chapter 9 Findings and Recommendations" U.S. Commission on Civil Rights, (n.d.) accessed March 22, 2022, https://www.usccr.gov/files/pubs/vote2000/report/ch9.htm.

16 "Voting Irregularities in Florida During the 2000 Presidential Election: Executive Summary," U.S. Commission on Civil Rights, (n.d.) accessed March 22, 2022, https://www.usccr.gov/files/pubs/vote2000/report/exesum.htm.

17 Ibid.

18 P. Mitchell Prothero, "Florida Supreme Court orders recount of undervotes," United Press International, last modified DEcember 8, 2000, https://www.upi.com/Archives/2000/12/08/Florida-Supreme-Court-orders-recount-of-undervotes/5410880151053/.

Reno also noted that even the Gore Campaign was requesting that the votes be counted only in the limited number of counties where it claimed to be winning due to the large numbers of undercounts.

This was the area where the civil rights community and the Gore campaign had differed early on in the process. A complete recount would reveal a fuller picture of what was disenfranchising voters, including the reasons why thousands of Florida voters had been falsely identified as ex-felons and denied their right to vote. A statewide recount would also reveal why students from several of Florida's Historic Black Colleges and Universities (HBCUs) were not allowed to vote because their registration forms had never been processed. The African American leaders repeatedly pressed Reno to use her office to bring actions against Bush campaign operatives who were holding boisterous rallies at vote counting centers seeking to disrupt the hand recount process. Initially sReno also refused this request. But by the end of the meeting, she begrudgingly agreed to send down one or two election monitors who would look into reported acts of intimidation of the vote recount, but even that gesture was seen as window dressing by the groups well after the fact. After much anticipation in preparing the briefing books and securing the big meeting, it was a great letdown that the Clinton/Gore administration's own Justice Department would not intervene—at least to the point of simply ensuring that the VRA had not been violated and taking steps to ensure that all the outstanding votes were counted.

At this point, the vote recount in the three counties was the last remaining remedy to get to the real results of the election. The longer the count went on, the smaller the winning margin of the Bush campaign became. Bush's lead, which did not include all the tens of thousands of contested and uncounted ballots in Devall County, fell from tens of thousands to just a few thousand. The Florida recount, even with its limitation of counting just the uncounted ballots from three counties, was beginning to reflect the true voter turnout. The main question was whether there would be enough time and manpower to finish the recount before the Electoral College met on December 13.

I reached out to my old friend Donna Brazile who had been named Gore's campaign manager, making her the first African American woman to head a major presidential campaign. She was still in Florida, trying to recruit volunteers to help with the recounts that the Florida Supreme Court had ordered. The counts were going slowly due to the massive number of ballots and the legal battles over those ballots that were being closely reviewed. I offered to help by mobilizing two busloads of Capitol Hill staffers and other supporters who could take a few days off to come down to Tallahassee and help with the vote count during the Thanksgiving break in Congress. It would be a long 18-hour bus ride, but it was no problem getting the first wave of volunteers to make the trip. Once that bus was filled, we sent it down right away to get started while we continued to work on filling the second bus. I had made plans to ride down with the second bus once it was filled.

One of the recruits on the first bus was Jocelyn Woodard, a former DNC staffer and labor activist who called me with her observations on a regular basis. On the day they arrived, in Miami Dade she phoned me in a panic, saying that provocateurs were outside the building where the votes were being counted. They were banging on the windows and doors and yelling epithets at the counters. She said the yelling got so loud, they had to stop the count and move to another location, as the local police had not been able to gain control of the situation.[19] The protests, would become known as the "Brooks Brothers Brigade" had been organized by operatives from the Republican National Committee (RNC) who sent down staffers to disrupt the recount process that had been ordered by the Florida Supreme Court. The protest proved to be successful in temporarily halting the recount and burning down the limited time there was to count all the ballots before certification deadlines.

It was a sad commentary on the state of affairs in Florida and the failure of our electoral system. The partisan nature of the campaign had turned from fierce to violent. The hyperbolic actions of the goon squads prompted Rev. Jesse Jackson and local Black clergy and labor leaders to plan a major march on Tallahassee to protest the violence against election workers, as well as demand a full recount of all the votes across the state and an end to the obstructive role that Secretary of State Katherine Harris and the Bush campaign were playing in trying to stop the recount.

On December 8 the Bush Campaign lawyers, led by former U.S. Secretary of State James Baker, decided to appeal to the U.S. Supreme Court to overturn the decision of the Florida Supreme court order for a statewide recount. Within days Rev. Jackson then called for a march in Washington in front of the U.S. Supreme Court, urging them to *not* intervene to stop the statewide recount. Both marches were successful and brought thousands of peaceful protesters to Tallahassee and Washington, D.C. I attended Rev. Jackson's rally at the Supreme Court in Washington along with several hundred supporters, who gathered on a cold, wintry day in December. The rally was energetic but non-violent and gained more media attention. However, I was becoming worried about all the attention being paid to getting people to rallies when we really needed to focus on getting more volunteers to Florida to help with the recount.

---

19 "Brooks Brothers riot," Wikipedia, last modified January 25, 2022, https://en.wikipedia.org/wiki/Brooks_Brothers_riot.

It was now early December and this battle had been raging in the courts, streets, and media for several weeks. Both sides had people in the streets, with tensions riding high. As time wore on, there seemed to be growing uncertainty over who actually won the presidential election and which votes should or shouldn't be counted. Gore's overall margin in the popular vote continued to climb nationwide, winning by well over one million votes. However, he was still trailing by a few thousand votes in Florida, which had yet to award its electoral votes.

In a show of confidence, Governor George Bush left his Texas ranch, where he had been since after Election Day, and flew into Washington, D.C., flanked by his highly visible Texas Rangers security detail to begin transition planning. It was a bold move to demonstrate his confidence in the final results, though the vote count was still going on and his lead in Florida getting smaller by the day, going from several thousand to less than 2,500 votes.

I called my friend Minyon Moore, who was now the White House Political Director, to see if the Clinton Administration had begun working with Gore on its transition efforts. She said that President Clinton did not want to be presumptive until all the votes were counted. Setting up a transition office in this atmosphere would be seen as provocative, and they did not want to stoop to Governor Bush's level. Besides, she said, "The two of them still have not spoken to each other."

Clinton and Gore, once close friends, had become estranged during the campaign due in large part to the fallout from the impeachment a year earlier. Gore had also uninvited Clinton to join him on the campaign trail and kept the lame-duck president at arm's length, though Clinton still enjoyed high approval ratings at the time. Gore had wanted to run his own race. According to Donna and Minyon, Gore wanted to be seen as his own man.

As the Electoral College vote inched closer in early December, Bush's lead in the ongoing Florida recount dropped to less than 1,000. At no time did he appear to be gaining votes during the recount and it was now clear that the vast majority of the tens of thousands of remaining uncounted ballots in Duvall County alone would yield the same results. The 27,000 uncounted ballots were largely those of Black voters who were voting over 90% for Al Gore statewide. [20] Despite all the setbacks, and despite Governor Bush's claims to be starting the transition, victory was still at hand for Vice President Al Gore. As the recount continued, the vote difference between Bush and Gore was now down to just over 500 votes.

---

20 "Election Digest," Orlando Sentinel, last modified December 5, 2000, https://www.orlando sentinel.com/news/os-xpm-2000-12-06-0012060211-story.html.

And then, on December 12, 2000, the U.S. Supreme Court convened in the Bush v Gore case and rendered its decision. In a historic 5 – 4 vote, the court broke precedent and intervened in a state election. It overturned the Florida Supreme Court's ruling to conduct a manual recount of votes in the three counties being contested. The court agreed with the Bush campaign that his Equal Protection rights were violated due to the lack of an existing statewide legal standard to recount the punch-card ballots.[21] Part of their rationale was that the process for the recount was not equal in all of the counties in Florida. I shuddered upon hearing those words, knowing that had the Gore campaign listened to the civil rights community and called for all the statewide ballots to be counted initially, the Supreme Court may not have had this additional issue to hang its legal justification hat on. The ruling set back the major steps forward that we had been making on expanding voting rights going back to Selma and the passage of the Voting Rights Act. Legal scholars including the Florida State University Law Review would assert that the *Bush V Gore* decision undermined the long held notion of a federal right to vote.[22]

* * *

The ruling came on a Saturday morning, while most people in Washington were at home or preparing for the holidays. I called Congressman Conyers at home in Detroit; he had not yet heard about the ruling. When he did, he chastised me for playing games with this announcement. "What are you talking about?" he exclaimed in total disbelief. "The US Supreme Court has no jurisdiction in state elections! They can't even do that!" He then hung up on me, enraged over the announcement. I didn't call him back. I knew that he would find out from other Judiciary Committee staff, Professor Lawrence Tribe, and other noted legal scholars he was conferring with that it was true. The U.S. Supreme Court had stopped the Florida recount.

My next call was to my friend Jocelyn Woodards to see where they were with the recount at her location. With now just over 500 votes separating the two candidates, it was still time for Gore to catch up and pull ahead, I thought, before the Supreme Court's ruling took effect. Jocelyn said they were in the middle of counting ballots when one of the Republican election monitors ran into the

---

21 "On this day, Bush v. Gore settles 2000 presidential race," National Constitution Center, last modified December 12, 2019, https://constitutioncenter.org/blog/on-this-day-bush-v-gore-anniversary.

22 Peter M. Shane, "Disappearing Democracy: How Bush v. Gore Undermined the Federal Right to Vote for Presidential Electors," *Florida State University Law Review* 29, no. 2 (2001): 535 – 585.

room, "yelling at the top of his lungs," that the U.S. Supreme Court had just ordered a halt to the recount.

"They told us to put our pens down, place our ballots down, and step away from the table!" she recounted. It was chilling. They reluctantly obeyed the election judge's orders. The pro-Bush supporters who had been protesting outside the Board of Elections erupted into cheers. The recount was over. Many of the volunteers whom we had recruited to come down to help with the recount were told to return to their buses and return to Washington, D.C.

By the time all the vote counting had stopped across the state, Bush's lead was only 537 votes: 2,912,790 to 2,912,252 or 48.84% to 48.83%.[23] Had the recount gone on for even one more day, Gore would have surpassed Bush and the recount would have stopped with Gore in the lead and the winner of the 25 electoral votes from Florida. Instead, the following day, Florida Secretary of State Katherine Harris, with an eerie grin on her face, announced that Governor George Bush had won the state of Florida by 537 votes and would be awarded the state's 25 electoral votes—enough to propel him to the presidency despite losing the popular vote.[24]

Conyers and the CBC were furious and requested a call with Vice President Gore to urge him to continue challenging the results of the Electoral College when it met on December 13. Gore, who had fought alongside his strongest and most fervent supporters, had finally had enough. He agreed to a call with the CBC members to explain his rationale to them. As Conyers' Chief of Staff, I was allowed to listen in and heard the CBC members make impassioned pleas for Gore to continue the fight. The uncounted votes in Florida, he conceded, included a large share of Black voters from across the state who were being disenfranchised. He could still theoretically be elected president but would have to invoke a rare challenge on the floor of the House of Representatives to the Electoral College votes from Florida. It was something that many members of the CBC strongly supported, but he was not inclined to do.

"Everyone watching knows what happened," Representative Corrine Brown from Jacksonville argued passionately. "They know that 27,000 Black votes from Duvall County were not counted and that the real winning margin for Gore is way past 537 votes!"

---

23 "Florida Secretary of State Rejects Counties' Appeal For More Time," ABC News Internet Venture, last modified November 12, 2000, https://web.stanford.edu/class/polisci179/ABCNEWS_com%20%20Secretary%20of%20State%20Rejects%20Recount%20Appeal.htm.

24 "2000 United States presidential election in Florida," Wikipedia, last modified March 3, 2022, https://en.wikipedia.org/wiki/2000_United_States_presidential_election_in_Florida.

Gore listened attentively and spoke in a soft and clearly exhausted tone. He had fought it as long as he could, he said. As much as he knew that they were all right, and that he had won the election in Florida, as well as the popular vote nationwide by over half a million votes, he said he would never be able to govern the country effectively under these circumstances. "If we keep on fighting," he said, "it will tear this country apart at the seams. And I'm just not prepared to do that." Gore said it was a gut-wrenching decision, "one of the hardest decisions I have ever made in public life." As painful as he acknowledged it was, he also said that, deep down in his heart, he knew "it was the right thing to do." He concluded by letting them know that he would be conceding the election the following day, much to the grave disappointment of the entire CBC and his millions of supporters across the US.

The Black vote had been effectively mobilized and the over 500,000 popular vote margins had helped give the potential president the margin of victory needed to win. But the nation's democracy had to survive, and to Al Gore, this was the best way to ensure that it would. Like the members of the CBC listening in, I too was disappointed. It had been a long, hard battle to pass the NVRA after the over-six-year legislative battle and the five additional years working toward its effective implementation. The major expansion of voter registration rolls that we had hoped for after the passage of the NVRA finally materialized in the 2000 election, and the massive Black voter mobilization undertaken by the NAACP proved it.

The earlier work of Rev. Jackson's two presidential campaigns had helped uncover many of the institutional barriers that we sought to correct with the legislation. The success of the NVRA was also due to the carefully executed litigation of the NAACP Legal Defense Fund (LDF), the American Civil Liberties Union (ACLU), the Mexican American Legal Defense Fund (MALDEF), and the policy and analysis work of DEMOS, the Brennen Center, People for the American Way, the League of Women Voters, Human Serve, the Center for Policy Alternatives, Common Cause, and so many other advocacy groups. All worked in concert to make the strongest case possible in the courts and in state legislatures all across the US. However, the major voter mobilization, the most effective voting rights litigation, and the collective policy work during implementation were still not enough to ensure that the person whom the majority of the people had elected as President of the United States was able to assume office in 2000.

For me, it was another sad reminder that the nation's democracy was still broken despite all the work that had been done to fix it. We had conquered one major hurdle by making voter registration easier and more accessible to all Americans. Voter participation was increasing. However, we had not re-created the system of administering our elections, which was still set up for a democracy in which only half of its citizens voted. I was reminded of Columbia University Professor Richard Cloward and Fransis Fox Piven's admonition from the 1980s: "What if we had an election and everybody showed up?"[25] That question was now being answered during the 2000 presidential election. We had closed this long chapter on voter registration reform and opened another one on the voter mobilization that would follow in 2000.

The cries of the NVRA being an unfunded mandate became clearer to me now. Our political calculation to not provide any funding for NVRA was designed to ensure the bill's passage against Republican attempts to defund it and undermine its implementation. Instead, states and counties were struggling to implement the new law and, in the end, were left holding the bag when it came to providing the resources to ensure that the reforms were properly implemented. By the end of 2000, it was clear that the battle to fix the nation's election administration system was just beginning. And there would be a need for even more federal legislation to set national standards for the counting of ballots and to protect the voting process. The debacle in Florida had proven that it was time to turn our attention to the battle for the fair and equitable *administration* of elections.

---

25 Frances Fox Piven and Richard A. Cloward, *Why Americans Don't Vote* (New York: Pantheon Books, 1988), 26–95.

Chapter 11
Post-2000 Election and the 9/11 Reconfiguration

Al Gore's defeat after winning the popular vote sent shock waves through the Democratic Party. Progressive activists and donors had hoped for another fresh four-year term in the White House, focused on important policy initiatives. They were hungry to move forward on a number of issue priorities without the drama, trauma, and scandals that had surrounded the Clinton White House. With the defeat of Al Gore, they were sorely disappointed. It was not to be, and most of the progress that had been made in the early years of the Clinton presidency would have to wait at least another four years.

Life on Capitol Hill was equally depressing. The loss of the White House meant that all the agencies that were working with Democrats in Congress on reforms like reinventing government, environmental justice, health care reform, election reforms, and criminal justice reform were now in the hands of a Republican Congress and a Republican president—the son of the president whom Democrats and progressives had just defeated back in 1992. It was now clear that the 21st century would begin with a conservative Congress and a conservative president whom many Democrats felt were more interested in looking backward than forward.

Meanwhile, progressive donors and organized labor who had invested tens of millions of dollars into the massive 2000 voter mobilization began to question the value of their investments. They commissioned major academic and data-centered research studies to analyze what had happened in 2000. This was followed by a yearlong series of briefings and second-guess meetings and retreats to reconfigure how to move forward into the next election cycle. Among the remedies was the need for new legislation for federal standards for election administration and campaign finance reform.

Many concluded that they had been outmaneuvered and outspent by the Republican Party's "big money in politics machine." They vowed to take on legislation to reform campaign financing and placed their hopes on a bipartisan measure being led by Bush's former rival Presidential candidate and Arizona Senator John McCain, and by Wisconsin Democratic Senator Russ Feingold. The McCain-Feingold Bipartisan Campaign Finance Reform Bill became the new rallying cry for a large segment of the good government groups and the donor community.[1]

---

1 "Bipartisan Campaign Reform Act," Wikipedia, last modified March 16, 2022, https://en.wikipedia.org/wiki/Bipartisan_Campaign_Reform_Act.

https://doi.org/10.1515/9783110742473-014

9/11 and the New Paradigm

On September 11, 2001, I awoke, like the rest of the country, to images of the World Trade Center ablaze. It was surreal to see that such an iconic building in the New York skyline was under attack. How could it have happened given all the well-established security in the United States? I stayed glued to the television screen as long as I could until I saw the reports of the second plane hitting the second tower. It was soon clear, at least to me, that this was no accident. Someone or something had intentionally flown those two planes into both World Trade Center towers. As I made my way to my job in Washington, D.C. from my home in Upper Marlboro, Maryland, I crossed over the Frederick Douglass Bridge coming down South Capitol Street and saw dark smoke billowing from a building in Northern Virginia. At first, I had not realized that it was in any way connected to the World Trade Center attack until I turned up the radio and heard reports of the Pentagon being hit by a third plane. It was not confined to New York. The nation's capital, Washington, D.C., was now under attack as well!

The traffic was horrible, which was not atypical for a Tuesday morning in Washington, D.C. However, this time the traffic was heavy in both directions, coming in and out of the district. My heart sank as I listened to reports of people jumping out of windows to their deaths at the World Trade Center while reports told of a massive inferno at the Pentagon and hundreds of people unaccounted for. As I witnessed the horror of the billowing smoke and heard the panicked reports from the radio, my first thought was to go to Capitol Hill to make sure everyone on our congressional staff was okay. I tried to call Congressman Conyers and the congressional office but my cell phone—like everyone else's—had stopped functioning and the traffic was barely moving. By the time I got into the city, the bulletin came across that Washington, D.C. was being evacuated!

When I finally got near the Rayburn House Office Building, U.S. Capitol Police were directing traffic away from Capitol Hill. As I looked at my gas tank, I saw that it was less than one-quarter full, so I had little choice but to head back home to Maryland. With traffic at a standstill, I rolled down my window to ask one of the Capitol Police for the latest information. He looked at me with some hesitation, then said, "There is a fourth plane and it's headed for the US Capitol. We don't know the time of impact yet." Once again, my heart sank. "You need to keep moving!" he said as he waved the stalled traffic away from the Capitol.

For the first time in my adult life, I experienced absolute fear. I was powerless to move any faster than the traffic. I was on First Street, just a couple of blocks from the U.S. Capitol building. With the Pentagon smoke in the background, I was fearful that I would not escape such a disaster were a plane to hit the Capitol Building. I tried again to make a call, but all cell service had been shut down. For over an hour, I sat in that stalled traffic, moving at a snail's pace near the Capitol and praying that God would deliver me from the sudden death that had befallen so many others on that fateful day.

Eventually, the traffic moved and I was able to make it back home. Later, I learned that the fourth plane never made it to D.C. It was taken down near Somerset, Pennsylvania due to the courageous acts of the passengers on Flight 93. From the moment I heard of their heroic act, I knew that Flight 93 was the plane that had been headed toward the Capitol—the one that the policeman had warned me about. Thanks to their sacrifice, we had been spared a fourth major hit on the US. As far as I was concerned, they had saved my life as well.

Eventually, I was able to use my landline at home to reach my two sons Greg, Jelani and the rest of my family in Ohio. Rep. Conyers was safe back in Detroit, while the rest of the staff made it out of the Capitol, or had never made it in. Most of them had made it out of the Capitol or had never made it in. I instructed everyone to go home and stay there until we knew what was happening. Over the next two days, Washington, D.C. became an armed camp with thousands of National Guard troops patrolling the streets surrounding all the major government buildings and much of downtown. Nothing in my life experience had prepared me for such an occurrence. Like so many others, I did not know what to think or which way to turn.

A few days after the attacks, President Bush went to New York City to stand among the rubble of the World Trade Center with firefighters and first responders, vowing that the perpetrators would hear from the US very soon. His defiant words rallied the nation and caused his approval ratings to skyrocket. By September 13th the country had been transformed and was now united behind the American flag and the still relatively new president.

I made another attempt to get back to Capitol Hill a few days after the attack. As I drove closer to the Capitol Office Building, I saw the National Guard troops and their Humvees stationed all around Capitol Hill and along the main thoroughfares surrounding it. The line of Guard troops and military vehicles went from the Capitol all the way down to the White House and downtown D.C. It was surreal to drive and walk past them.

When I walked into the congressional office, an eerie silence reigned among the staff assembled. Congressman Conyers was in Detroit, and the staff was waiting on some sense of direction. It was clear that none of us had any idea what was coming next. The one thing we did know, without anyone saying it, was that the work we were undertaking—and, really, the world we were living in—were no longer the same. In fact, it was hard to see how we could go forward when the nation was facing a crisis like this, one that we had not experienced before: An attack on the American homeland, including the nation's capital. Nothing was the same anymore and it was hard to see how we could go forward with major issue advocacy or an electoral program in this atmosphere.

A few days later, when we were still working in the aftermath of the 9/11 attacks, several members of Congress received letters in the mail containing the deadly chemical agent anthrax. As a result, all congressional offices and access to Capitol Hill were closed off indefinitely. Congressional staff were asked to work from home or auxiliary government buildings in Washington, D.C. For the most part, major legislative initiatives ground to a halt while Congress and the White House placed their entire focus on securing the nation's borders, getting to the bottom of what had happened on September 11th, and preparing for a long, protracted war in Afghanistan and Iraq that would commence in 2002.

Being detached from the Capitol Building and staff dramatically changed everything, including my belief on where and how I could best continue to make a difference in voting rights and voter mobilization. A few weeks after the anthrax scare, I decided to move on from Capitol Hill and accepted a job offer from the NAACP National Voter Fund to become its new executive director. It was a very difficult decision to leave Congressman Conyers and all my many congressional duties, this time for another full-time job. The extended Capitol shutdown meant that I would not be able to return to my office on Capitol Hill before starting the new job. As I would soon discover, the challenges of living and operating in a post-9/11 Washington created a new paradigm in the United States that went far beyond Capitol Hill and would affect every aspect of organizations and advocacy across the US into the future.

For many policy and non-profit organizations in Washington, major funding for ongoing advocacy campaigns dried up within months due to the 9/11 attacks. New heightened security measures were being put into place across the society and culture. The economic downturn in the US caused financial commitments and projects that had been in the pipeline to be postponed or canceled. By the end of the year, many organizations were laying off non-essential staff and cutting back expenditures to the bare bones. At this point, our main jobs were no longer about mobilizing voters or advancing new major policy initiatives. Instead, we focused on surviving a major economic downturn and living in a country preparing for a major war. It would be the beginning of a long and protracted vengeful war in Afghanistan and Iraq that would last for the next two decades.

The 2002 election cycle was now seen simply as a rebuilding year in the aftermath of the 2000 elections and 9/11. For many nonpartisan and civil rights organizations, the challenge was rebuilding an infrastructure for mobilizing voters in time for the 2004 elections. A major part of that strategy was building a national "Election Protection" network composed of lawyers and membership groups on the ground that would offer training on procedures to protect the vote in future elections. These efforts were spearheaded by the Lawyers Committee for Civil Rights Under Law, People for the American Way, and a large network of over 30 organizations. A national toll free hotline, 866-OUR-VOTE was re-established and expanded nationally. Voters could now call in with any complaints or report problems they were experiencing leading up to and on Election Day. The data from those thousands of calls in future elections would help peel back the layers on what was clearly an election administration apparatus in great need of fixing to ensure that the Florida debacle was never repeated.

At the same time, reform efforts were underway to address the election administration issues that had been revealed in the 2000 Florida elections. The lack of federal standards for *counting votes* and election administration was finally being addressed by Congress, with the 2000 election debacle being Exhibit A for what states needed to avoid in future elections. In late 2001, in response to the 2000 election debacle in Florida, Representative Bob Ney, a Republican from Ohio, took the lead in drafting new federal legislation designed to assist states in addressing the issues of outdated voting machines and election administration procedures. On November 14, 2001, Representative Ney introduced the Help America Vote Act (HAVA), H.R. 3295, on a bipartisan basis with 76 other members of Congress, with almost half being Republican co-sponsors.[2] As chair of the powerful House Administration Committee, Representative Ney was able to help build Republican support for the bill while Representative Stenny Hoyer from Maryland led Democratic efforts to steer the new bill through Congress one year after the controversial 2000 election. The HAVA created new mandatory election administration minimum standards that states were required to follow in carrying out vote-counting procedures. Unlike the NVRA, the HAVA provided much-needed funding to states to implement HAVA mandates including the replacement of outdated voting lever machines and the widespread elimination of the punch card machines that had led to the Florida debacle.[3]

Civil rights organizations, led by the disability community and election integrity groups, began to coalesce around the legislation, which set forth new federal guidelines and standards in election procedures. They were particularly supportive of mandates that would, for the first time, establish or strengthen federal guidelines for the counting of votes in states, as well as overseas voting and pro-

---

2 "H.R.3295 – 107th Congress (2001–2002): Help America Vote Act of 2002," Congress.gov, last modified October 29, 2002, https://www.congress.gov/bill/107th-congress/house-bill/3295.
3 Ibid.

viding protections for voters with disabilities. Despite this widespread support, there was opposition to the bill due in large part to pockets of resistance on both sides of the aisle. Republicans who opposed the bill were leery of yet another federal bill imposing new mandates on states and creating a new federal agency, the proposed U.S. Election Assistance Commission, (EAC) that would serve as a clearinghouse for election administration undertaken in states. In particular, there were concerns about changes to voting technology and potential confusion surrounding the voter registration process. Republicans insisted on some form of photo ID being required for first-time postcard registrants.

On the other hand, a small contingent of Democratic lawmakers and some allied groups were concerned about the addition of ID requirements for first-time postcard registrants, which was viewed as complicating the voting process. Technical voter integrity experts were also critical of the new law requiring the widespread use of new electronic voting machines that might be suspectable to manipulation from nefarious actors on the newly emerging World Wide Web. Testing and certification standards became major areas of negotiation that were eventually addressed with further modifications to the bill's language. Also, the HAVA created new sub-agencies to address many of these concerns, including a standards board made up of election administration technical experts and a national board of advisors made up of stakeholders in the various levels of government and the non-profit sector.

The HAVA was able to avoid much of the long, drawn-out partisan wrangling that characterized the five-plus-year battle to pass the National Voter Registration Act. On December 13, 2001, exactly one year after Congress certified the 2000 election results, the original version of the Help America Vote Act passed the U.S. House of Representatives by an overwhelming bipartisan vote of 362– 63.[4] A modified version was passed in the U.S. Senate on April 11, 2002, under unanimous consent. A conference committee was formed to work out the differences between the two versions. Allied groups and congressional members and staff worked through many of the differences within a matter of months —not years. The final conference reported bill was passed on October 16, 2002, by a vote of 357– 48 in the House and by a vote of 92– 2 in the Senate. Finally, on October 29, 2002, President George W. Bush signed the election reform bill into law with little fanfare.[5]

---

4 Ibid.
5 "Actions – H.R.3295 – 107th Congress (2001– 2002): Help America Vote Act of 2002," Congress.gov, last modified October 29, 2002, https://www.congress.gov/bill/107th-congress/house-bill/3295/all-actions?overview=closed#tabs.

It was somewhat ironic that President Bush would sign the bipartisan bill, which was a fitting conclusion to the highly partisan battle that had taken place in the aftermath of the 2000 presidential elections. The September 11 attack had also sobered the nation and helped build support across party lines. HAVA was a new law that would strengthen our democracy after one of the greatest attacks on it from overseas, and in the face of the challenges to democracy that had emerged following the Florida debacle and the Supreme Court's intervention in Florida.

I was ecstatic with the passage and the fact that it was done on a bipartisan basis. It was the last bill I had been working on when I left Capitol Hill, and I had been feeling a little guilty about not being there to help push it through the final passage. It was a departure from my last decade of advocacy for voting rights and electoral reform bills. On this go-round, I found myself on the outside in the final months of political maneuvering to pass this landmark federal legislation. In this instance, I was now at the NAACP National Voter Fund, away from all the maneuvers on Capitol Hill, but still working to build grassroots support for the new HAVA bill. We were also working to build support for new legislation to stem the growing influence of money in politics. This effort involved another bipartisan approach called the McCain-Feingold Bipartisan Campaign Finance Reform Act.[6] The bill had broad support in the good government and election reform community, but virtually no support among Republicans and even Democrats who were benefiting greatly from the current system of campaign financing. There was also little awareness of this issue in the African American community.

While I supported both efforts, I sought to resolve the unfinished business of the NVRA, pushing for universal voter registration by advancing same-day registration (SDR) bills in reform-friendly states like California, Michigan, and New Jersey. In California, an heir to the Taco Bell company, Rob McCay, was advancing an SDR bill and reached out to me in an effort to take the effort national. A number of other like-minded donors were looking to advance campaign finance reform, rather than EDR. A growing number of financially well-off champions were willing to invest in worthwhile causes in support of Democratic reforms. However, the vast majority of progressive donors were focused primarily on investing in a progressive infrastructure in states as the new national imperative. Strengthening the grassroots and engaging underrepresented constituencies to-

---

6 "Bipartisan Campaign Reform Act," Wikipedia, last modified March 16, 2022, https://en.wikipedia.org/wiki/Bipartisan_Campaign_Reform_Act.

gether in states was seen as the best remedy for change in the post-Florida 2000 and the post-9/11 era.

Chapter 12
The 2004 Ohio Election Debacle, Katrina and VRA Reauthorization

In July 2004, the Democratic Party nominated Massachusetts Senator John Kerry as its 2004 presidential nominee and North Carolina Senator John Edwards as his vice-presidential running mate. Kerry wrapped up the nomination shortly after the New Hampshire primary by beating Vermont Governor Howard Dean and other lesser-known candidates. The campaign was also notable as two African American candidates launched largely symbolic campaigns for president: Rev. Al Sharpton, a longtime civil rights activist and leader of the New York-based National Action Network (NAN), and former Illinois U.S. Senator Carol Moseley Braun. Sharpton ran a campaign closely modeled after the progressive issue-based campaign that Rev. Jesse Jackson had run in the 1980s. Though it lacked the energy and enthusiasm of the Jackson effort, it elevated Sharpton's status as a national civil rights leader.

Moseley Braun had been defeated for re-election in 1998 by Republican Senator Pete Fitzgerald and had accepted appointments as the US Ambassador to New Zealand and Samoa during the final years of the Clinton Administration. In late 2003, she opted out of running for her old Illinois senate seat and instead decided to run for the Democratic nomination for president. After serving only one term, the low-key incumbent Republican Senator Fitzgerald chose not to run for re-election in 2004. Both former Illinois senators opting out of a run for the Senate opened the door for a little-known Illinois state senator, Barack Obama, to seek the open U.S. Senate seat in 2004.

Kerry chose Obama, still just a state senator, to give the keynote address at the 2004 Democratic Convention. Obama electrified the convention hall with a speech that sought to unify the convention and the country. His most memorable line was, "There is not a Black America and a White America and Latino America and Asian America—there's the United States of America!"[1] The speech and his unifying message resonated with millions of viewers across the country who got their first glimpse of the person who would go on to win his U.S. Senate seat in November. The speech and his winning senate campaign helped set the stage for Obama's emergence as a future leader of the Democratic Party.

---

[1] "Barack Obama's Remarks to the Democratic National Convention," The New York Times, last modified July 27, 2004, https://www.nytimes.com/2004/07/27/politics/campaign/barack-obamas-remarks-to-the-democratic-national.html.

https://doi.org/10.1515/9783110742473-015

On the nonpartisan side, a loose confederation of over twenty 501(C)(3) groups gathered in Washington in the summer of 2004, convened by Minnesota progressive activist Mark Ritchie. The group drew up early plans for a more co-ordinated national strategy for nonpartisan groups to share resources, research, data, and voter engagement best practices. Much like the *America Votes* (C)(4) effort, it had the support of some of the most progressive donors, but on a much smaller scale. The group of national organizations agreed to coordinate its efforts at the state level under the banner "November 2nd Coalition," named for the 2004 Election Day.

As I had done in 2000 and earlier since the 1990s, I returned to my home state of Ohio in the final few weeks to help navigate GOTV efforts there. Ohio was one of the NAACP NVF's largest state programs. From February to October, the field effort, led by NVF State Director Thaddeus Jackson, registered over 82,000 voters, and trained and recruited over 300 canvassers to go door to door in Ohio's five major cities: Cleveland, Columbus, Cincinnati, Akron, and Dayton. Collaboration with other partners in America Votes and the November 2nd Coalition resulted in a massive turnout of voters on November 2 with a turn-out of 71.7% the second-highest turnout of voters ever recorded in the state of Ohio. [2] The mobilization campaign in 2004 in Ohio felt strangely like the 2000 effort in Michigan. It felt good to be back on the battlefield: knocking on doors, writing up newsletters, distributing thousands of voter guides to churches and community centers. The campaign also included placing major ads on Black radio and in the Black press, helping to carry the message about the importance of the 2004 election between Senator John Kerry and President George Bush. While not endorsing any candidates, we reminded voters about the election de-bacle in Florida in 2000 and that every vote counted.

At first, I was struck by the similarities between Cleveland in 2004 and De-troit in 2000. Both had long lines everywhere. However, in Ohio, voters faced more bitter cold and constant rain, which made standing in line outside the poll-ing place a much more miserable experience. Several hours of long lines were recorded in Cleveland, Columbus, Cincinnati, and college towns all over the state, including my home campus of Ohio University. At Dennison University, several students were reported to have stood in line for over nine hours before finally voting close to Midnight. By contrast, in rural areas of the state, voting wait times were measured in minutes, not hours, with waits as short as five mi-nutes. In many urban centers across the state, voters who had been registered to

---

2 "Experts confounded: Turnout higher in Ohio in 2004," The Columbus Dispatch, last modified November 7, 2008, https://amp.dispatch.com/amp/23962130007.

vote shortly before the deadlines were turned away because their names never made it to the voter rolls. Others showed up only to discover that their polling place had been moved since the last election, without their ever being notified. Many others took one look at the long lines, turned around, and headed home. Some never bothered to get out of their cars or buses; they simply took a pass on voting rather than waiting for hours in the cold rain.[3]

This was the election debacle of 2004 that we had all feared. The Ohio secretary of state this time was a Black Republican, Ken Blackwell. He had gained notoriety in the national press for rejecting voter registration cards from grassroots advocates because the weight of the paper used for the forms was not heavy enough to be accepted.[4] Blackwell had rejected thousands of voter registration forms collected by groups like the NAACP, the League of Women Voters, churches, student groups, and others that had a long history of conducting voter registration drives in Ohio. Additionally, Blackwell challenged the provisions of the Help America Vote Act (HAVA) law that regulated the counting of provisional ballots.[5] Like Florida Secretary of State Katherine Harris in 2000, Blackwell was a staunch supporter of President Bush and for months proudly promoted his status as one of the co-chairs of the Bush for President Campaign.[6] This one act alone was a warning sign to voting rights groups that there could be even more trouble on Election Day.

On election night, there were still over 155,000 uncounted provisional ballots in the state of Ohio; Blackwell and his administration did not make it certain whether those ballots would ever be counted toward the final tally. His directives to his county board of election on the counting of provisional ballots did not line up with the new federal standards set forth in the Help America Vote Act which caused widespread confusion at polling places.[7] Thousands of the provisional ballots were from voters who had shown up at the right polling place but had stood in the wrong lines for their precincts for several hours. Rather than being sent to the back of the correct long lines, they opted to vote "provisionally," which meant that their votes would be segregated from the other ballots and

3 "Preserving Democracy: What Went Wrong in Ohio," The Green Papers, last modified January 5, 2005, https://www.thegreenpapers.com/G04/ohiostatusrept1505.pdf.
4 "Ohio rejects 1000s of voter registration applications due to paper weight," Daily Kos, last modified September 27, 2004, https://www.dailykos.com/stories/2004/9/27/53984/-.
5 Peter Shuler, "Ken Blackwell's Disgraceful Election Machinations," CityBeat, last modified December 8, 2004, https://www.citybeat.com/news/ken-blackwell-s-disgraceful-election-machinations-12229108.
6 Ibid.
7 Ibid.

counted only later down the road if there was a need.[8] Post-election analysis would reveal that a disproportional percentage of Ohio provisional ballots were cast by young voters, frequent movers, urban and African American voters.[9] The failure to not count these provisional ballots would mean that the true will of the voters on election night was not represented in the media and that the election, in fact, was much closer than the Bush campaign or Blackwell's Secretary of State's office was reporting. In addition to the long lines, there were reports of machine breakdowns and malfunctions, newly registered voters' names not appearing on the voter list, voters being forced to stand outside in the rain rather than being let into the heated buildings, widespread shortages of paper ballots, and rumors of Black voters being challenged at the polls by Republican election observers. It was a chilling replay of all the problems that Black and Brown voters encountered in Florida.

Shortly after our canvases ended and the polls closed in Ohio, I met with the two-person delegation of international election observers from Europe that had been part of the nationally coordinated effort led by Keith Jennings as part of the *Count Every Vote* Election Observance program. The observers had flown into Ohio to closely monitor the Election Day activities. By the time they reached me late that evening, I was completely exhausted but gave them an earful, recounting all the areas of concern I was picking up from across the state. They took plenty of notes but did not seem poised to intervene in any way. This was somewhat of a surprise because I believed they would have been the most appropriate people to raise many of these concerns with local election officials. Instead, they conceded that they were only observers and would be making a full report—in the coming months—on what they observed in all the targeted states to which their full delegation had been dispatched across the US. I was glad they were there to witness what we had seen, but somehow, felt we were still on our own.

It was another long and difficult night of waiting for more returns and for the newscast to make a call as to who was winning in the key battleground states. After the results of the other states, like Michigan, Wisconsin, and Pennsylvania, were called late into the night, it was down to the state of Ohio. As the night wore on, it soon became clear that Bush and Kerry were almost tied in the Electoral College despite Bush's slight lead of 50.7% of the popular vote. With 270

8 Jim Bebbington and Laura Bischoff, "Blackwell rulings rile voting advocates," MIT, (n.d.) accessed March 22, 2022, http://www.mit.edu/people/fuller/peace/league_women_voters.htm.
9 Shuler, "Ken Blackwell's Disgraceful Election Machinations," CityBeat, last modified December 8, 2004, https://www.citybeat.com/news/ken-blackwell-s-disgraceful-election-machinations-12229108.

electoral votes needed to win the Electoral College, Bush had won 266 to Kerry's 251. Whoever was declared the winner of Ohio's 20 electoral votes would win the presidency regardless of the popular vote, as was the case in 2000. This time, the shoe was on the other foot, with Democrats looking to the Electoral College as the only way to pull out a win. By 3:30 AM Bush still had a lead in Ohio of just over 118,000 votes with a shrinking percentage of votes still waiting to be counted—including thousands of absentee and provisional ballots. Like millions of other Americans, I went to bed that night not knowing who won the election.

When I woke up after just a few hours of restless sleep, I heard early news reports that Senator Kerry was preparing to make an announcement conceding the election at a 10:00 AM press conference. I sprang from my bed and started making calls to Washington, to the DNC, to Capitol Hill, to the Nov. 2nd Coalition, to America Votes, and to the Election Protection coalition. On each call, I asked the same question: Why was the candidate planning to concede the election on the morning after Election Day when, clearly, over 155,000 votes had still not been counted in Ohio—not to mention several other states on the West Coast where millions of votes were still being counted and could add to the popular vote totals.

I repeatedly argued that whoever was called the winner in Ohio would be declared the new president. Although John Kerry was not winning the popular vote, it was still possible that he could win the electoral vote as Bush had done in 2000—but only if Ohio were called for him. Ohio had reported a historic 70% turnout that year and, once again, the election administration apparatus was not able to fully ensure that all of its voters could vote without unnecessary barriers. Once again, voting machine breakdowns, malfunctions, long lines, missing registration forms, and hundreds of thousands of uncounted provisional ballots made the Ohio election something that I felt needed to be investigated by the Justice Department. At a minimum, there needed to be a full-scale effort to ensure that all the 155,000 provisional votes were counted before anyone should concede and before we knew the actual tallies, not projections.

"It's way too early to concede!" I would yell over and over, louder, and louder, into the telephone as the 10:00 AM hour approached. No one I reached knew what to do or how to respond if the decision was already being made by the candidate. I pleaded to the DNC that a simple follow-through with the election protection contingency plans laid out by the candidate should be followed. I reminded them that there was a game plan that the candidate and the DNC had agreed to with many of their Black Caucus members and African American leaders across the country. I argued, to no avail, that the DNC needed to intervene and start the process of delaying the concession announcement until all the provisional votes were counted.

Like most voting rights advocates, I believed that the scores of Democratic lawyers who had been flown into Ohio from all over the country would file multiple lawsuits the next day to ensure that all the 200,000-plus provisional ballots were counted. Instead, at a 10:00 AM press conference, the Democratic nominee, Senator John Kerry of Massachusetts, conceded the election to President George Bush. The concession came even though the race was still close, and votes were still being counted in many states. By the time of the press conference Bush's margin of victory was now over 135,000 votes, with over 155,000 uncounted provisional ballots.[10] We knew that most of these provisional ballots were from the urban centers and college campuses where Kerry had overwhelming support and where most of the election administration problems were concentrated.

Senator Kerry's announcement at 10:00 AM was a betrayal of his widely proclaimed promise, made during his acceptance speech at the Democratic National Convention that he would not concede until every vote is counted.[11] He had repeated that pledge in speeches across the country to cheering crowds including civil rights groups and voting rights advocates. Now here we were with hundreds of thousands—if not millions—of votes cast on Election Day that were not counted in Ohio and other states. Many of those votes were from Black, Hispanic, poor, and student voters who had stood in long lines, in the cold, pouring rain for hours, only to find that their names were not on the list or that they were in the wrong line. Kerry's broken promise and "I just wanted to get it over with" attitude in statements after his concession made a mockery of the American citizens who had been committed to voting for him and to participating in our democracy. This time, there would be no six-week battle, no litigation filed, and no candidate standing up for the people who had stood in line for hours for him and the Democratic party as Al Gore had done in 2000.

The following day, I was literally sick to my stomach. It was happening again! Another election was being taken from the true elected leader—and, once again, the Democratic Party candidate and the media (not the voters and voting rights advocates) were the arbiters of when the election would be called. Kerry's earlier than expected concession ended any hope of success for the major election protection efforts that were in place. Many of us who had seen the long lines of people standing in the cold rain for hours experienced an overwhelming sadness over the fact that we still had not fixed what was wrong with our elec-

---

10 Adam Liptak, "Voting Problems in Ohio Set Off an Alarm," The New York Times, last modified November 7, 2004, https://www.nytimes.com/2004/11/07/politics/campaign/voting-problems-in-ohio-set-off-an-alarm.html.
11 "Kerry lawyers scrutinize voting in Ohio," nbc News, last modified August 4, 2012, https://www.nbcnews.com/id/wbna6460869.

tion system. Instead of staying to wage the next phase of the election protection battle and ensure that all the votes were counted, as it had promised, the Kerry campaign closed its doors and began to dismantle. There would be no long protracted fight for the right of every vote to be counted. In the end, it was all about politics.

I left Ohio the next morning on a plane heading back to Washington, D.C., where I saw several Democratic party lawyers who had flown in to handle election protection problems. Many of them, whom I had met in the trenches, had reverted to mere passengers in line, boarding a plane. No one talked about the election or even looked my way to connect. They held their heads down, almost to a person, not even talking among themselves. They were flying back to Washington, New York, and Chicago. Their law firms had released them to help with the campaign, to be on hand to file temporary restraining orders (TSOs) as needed in the post-election period, and to defend voters who were being disenfranchised. But, like mannequins, they reverted to their stance as members of the firm who had lost the case in court and were exiting the courtroom and moving on to the next case. Suddenly, it was all over, and we were on our own... again.

Back in Ohio, a couple of weeks later, a number of local grassroots election lawyers and activists led by attorneys Bob Fitrakis and Cliff Arnebeck, as well as the group CASE-Ohio, convened a series of hearings in Columbus and around the state that offered voters an opportunity to share their stories about what they had experienced on Election Day. I was asked to serve as one of the panel members who heard their testimonies. At each hearing, people showed up by the hundreds, recounting the harrowing struggles they had experienced while voting. Many called for an official congressional investigation, but with Republicans still in control of Congress, their requests fell on deaf ears. However, Congressman John Conyers (by now a legendary champion of voting rights) and Cleveland Congresswoman Stephanie Tubbs Jones convened a Democrats-only hearing in Columbus, Ohio. They were joined by State Representative Charleta Tavares representing the Ohio Legislative Black Caucus. The panel heard witness after witness testify in detail about their problems, which had occurred not just on Election Day but also on the days and weeks leading up to the election.

Expert witnesses who worked on voting machine integrity were brought in to testify, giving credence to claims of machine malfunctions that had been reported in several locations. Vote flipping from Kerry to Bush, as well as machine counts that did not match the official voter rolls, were questioned. The hearing's extensive findings were collected in a document that came to be known as *The*

Conyers Report on the 2004 Election in Ohio.[12] The report was used by Congress-woman Tubbs-Jones and key members of the CBC to call on Congress to address the voting irregularities from Ohio. She was joined in her appeal by Rev. Jesse Jackson, Rev. Otis Moss and numerous Ohio faith leaders, Green Party activists, and election lawyer advocate Jon Bonifaz of the group Voter Action.

As pressure from grassroots voting activists in Ohio continued, the Kerry campaign sent a team of their election lawyers back into Ohio in mid-November on what they described as a "fact finding mission," to help identify voting problems but also to put to rest any doubts about the legitimacy of the Ohio vote totals.[13] It was not designed to challenge the results, but an effort to "keep their commitment" to ensure that every vote was counted. After a review of the numerous issues Kerry's lawyers concluded that despite the widespread problems experienced by Ohio voters, it was not enough to overcome the 135,000-vote deficit against Bush.[14]

On the day of the Electoral College vote in December 2004, two busloads of voters traveled to Washington, D.C. from Ohio to protest outside the Capitol against the Electoral College vote. The small rally of barely one hundred protesters gained little notice at the foot of the lawn on the west side of the Capitol Building. Inside, on the floor of the Capitol, while some members of the CBC supported Tubb-Jones' challenge, only one Democratic US senator, California's Barbara Boxer, would raise her objection on the floor of the Senate, a step that was required to launch a formal challenge.[15] While the challenge was given floor time and allowed an opportunity to showcase the problems in Ohio's election, it met with the same result as the congressional challenges in 2000. They were ruled out of order, this time by Vice President Dick Cheney, who chaired the Electoral College proceedings. In the end, Ohio's 20 electoral votes were awarded to Bush, giving him the 272 electoral votes needed.[16] The re-election of President George Bush was now complete, and the Ohio challenge came to an abrupt end.

---

12 "Preserving Democracy: What Went Wrong in Ohio," The Green Papers, last modified January 5, 2005, https://www.thegreenpapers.com/G04/ohiostatusrept1505.pdf.

13 "Kerry lawyers scrutinize voting in Ohio," nbc News, last modified August 4, 2012, https://www.nbcnews.com/id/wbna6460869.

14 Liptak, "Voting Problems in Ohio Set Off an Alarm," The New York Times, last modified November 7, 2004, https://www.nytimes.com/2004/11/07/politics/campaign/voting-problems-in-ohio-set-off-an-alarm.html.

15 Maura Reynolds, "Boxer Poses a Challenge, Briefly," The Los Angeles Times, last modified January 7, 2005, https://www.latimes.com/archives/la-xpm-2005-jan-07-na-electoral7-story.html.

16 Rich Exner, "2004 Ohio presidential election results; George W. Bush defeats John Kerry (photo gallery)," Cleveland.com, last modified January 11, 2019, https://www.cleveland.com/datacentral/2016/06/2004_ohio_presidential_electio.html.

Nowhere was the disappointment greater than in the state of Ohio. Had John Kerry carried Ohio and secured its 20 electoral votes, despite losing the popular vote nationally, he would have won the presidency by winning 271 Electoral College votes. Instead, he ended up with only 251 electoral votes, which he had secured primarily by winning every state in the Northeast, the entire West Coast, and the three upper Midwest states of Minnesota, Wisconsin, and Michigan. Despite Ohio's over 71% turnout and high Black voter mobilization, which gave Kerry nearly 90% of the Black vote, African Americans were again blamed for the Kerry loss because the Black support did not reach closer to 95%. It was the high water mark that political pundits claimed would have secured a victory in the close Ohio contest in which Bush was declared the winner, 51–49%.[17]

The one consolation prize in 2004 was the election of Barack Obama as the senator from Illinois. His electrifying speech at the 2004 Democratic Convention had started speculation of his being a presidential candidate as early as the spring of 2005. With Obama's Senate victory, there was at least some hope that the upcoming 2006 and 2008 elections could help usher in a new generation of Democratic leaders. This hope helped many who questioned the 2004 results move on from that election and refocus their efforts on future opportunities that the country would have—as well as future challenges.

Katrina Displacement and the 2006 VRA Reauthorization

In the late summer of 2005, a natural disaster fell upon the Gulf Coast with two major super hurricanes: Hurricane Harvey and the unprecedented category 5 Hurricane Katrina, which hit New Orleans with a vengeance on August 29, 2005. The National Hurricane Center estimated a total of 1,856 people from Louisiana, Mississippi and other states along the Gulf Coast were killed by the effects of Hurricane Katrina alone.[18] On the days leading up to the storm New Orleans Mayor Ray Nagin and parish officials ordered an evacuation of over 1.3 million residents from the city and surrounding areas. With over 80% of New Orleans under water, over 250,000 residents were displaced from their homes and forced to relocate and be transported to evacuation centers throughout the South and major urban centers.[19] The displacement of these citizens also meant the displacement of over 200,000 voters. Tens of thousands lost their homes and would

---

17 Ibid.
18 "Hurricane Katrina," Wikipedia, last modified February 5, 2022, https://en.wikipedia.org/wiki/Hurricane_Katrina.
19 Ibid.

be unable to return home to vote or even have a say in the upcoming 2006 municipal elections.

I made a number of trips to New Orleans and saw firsthand the devastation that the storm had wreaked on the city. On one occasion, I was able to share a cab ride with an old friend, Democratic pollster Cornell Belcher, who gave the driver a $50 bill and asked him to show us the real effects of Katrina from the lower 9th Ward. Even months after the storm, cars were still piled on top of each other and homes were flattened, with trailers parked on their front lawns by homeowners. Large segments of the city still had no electricity, no street-lights, and no running water or functioning sewage system. There were literally thousands of shuttered homes, shuttered large and small businesses, shuttered schools, shuttered churches, and even shuttered cemeteries. It was a disaster zone that looked apocalyptic and deeply sobering to me and Cornell. The taxicab driver was almost in tears as he graphically described the devastation of the storm and its aftermath. It was clear that voting was not the most important thing that New Orleans needed. Instead, it needed real relief that was being promised by the Bush Administration and the Federal Emergency Management Agency (FEMA). It was clear that even three months after the hurricane, the federal response was lacking, despite pledges by President Bush for a speedy recovery. It was also clear that the city, state, and federal governments were woefully unprepared for such a catastrophic climate event.[20]

I was so moved by the experience that I decided to take an extended leave of absence from the NAACP National Voter Fund in late 2005. I began working with the National Coalition on Black Civic Participation (NCBCP) and other Katrina recovery groups in their efforts to undertake a *Rebuild Louisiana* initiative. The initiative was launched by NCBCP president, Melanie Campbell, with support from National Urban League President and former New Orleans Mayor Mark Morial, Hip Hop Caucus Leader Rev. Lennox Yearwood, fraternities, sororities, labor leaders, business leaders, faith leaders, and other coalition partners. The programs they initiated with local leaders like online publicist Vincent Sylvan helped to place a continued focus on hurricane relief efforts during and even after the election campaign for mayor was over.

Rebuild was an effort to move beyond the voting issue and keep the political spotlight on many systemic problems that had continued to plague the city and region even after the election. This included scheduling numerous town hall meetings with elected officials to discuss the state of relief efforts and programs

---

20 "Hurricane Katrina," History, last modified August 9, 2019, https://www.history.com/topics/natural-disasters-and-environment/hurricane-katrina#political-fallout-from-hurricane-katrina.

to hold the Bush Administration, state, and local elected leaders accountable for speeding up relief efforts. The forums focused on immediate shortages of funding for temporary housing and support for human needs programs to protect children and families trough nutrition, health care, childcare, and other family services that had been disrupted. They lacked a focus on long-term investments needed to fix the broken levees, to rebuild schools, local small businesses, and residential housing units for displaced residents.

In December 2005, I received a call from my old friend Donna Brazile, who was now a vice-chair of the Democratic National Committee. She was seeking my help with a herculean effort to get the displaced voters of her hometown, New Orleans, and Louisiana in general to vote absentee in the upcoming spring primary elections. Hurricane Katrina was unprecedented in its massive force and death toll of over 1,800 people and the over $130 Billion in damages to the region.[21] However, it also ushered in the largest displacement of voters in US history with over half of the city's 500,000 residents forced to evacuate. There had never been a massive absentee voter outreach effort that crossed state lines. FEMA had dispersed Katrina's evacuees throughout multiple cities including Atlanta, Houston, Dallas, and other urban centers. I was sympathetic to the problem that Donna presented but did not think that I could answer the call of the party this time. The problem seemed too big to solve and I wasn't sure if the party was the best place to get this work done.

Donna was a New Orleans native with a large family still living in the aftermath of the hurricane. She was determined to move the displaced Katrina voter outreach program forward, believing that the DNC had an obligation to ensure that voters who had lost everything did not also lose their right to vote. Even after I had declined the offer, she approached me again with an impassioned plea. She stressed that my expertise in voting laws and elections was just the kind of support and leadership the party needed to work with the secretaries of state and election officials in multiple states where voters had been displaced. Her final appeal was that the mayoral election in New Orleans was quickly approaching, and she needed someone who could start right away in implementing the plan and steering the party's election protection efforts at the DNC and with state parties.

I always found it hard to say "no" when duty called. In this instance, it was something that I saw as part of the disaster relief effort that few, if any, organizations were taking on. I regarded it as an unprecedented opportunity to develop national processes for conducting an absentee ballot program in the aftermath of

---

21 Ibid.

a national disaster. The right to vote was at stake and once again, I turned to the NVRA and the Help America Vote Act to determine which of its provisions we could use to assist in the effort. As it turned out, the provisions for agency-based registration and use of the national postcard registration were the two components that became the least challenging and most reasonable efforts to be incorporated into a national program.

I agreed to support Donna's efforts on a short-term basis as a consultant only, though as part of that assistance, I also agreed to temporarily fill a vacancy at the DNC as director of the DNC's Voting Rights Institute (VRI). Former Vermont Governor Howard Dean, who had unsuccessfully run for president in 2004, had run and won for chair of the DNC. Donna approached Dean about my coming on board temporary to help her get through the Katrina absentee voter program. Chairman Dean agreed but only if I would also take responsibility for building an election protection (EP) program in all 50 states within the party infrastructure.

While the DNC had a national election program, only a handful of state parties had incorporated any EP program into their state party apparatus. It was part and parcel of Dean's plan to run a "50 State Campaign" in the 2006 midterm elections rather than concentrating on the handful of battleground states —a failed strategy that had been done over and over again by party leaders with the same unsuccessful results. The extra-heavy assignment seemed like double-duty to me! I was placed within the DNC Political Division headed up by Political Director Pam Womack from Virginia and worked as her Deputy Political Director again with my old colleague Maureen Garde. She had stayed committed to the DNC the entire 10 years since I had last worked there. We all worked under the leadership of Leah Daughtry who served as the DNC Chief of Staff. Leah helped ensure there was inter-party and financial support for the new election protection effort that still faced some institutional resistance from some state parties.

I still harbored reservations about leaving the advocacy world and going to work again for the party. However, I was reminded of the 2004 election debacle in Ohio and how much difference it could have made if the party *itself* had established election protection plans and guidelines within its own state structure. Maybe it would make a difference the next time we had a presidential election? And maybe this was the right time for me to offer my services to the party for what would be my second tour of duty. After experiencing all the difficulties and heartaches of the 2000 and 2004 elections, I was now a wounded but still active duty voting rights soldier who could offer the DNC new perspectives on programs to protect voting rights

For the next several months in 2006, we were successful in assisting over 70,000 displaced voters in casting absentee ballots that allowed the mayoral elections in Louisiana to take place with the participation of large segments of absentee votes from displaced voters. Despite the loss of over 250,000 residents, and all of the problems that continued to plague the city, New Orleans held a successful election. But even more importantly, the Democratic party established the first national contingency plans and best practices for conducting a massive absentee balloting election in the aftermath of a natural disaster. The effort to re-enfranchise the displaced voters of Louisiana was hailed as one of the most important milestones in the rebuilding of New Orleans and Louisiana after the deadly Katrina Hurricane.

At the DNC, the Voting Rights Institute consisted of me, former DOJ Attorney Anna Martinez, longtime DNC Legal Counsel Joseph Sandler, and scores of volunteer lawyers who made up the DNC National Democratic Lawyers Council. Despite our small staff, we got several new initiatives up and running. We first convened all the state party leaders in cooperation with the Association of State Democratic Chairs (ASDC) and laid out a roadmap for instituting their first-ever state-run and national party-supported election protection program. To facilitate this effort, we set up a national election protection hotline, 866-DEM-VOTE, for all states to use in reporting problems with voter suppression, voting machine malfunctions, or other election irregularities. We also provided 18 key battleground states with funding to hire their first ever election protection coordinator. To smaller states, we provided less funding to develop a voluntary system to ensure newly established election protection guidelines would be followed.

While being respectful of their roles on the nonpartisan side, I convened the Voting Rights Institute and National Democratic Lawyers Council for a first-of-its-kind summit between voting rights advocates, volunteer lawyers, and experts in election administration. The goal of the summit was to discuss the importance of protecting the impartiality and integrity of the election process and work together to ensure that there were no repeats of the election debacles of Florida in 2000 and Ohio in 2004. This was significant in that these divergent groups were often at odds. On the DNC side, there were often hundreds of Democratic party lawyers who were flown into states in the final days before an election, ready to go to battle in the courts, without having much information about, or appreciation for, the work that voting rights advocates were already doing on the ground.

For many of the advocates, it was an opportunity to better appreciate the concerns of election officials and administrators, who were often subject to lawsuits and claims of voter suppression and intimidation. It was also an important opportunity for advocates to impress upon on the party the importance of supporting the full implementation of the National Voter Registration Act and the newly minted provisional voting components of the Help America Vote Act. The summit was a success in that it helped set the landscape for future election administration programs on both the partisan and nonpartisan sides. These on-going party election protection efforts and the non-coordinated but parallel non-partisan efforts would go a long way toward ensuring that the 2006 midterm elections and the 2008 presidential election were free from many of the election mishaps of the previous two presidential election cycles.

In just a few weeks, we received another major victory in Congress when efforts to reauthorize the Voting Rights Act in 2006 was passed on an overwhelmingly bipartisan basis. Initially, Republicans, primarily from Southern states, raised numerous objections to reauthorizing the bill that kept many of their states covered under the pre-clearance provision. Without major changes, they threatened to filibuster the bill until a new formula was devised that would bail out their states or have the law apply equally to all states. Their opposition was muted when President George W. Bush spoke at the national convention of the NAACP in Washington, D.C. Still under fierce criticism for his administration's mishandling of the Hurricane Katrina relief efforts, Bush gave a surprisingly full-throated endorsement of the reauthorization of the Voting Rights Act, to the thunderous applause of 8,000 NAACP convention delegates gathered at the Washington Convention Center.[22] He urged the senate to pass the bill without delay or any amendments that had been called for by a number of Republican senators and promised to sign the bill into law if it reached his desk.

Bush's speech was followed the next morning by a full NAACP Lobby Day on Capitol Hill organized by veteran NAACP Washington Bureau Chief Hillary Shelton. The effort included buses from around the country filled with hundreds of more NAACP members who converged on Capitol Hill offices for one of the most effective lobby days in the association's history. In all my years in Washington, I had never seen so many African Americans on Capitol Hill! It overwhelmed congressional offices and the Senate Judiciary Committee room where the VRA was being marked up. Alabama Senator Jeff Sessions had initially sought changes in the bill to make it easier for Alabama and other southern states to bail out of Section 4 pre-clearance provisions. Republican senators had earlier threatened to filibuster the bill for the same reasons.

---

22 "President Bush Addresses NAACP Annual Convention," George W. Bush Archives, last modified July 20, 2006, https://georgewbush-whitehouse.archives.gov/news/releases/2006/07/20060720.html.

The bill H.R. 9 had been renamed the *Fannie Lou Hamer, Rosa Parks and Coretta Scott King Voting Rights Act Reauthorization and Amendments Act of 1998*[23]— all three pioneers of the civil rights movement with Parks and King having recently passed away. With a committee room jammed full of NAACP leaders from around the country, Sessions and other opposing senators did a sudden about-face and withdrew their opposition to the bill. Even while supporting the bill in the final vote of the Judiciary Committee mark up, Sessions warned his colleagues that the failure to update the preclearance formula may not survive a Supreme Court challenge in the future. The final vote on the bill in the Senate was 98 – 0 on July 20, 2006. True to his pledge to the NAACP, President Bush signed the bill into law on July 27, 2006.[24]

With the Voting Rights Act now reauthorized and secured, and with the NVRA and Help America Vote Act laws finally being fully implemented in the states, prospects for a smooth administration of the 2006 elections improved dramatically. Finally, I began to see more clearly how all of the advocacy efforts since the mid-1980s had created an almost unbroken thread of progress in the area of voting rights legislation. They were not the bloody battles that had marked the path to passage of the original VRA in 1965. They were however intense legislative battles that were won amidst our struggles through two election debacles, the 911 terrorist attacks, hurricanes, and other national disasters.

Howard Dean's "50 State Campaign" strategy eventually paid off for the Democratic Party. Across the country, Democrats regained control of the US House of Representatives for the first time since their devastating defeat in 1994. House Minority Leader Nancy Pelosi became the first female Speaker of the House of Representatives in US history. History was also made when 22 members of the Congressional Black Caucus became chairs of key congressional committees and sub-committees for the first time in US history. This included Congressman John Conyers, who would become the first African American chairman of the powerful House Judiciary Committee, a lifetime goal of his since first being elected to Congress in 1964; Representative Charlie Rangle from Harlem, who became the first African American chairman of the powerful House Ways and Means Committee; and William Clay who became the first Afri-

---

23 "H.R.9 – 109th Congress (2005 – 2006): Fannie Lou Hamer, Rosa Parks, and Coretta Scott King Voting Rights Act Reauthorization and Amendments Act of 2006," Congress.gov, last modified July 27, 2006, https://www.congress.gov/bill/109th-congress/house-bill/9.

24 "Actions – H.R.9 – 109th Congress (2005 – 2006): Fannie Lou Hamer, Rosa Parks, and Coretta Scott King Voting Rights Act Reauthorization and Amendments Act of 2006," Congress.gov, last modified July 26, 2006, https://www.congress.gov/bill/109th-congress/house-bill/9/all-actions?overview=closed#tabs.

can American Chair of the Education and Labor Committee. The major victories in 2006 helped take the sting out of the 2004 election debacle in Ohio and across the country. Navigating the waters between voting rights activists, election officials, state party leaders, and hundreds of lawyers was no easy task. However, it helped lay the foundation for the peaceful co-existence of the various election protection programs on both the partisan and nonpartisan sides for future elections and voting rights challenges that were still to come.

Chapter 13
The Obama Phenomenon and the Historic 2008 Mobilization

Donna's Brazile's request that I help her with the Katrina effort came at a big cost personally and professionally. I had to cease most of my formal work with nonpartisan efforts due to my party affiliation. I was also required to remain neutral in the upcoming 2008 presidential election, which had gotten off to an early start right after the 2006 general election. Among the 2008 hopefuls eager to jump out and get the campaign started was the newly elected senator from Illinois, Barack Obama. The media focused nonstop on his potential 2008 presidential candidacy. I had been a staunch supporter of Obama in his senate race. A good friend of mine from Detroit, Spencer Overton, was a law school classmate of Obama and had urged me to collaborate with him on a fundraiser and a staff recruitment effort. That request was also made by another friend, Darryl Thompson, a former staffer at the DNC building who worked for the Democratic Senatorial Campaign Committee (DSCC) and later as a top aide to Nevada Senator Harry Reid, who was the Senate Minority Leader.

I had met Obama once during a Congressional Black Caucus Weekend's Black Tie Dinner, when he was a young Illinois state senator. It was one of those events where you greeted and talked to scores of people throughout the night, collecting business cards from everyone. Among the cards I collected was that of the Illinois state senator who had made a failed bid for a congressional seat in Chicago held by a former Black Panther leader, Bobby Rush. One day, unexpectedly, Obama telephoned me while I was in the middle of a major legislative project for Conyers. It was a rare follow-up call after our brief meeting at the CBC weekend event. He talked very confidently and almost without ceasing about his plans to run for higher office in Illinois and possibly the U.S. Senate. At the time, I regarded him as an ambitious local elected official who had big dreams but was not ready for prime time.

I was surprised just a few weeks after the November 2006 general election when one of my Hill friends, Mike Stramanus, an Obama Senate staffer, approached me to see if I would be interested in coming to Chicago for a meeting with a number of advisors to Senator Obama. It would be a very small gathering that would discuss Obama's plans to run for president. I immediately said no, as I thought it was way too premature for such a meeting. It had been just a few weeks since the Democrats had taken back control of the U.S. House and I thought it made no sense to be in a strategy session for a 2008 election when

https://doi.org/10.1515/9783110742473-016

the new Democratic Congress had not even been sworn in! After repeated requests from Mike, I gave him a final no and said that it was probably not possible because I was working at the DNC and was required to remain neutral.

In the back of my mind, I knew that turning down the meeting might be a mistake that I would regret later. However, there was a real chance that I could lose my job at the DNC and being unemployed was not a good idea for me at the time. Although I missed out on the meeting, I later learned that it included David Axelrod and David Plouff, for whom I had worked at the DCCC back in 1998. I began feeling that I had missed a good opportunity but was later informed by Mike that he could still arrange a one-on-one meeting with Obama so that I could give him my own ideas about a 2008 run for president. It took some time, but we were finally able to arrange an opportunity for me to meet with the senator when he would be coming over to the US House of Representatives for an annual holiday reception hosted by my old boss, Representative John Conyers. At the time, it was the *go-to* event, including hundreds of key members of Congress, industry leaders, advocates, and key Hill staffers. Mike arranged for me to meet with Obama on his way to the Rayburn Office Building before the reception.

Expecting a sit-down meeting, I scrambled to find a place to meet off Capitol Hill so that we would not be discussing politics in the halls of Congress. As it turned out, there would be no sit-down meeting; I would have to settle for talking to him en route to the reception. I took it, not knowing when and if I would get another chance to connect. I waited outside the Cannon Office Building to catch the senator as soon as he came across from the Senate side. As he quickly walked alongside Mike, I noticed that he was smoking a cigarette. He stopped briefly to warmly greet me and then continued his stride toward the Rayburn House Office Building.

"Is this the way?" he asked, looking at me for logistical direction, "I'm just following you." The three of us walked down the long mostly empty street while we made small talk about the latest legislative activity on the Hill. After a few minutes, the issue of him running for president had not come up. As we got closer to the venue, I decided to bring it up myself. "I'm sorry I couldn't make the meeting in Chicago," I said.

"That's OK," he said. "We're talking now." At that point, he stopped to tie his shoelace, which gave me a few seconds to catch my breath and collect my thoughts.

"Mike says you're thinking about running for president," I said to break into the conversation. "Isn't it a bit early? I mean, it's mid-December 2006 and we haven't even sworn in the new Congress we just elected."

"I haven't made any decisions about anything," he said somewhat defensively as he continued his stride toward the reception. "Mike tells me you have a lot of experience in presidential elections working with Jesse Jackson and the DNC."

"Yes," I said. "Have you had a chance to talk to Rev. Jackson yet?"

"No," he answered, "it's been really busy."

"Well, "I said, "it's probably more important to talk to the Clintons. They really still run things related to the party since Gore lost. " He was suddenly silent, with only the sound of our feet walking down the long corridors. "Have you had a chance to talk to President Clinton yet?" I asked, almost to break the ice and keep the conversation going.

The young senator gave me a resounding "Nope."

"What about Hillary Clinton?" I probed further. "She is thinking about running for president, you know. And all the odds say she's kind of a shoo-in."

My line of questioning seemed to irritate him. I could feel the earlier warmth slipping away. "I just know they have a lot to say about what goes on in the party," I said, almost as if he did not know that inside Washington fact.

He finally stopped his stride and turned to me. "I'm not trying to run that type of campaign," he said rather abruptly. Sensing my tension, he paused and added, "I'm really looking forward to meeting John Conyers," almost as though he was changing the topic. "He's been a hero of mine for years."

"I'm sure he's looking forward to meeting you as well. Everybody is excited about your being the only Black senator. We are going to be able to do a lot next year with a Democratic House of Representatives. Hopefully, we can now get some things through the Senate in the next couple of years."

He did not respond, just continued his quick pace.

We were swiftly approaching the Judiciary Committee hearing room where Conyers' holiday party was in full swing, fully packed with people wall to wall. I knew they would be pulling on him the moment we entered the hearing room. Our brief meeting was suddenly over.

"I was hoping we could talk more," I said as I opened the door to the reception. Before he could answer, the crowd of attendees began approaching him for handshakes and side conversations. It took him a full 20 minutes to get to Conyers across the room. When they finally met up, Obama gave a customary honorary bow to the incoming chair of the House Judiciary Committee. Conyers was elated to greet him and barely noticed that I was standing next to the senator. They talked briefly and took pictures. However, the push of the excited crowd pulled Obama out of Conyers' orbit within the first few minutes. I looked at Mike and said that this was probably the worst place to meet Conyers or for us to have a real conversation with the senator about his plans.

The reception was also a time for me to see a lot of my old friends from Capitol Hill, so I soon went back to enjoying the gathering myself. Obama stayed for another half an hour before making his way toward the door. I decided to give it one more try and went over to him before he left. I asked if we could meet another time. He said he would try but things were "really busy." I then let him know that I had been working with his old classmate Spencer Overton on some events in support of him. He stopped en route, placed his hand on my shoulder, and gave me a warm smile. "Spencer is a really great guy! Please tell him I said hello." At that point, a Conyers staffer took a picture of us talking as Obama walked out the door. Suddenly, the long-awaited meeting was over.

After a couple of days had passed, I called Mike and thanked him for the meeting. I also let him know that I thought that I had bombed with Obama by spending too much time lecturing him on inside party politics and not enough time on what he was trying to do and how I could help. "Don't worry about it," Mike said reassuringly. "It was probably stuff he really needed to hear."

I pressed for a follow-up meeting a few times but was never able to get a hard commitment. Finally, in February 2007, I got Mike to commit to another meet-up. This time it would be at the DNC winter meeting at the Washington Hilton Hotel. Obama was scheduled to speak there as a potential 2008 candidate and Mike thought I could get a few minutes with him before or after the speech. As it turned out, he arrived only in enough time to make it to the podium and give remarks that electrified the crowd. Between the media and the people rushing to take his picture, it became almost impossible to expect that I would get a chance to meet with him before the speech.

After the speech, there was a reception for the DNC Black Caucus that he said he would stop by. I arrived early to make sure I caught him before the crowd grew. But it was already too late. Word had spread throughout the hotel that Obama was coming to the reception, and the reception room was jam-packed. I parked myself by the door of the reception room, hoping to catch him before he entered—an old trick I often used with members of Congress during my days on Capitol Hill. My strategy worked, even if only for a few minutes. I caught Obama before he walked in. He stopped and greeted me warmly. Then I blurted out half-heartedly, in a sarcastic refrain from our last conversation, "So, have you talked with Hillary Clinton yet?" I yelled it out above the buzz of the crowd gathering by the door.

He flashed a broad grin and again answered in the same refrain: "Ah, nope!"

"I've been hearing you out there," I continued. "You really have people psyched up! You did great in there at the DNC meeting! You're really raising everybody's expectations about your campaign." He thanked me for the compliments, then moved on into the room. I followed him this time and stood close by while he made very brief remarks to the assembled crowd that was ecstatic! As he made his way back toward the door, I asked him, "Have you thought about how we keep people this excited all the way through the campaign? The primaries are almost a year away." He didn't say anything as the crowd trailed him out the door. He tried to respond further but kept greeting an endless flow of people rushing toward him.

Before he pulled away, he turned back and spoke. "Don't worry, Greg. It's going to be a very different kind of campaign." It was a repeated refrain from our last conversation. At that point, the rush of the crowd overtook him as he made his way through the hotel lobby. At that point I almost knew that I had blown it again. Not only had I come across as a Clinton person, but I also suggested that he was raising expectations too high among Black voters and that he might not be able to sustain the momentum. I would be proven wrong in the months to come.

From that point on, I didn't make further attempts to meet him. Within a few weeks, he was on the front pages of every news magazine and becoming a star attraction everywhere he went. He clearly knew what he was doing and how he could put together a winning campaign. He was a community organizer (like me), not a politician, and he was right. It would not be the kind of campaign we had seen in the past.

With the early presidential primary season well underway in early 2007, tension within the party begin to build around two main factions: Obama supporters who were fervent in their support of him, and old-line Democratic party leaders and regulars who were looking to Hillary Clinton as the all-but-certain Democratic nominee. As I had told Obama, supporters of the Clintons were still in firm control of the party, but the energy and excitement that swirled around the potential of an Obama campaign began to grow *outside* the party apparatus.

Within the African American community, where Hillary Clinton enjoyed her strongest support, polls began to show slippage in her support among her strongest constituency base. Additionally, progressive forces within the party began to coalesce around Obama, with large crowds greeting him everywhere he went, accompanied by wall-to-wall media coverage. While Clinton began building her traditional support within the party, Obama's campaign was bringing in thousands of new voters searching for something different this time around.

As the race for president heated up and Obama and Clinton formally announced their candidacies, the rules for DNC staffers and consultants to remain neutral became much stricter. As a strong personal supporter of Barack Obama, I was told in no uncertain terms by senior staff at the party that there could be no more private or even semi-public meetings between me and the candidate or his staff. I was to stay as far away from it as I could. While I never seriously sought a campaign job or key position, I wanted to be somewhere else where I could at least help mobilize Black voters.

My job at the DNC in setting up the election protection apparatus within the party was now virtually on autopilot operating out of state parties. With most of the energy and attention now moving toward the presidential campaigns, I began having thoughts of leaving the party and going back to my work mobilizing voters on the nonpartisan side. I was concerned that not enough was being done on that side to prepare for an election cycle in which the Black vote would be one of the most decisive factors during both the primary and general elections.

Since I had left, the leadership of the NAACP parent company had changed. I arranged a meeting with the interim president, the long-time General Counsel Dennis Hayes about reviving its C 4 civic engagement arm that had been without a director since my departure. He welcomed the opportunity for me to return and provided me the support to re-build the staff and carry out a full and impactful voter engagement program. It seemed like the best option to move forward into the 2008 cycle given the well-established brand name of the NAACP and the hard work that the NAACP-National Voter Fund had carried out in 2000 and 2004.

Once again it felt like I was starting from scratch, similar to the way it felt after the 9/11 attacks. But I was quickly able to re-establish my ties with the America Votes coalition and progressive allies undertaking voter mobilization efforts. With their technical and financial support, we began developing plans for a major data centered 2008 Black voter outreach program. Shortly thereafter I met with the Voter Fund's 2000 data vendor about the possibility of creating a completely standalone version of the election protection hotline that would serve the same function as the 866-DEM-VOTE hotline on the non-partisan side. To make the hotline worthwhile and impactful it needed to be promoted by a celebrity who could help get the word out to a larger African American audience.

We pitched the idea to Tom Joyner of *The Tom Joyner Morning Show,* (TJMS), and his Business Manager son, Oscar Joyner. TJMS was broadcast on *Radio One* on over 165 Black and urban radio stations across the US. At the time it was the most popular radio show and on-air personality on black radio. Joyer's live morning show on election days for the past several years were besieged with hundreds of calls into his station from listeners who were experiencing problems at the polls. Oscar Joyner initially just wanted an outlet for all the call traffic to free up their telephone lines through all the primaries. Tom Joyner was a huge fan of promoting the importance of voting in every election. But he was an even bigger fan of Barack Obama and the prospect that an African American could actually be elected president. Our data teams were focused on the expansion of the call traffic for the hotline and the collection of reoccurring complaint data that could be analyzed for more effective election protection programs.

While supportive of all those goals, I was a strong proponent that the hotline be somehow configured to register voters throughout the election year—and not just to report problems on election day. Both Joyners were enthusiastic about what became a now multi-dimensional project. Tom not only brought into the idea he reached out to famed Black creative modern artist Annie Lee to develop artwork around the theme of voting that we could use to promote the project. He also helped with the initial financial investment to get the technical and promotional aspects of the project off the ground and put into practice.

The overall project would become known as the TJMS 866-MYVOTE Hotline, a first of its kind all- purpose toll-free number. In addition to being a non-partisan toll-free line to call in with election day complaints, MYVOTE1 callers could find their poll location, register to vote, and leave an incident report message to record problems encountered throughout the entire primary election season and during the early vote period in the fall. Joyner would report some of the major problems on election day live on the air, while we would direct volunteers on the ground to those locations for assistance. The effort became known on the air as the *TJMS Trickery Report* with the Voter Fund providing on the ground assistance with occasional on-air commentary on any voting rights related issues. Additionally, we were able to build out a data collection component that allowed the partnering University of Pennsylvania Toll School of Public Policy to analyze the data and track trends in states where election irregularities were taking place.

With the MYVOTE 1 program in full swing, it became the central program focus of what was now the NAACP-NVF's *Empowerment 2008 Campaign* for the general election. Voter registration and mobilization efforts were led by National Field Director Claude Foster and Dallas Jones and undertaken in seven battleground states; Ohio, Florida, Michigan, Pennsylvania, Virginia, Nevada, New Mexico, and four non-battle ground states of Texas, New Jersey, Louisiana, and Alabama. Through the MYVOTE 1 program we were able to add 63,000 new registered voters to the 216,000 voters we had registered in 2004. These efforts however were modest compared to the millions of voters who were being registered by Project Vote, Labor, women's groups, environmental groups, and others. Many of the advocacy groups saw the 2008 election as a bell weather opportunity to advance their many issues that had been laid dormant during the 8 long years of the Bush Administration.

The success of NAACP-NVF and Tom Joyner's 866-MYVOTE1 on air program created some internal conflicts within the election protection coalition in 2008.

The original national hotline 866-OUR-VOTE, created by the Lawyers Committee for Civil Rights Under Law and other voter protection groups in the aftermath of the Florida 2000 election had been providing legal assistance to voters across the country for years. Although we provided different functions and services to voters, many donors and allies believed having two hotlines were duplicating efforts and urged Joyner to take his popular number down. With over 300,000 calls coming into the MYVOTE1 hotline during the primaries alone, I was reluctant to shut down anything that was meeting the needs of so many voters across the US. After several months of wrangling, in an effort to better collaborate between the groups and avoid duplication, I worked with the MYVOTE1 and OUR-VOTE vendors on a compromise to keep both numbers up but ensure that callers seeking legal assistance would be patched directly to the 866-OUR-VOTE number.

Across the US, voter registration rates were skyrocketing in the Black community and on college campuses. The Obama campaign phenomenon was real and was inspiring a whole new generation of voters to participate. The reforms we had instituted with the National Voter Registration Act (NVRA) and the Help America Vote Act (HAVA) were now in full bloom with both partisan and nonpartisan efforts swelling voter registration rolls across the US. Obama continued drawing unprecedented crowds and media at all of his events. Through very effective use of social media and internet giving, the campaign raised record levels of funds from small donations from millions of regular voters and built an unprecedented volunteer base of millions. The combined efforts eventually overtook Hillary Clinton's traditional campaign apparatus as the primary season came to an end. It *was* a different kind of campaign, just as he had told me.

Obama's support had easily superseded the vote totals that the Jesse Jackson campaigns had accomplished in his two runs for president in the 1980s. The rule changes Jackson had fought for helped to build Obama's delegate totals in a number of states. The Obama's campaign built a massive broad-based coalition of progressive, African American, and young people that eventually appealed to a surprisingly significant number of suburban white women voters who had been strongly committed to Clinton. It turned out to be an unexpectedly long, tough, and sometimes bitter campaign for the Clinton dynasty. By the end of an extended campaign fought to the last primary, Obama triumphed over Hillary Clinton in the delegate count. Clinton graciously conceded the race at the end of the primary season. By the end of the DNC convention, her enthusiastic endorsement of Obama's campaign and vigorous campaigning in the following months paved the final path toward a historic fall campaign. This time, everyone vowed to stay united until all the provisional ballots were counted, as was provided for by the newly enacted Help America Vote Act of 2002.

Back at the DNC, the DEM-VOTE hotline was finally being fully utilized by the Democratic state parties. The 50 State election protection program that I had established while at the party in 2006 was now fully operational and working with an experienced team of party lawyers who had learned the lessons from 2004 and vowed not to repeat it. Their efforts dovetailed with the Obama campaign's Election Protection program that was embedded into the campaign apparatus, armed with their own team of lawyers as well.

In most national polls, Obama and his running mate Senator Joe Biden led his Republican rival John McCain and McCain's ultra-conservative vice-presidential nominee Alaska Governor Sarah Palin by just a few points. Statistically, this was a dead heat. In the state of Ohio, Obama went back and forth, with his lead never more than one or two points. We knew from history that the undercount of the Republican vote in Ohio was always a factor. Being one or two points ahead meant the race could go either way. It was the same in other states. Obama was slightly ahead in New Mexico, Nevada, Pennsylvania, Virginia, and Michigan. The McCain and Republican Party forces on the ground in those states were simply no match for the historic Obama phenomenon and volunteers that numbered in the millions across the US. His surge of support from diverse voters across the spectrum were supporting Obama's message of HOPE and CHANGE.

As the 2008 campaign moved on it became clear the election would again come down to a handful of states including Ohio. True to form I spent the last week of the campaign in my home state helping to direct the NAACP-NVF GOTV field operations being led by the state coordinator Thaddeus Jackson. The GOTV efforts consisted of over 150 canvassers on the ground and a full-scale voter registration, voter education campaign through a voter guide and door to door canvassing of the lowest performing voter turnout precincts. It was not unlike the efforts in 2004 except this time we were prepared for any chicanery. Tom Joyner was alerted to keep his eye on Ohio and Florida and all the lawyers were in place for a long battle that they vowed would not end abruptly as it did in 2004. This time everyone vowed to stay united until all the provisional votes were counted as was required by the newly enacted Help America Vote Act of 2002.

All our operatives were giving it everything they had to turn out Black voters in all of our states. Despite the long hours and non-stop voter outreach work, the level of enthusiasm was high everywhere with scores of volunteers and support building up the closer we got to election day in all of our targeted states. I was personally exhausted from all of the many months of preparation and execution and was glad when election day finally arrived.

After our efforts were completely shut down, I went to downtown Cleveland, where the Obama campaign's hotel was located. I had planned for a long night that would go into the next day or the next week until we knew the outcome. After all the drama and trauma of 2000 and 2004, I braced myself for what could be another disappointing election night. Instead, it looked like Obama was slowly but surely amassing the electoral votes he needed to win the election. What had been reliably solid red states in past presidential elections began falling into the Obama column. States like North Carolina, Virginia, and even Indiana, the traditionally solid Republican neighboring state to Illinois, were called for Obama.

As the states began to be called into the early evening, it looked like the prospect of a Democratic victory was within reach. On election night, the media and campaigns awaited the result of one more battleground state. It was approaching 11:00 PM and we were awaiting the latest CNN projections that would be revealed at the top of the hour on large television screens in the hotel ballroom. Most people were not even looking at the screens when CNN Anchor Wolf Blitzer announced that the state of Ohio was being called for Barack Obama, giving him the electoral votes needed to be elected the next President of the United States.

Suddenly, time seemed to stand still as the crowd of several hundred people erupted in the loudest roar I had ever heard at an event. I recall leaping several feet off the ground and shouting in excitement along with the other revelers. It did not seem real this time. We had elected the first African American as President of the United States! Long hugs were exchanged with complete strangers, virtually any and everyone in my vicinity, as tears of joy began pouring out all over the ballroom. It *was* really happening. We had done it! The multi-year battle for voter registration reform, election protection, litigation, door knocking, and years of work had finally paid off. It did not even seem real until Senator John McCain came out and gave one of the most gracious concession speeches anyone could remember. He congratulated his opponent and told the entire nation that Barack Obama would be "my president" and that all his followers should get behind the new president-elect for the sake of the country.

The strength of the massive turnout of Black voters in 2008 reached historic highs of 62.5%, a rate unseen in a general election since the passage of the Voting Rights Act or the NVRA, even surpassing the massive turnouts we had witnessed in Florida in 2000 and Ohio in 2004.[1] The 2008 election also saw the most racial and ethnically diverse turnout of voters in US History with one of

---

1 Tasha S. Philpot, Daron R. Shaw, and Ernest B. McGowen, "Winning the Race: Black Voter Turnout in the 2008 Presidential Election"*The Public Opinion Quarterly* 75, no. 5 (2009): 995– 1022.

every 4 voters being a person of color.[2] The massive turnout was matched by the second-highest turnouts for people 18–24 since the enactment of the 26th Amendment.[3] A post-election report by CIRCLE, a nonpartisan research center at Tufts University revealed that up to 24 million young Americans age 18–29 voted, resulting in an estimated youth voter turnout of 54.5%, according to an exit poll analysis. The turnout rate edged out the all-time highest youth turnout of 55.4%, in 1972, the first year that 18-year-olds could vote in a presidential election.[4]

After all my early years of organizing student voters and young people, this was the election in which that youth vote finally broke free and flexed its political muscle to the maximum. Over 66% of young voters supported Obama—another record level of support for a single candidate.[5] Suddenly, it was all coming together: youth, Black, Brown, and even women voters turned out in record numbers and let their voices be heard in this historic election. Overall, in the 2008 election, over 71% of the 206 million eligible voters were registered to vote, with over 90% of the registered voters reported to the US Census as having voted in the 2008 election. The overall turnout of 64% ranked among the highest turnouts ever reported. [6]

Being a part of this historic voter mobilization was the greatest sense of accomplishment that I had experienced in my lifetime. The fact that Ohio, a reliably red state, had put Obama over the top had not been lost on me or on any of the people in that room. After all the success and defeats, great strides, and many setbacks, all the hard work over the years had come together to produce this victory. And it was poetic justice that the celebration was taking place only four blocks from the Cleveland Public Library, where I had made my first attempt to register to vote. The passive resistance the registrar had shown me

---

2 "Dissecting the 2008 Electorate: Most Diverse in U.S. History," Pew Reserach Center, last modified April 30, 2009, https://www.pewresearch.org/hispanic/2009/04/30/dissecting-the-2008-electorate-most-diverse-in-us-history/.
3 "Youth Turnout Rate Rises to at Least 52%," CIRCLE (The Center for Information and Research on Civic Learning and Engagement), last modified November 7, 2008, https://archive.civicyouth.org/youth-turnout-rate-rises-to-at-least-52/.
4 Ibid.
5 "Featured: Voter Turnout Among Young Women and Men in the 2008 Presidential Election," CIRCLE (The Center for Information and Research on Civic Learning and Engagement), last modified October 29, 2010, https://archive.civicyouth.org/featured-voter-turnout-among-young-women-and-men-in-the-2008-presidential-election/.
6 Thom File and Sarah Crissey, "Voting and Registration in the Election of November 2008," U.S. Census Bureau, last modified July 30, 2012, https://www.census.gov/history/pdf/2008presidential_election-32018.pdf.

that day was melted away by the warmth that I witnessed in that ballroom. Black, white, Brown, LGBTQ, rich, poor and people of all backgrounds and economic strata were all celebrating together—this time seemingly with no regard to race. In some strange way, even the old-guard white political operatives were released from America's brutal past. They seemed to know, perhaps even more than we did, how much of an accomplishment it was for a Black man to assume that position, as they knew how much the Black vote had been suppressed for so many years, for so many decades, for so many centuries.

Far too much credit is given to political strategists and campaign managers who write books and talk about the great wisdom they exhibited in the candidates whom "they got elected." Most of what they can account for is the 6 to 10 months that they spent managing their one campaign. Credit is rarely given to the long haulers who woke up every day for years and sometimes decades with a singular focus on fixing and administrating our broken democratic system. Some people have fought to preserve and expand the democracy that we have carved out of the United States' tainted legacy. This was a story about those nameless and faceless people who made a major contribution mostly behind the scenes. It was a multi-year, multi-decade, multi-century struggle that continues to this very day.

In 2008, it felt like we had finally gotten the democracy we had been promised in the Declaration of Independence, the US Constitution, and the Bill of Rights. Our African American ancestors and scores of citizens fought and experienced great pains—and even death—to get this right guaranteed to every American citizen. It was worth the fight despite the many sacrifices. They all moved this movement further toward the democratic promise that perhaps, for this one time in history, seemed to be unbroken and maybe even fulfilled.

The Obama Election Backlash and Resistance

With the election now behind us I was able to finally exhale after so many years of non-stop work on voting rights and voter mobilization. I wanted to pivot to a new line of work and allow the new administration to carry out all their important goals including the recovery from the major economic collapse that had taken place in the closing months of 2008. In the final days of the Bush Administration a major multi-billion-dollar bank bailout package was being carefully negotiated between Wall Street and Washington.[7] It was hailed as a "do or die" rescue of the American economic system necessary to save the overheated banking and mortgage system from further economic collapse. Amid all our focus on voting and democratic reforms, the United States had entered the era of the "Great Recession," second only to the "Great Depression of the 1930s[8]. The economic suffering was widespread across the US in urban areas and in small towns. Home foreclosures, bankruptcies and business failures were rampant, and it soon dampened much of the enthusiasm that many had felt for the new incoming Obama/Biden Administration. With the support of the new incoming and outgoing presidents, the massive bailout passed on a bi-partisan basis just a few weeks before the Obama inauguration on a partisan basis.

Despite the crippling economic conditions, the country faced, and the generosity of the mega Wall Street bailout that had just occurred, there was little bi-partisan support in Congress for Obama's over $819 billion economic stimulus and recovery package for "main street."[9] The economic remedies proposed by the new president faced fierce opposition from right wing media on radio and television. His plans for a universal health care system were labeled as "socialism," and even his modest plans to address issues related to climate change, criminal justice reform and even foreign policy were opposed from the moment they were announced. Republicans used the filibuster to block many of Obama's early judicial appointments and even sub cabinet level appointees. Obama's admonition that there were no red states and blues states...only a United States soon proved to not be the case.

The stimulus bill was navigated through the Congress by Vice President Joe Biden. Despite his years of work on the hill, not a single republican supported the Obama $831 billion stimulus package that passed the House of Representatives 244 – 188 after a long and hyper partisan and divisive debate. In the Senate only 3 republicans crossed party lines to support the bill that passed 60 – 37 in the US Senate.[10] Having learned its lesson early in the administration, President Obama fought back by converting his massive 2008 campaign structure into a

---

7 "Troubled Asset Relief Program," Wikipedia, last modified February 18, 2022, https://en.wikipedia.org/wiki/Troubled_Asset_Relief_Program.

8 Ibid.

9 Kimberly Amadeo, "Obama's Stimulus Package and How Well It Worked," The Balance, last modified December 31, 2021, https://www.thebalance.com/what-was-obama-s-stimulus-package-3305625.

10 "Roll Call Vote 111th Congress – 1st Session," United States Senate, (n.d.) accessed March 22, 2022, https://www.senate.gov/legislative/LIS/roll_call_votes/vote1111/vote_111_1_00061.htm.

new grassroots organization, *Obama for America, (OFA).*[11] The new stand-alone group led the way with a full-fledged defense of the administration's legislative goals and objectives in partnership with its many progressive allies across the US. The massive grassroots effort was initially built inside of the Democratic party apparatus which allowed OFA to be assembled more quickly and efficiently, but with (at the time) unknown ramifications for the party down the road.

Despite now having a Democratic President, a Democratic Congress and more Democratic governors and state legislatures, we soon discovered that the resistance to moving forward with a progressive agenda was growing fiercer. The presence of Obama, the first African American president seemed to fan the flames of racism and resentment on the right even stronger than they were in years past. The fierce partisanship grew more cutting edge, moving even beyond the Bill Clinton Impeachment era. It was fed by Fox News' 24-hour cable TV barrage, Rush Limbaugh's daily talk radio broadcasts and a growing litter of hard right talk show hosts. These radio talk shows proliferated on AM and now even FM radio in rural areas of most states. As social media began to grow in its usage, fierce anti-Obama resentment spread throughout the internet.

This new wave soon became defined as "The Tea Party movement."[12] Folklore would hold that it began with an impromptu rant on a business cable news show. But it was also seen in packed town hall meetings opposing the single payer national health care bill being proposed by Obama and the Democrats. Local gatherings of primarily small-town white homeowners angry at the economic conditions they faced, soon grew into a larger organized opposition to the economic bail out of wall street and later health care reform and immigration reform.[13]The Tea Party movement was also fed by a National Rifle Association (NRA)[14] led media campaigns to "protect the 2nd Amendment" against perceived and Tea Party manufactured threats by the federal government against gun owners and gun ownership.[15] The Tea Party movement soon became identified with yellow and black flags featuring a coiled snake with the battle cry mantra of

---

11 "Organizing for America," Wikipedia, last modified March 19, 2022, https://en.wikipedia.org/wiki/Organizing_for_America.

12 Michael Ray, "Tea Party movement," Encyclopedia Britannica, last modified February 7, 2022, https://www.britannica.com/topic/Tea-Party-movement.

13 Ibid.

14 "National Rifle Association," Wikipedia, last modified March 15, 2022, https://en.wikipedia.org/wiki/National_Rifle_Association.

15 Alan Berlow and Gordon Witkin, "Gun lobby's money and power still holds sway over Congress," The Center for Public Integrity, last modified May 1, 2013, https://publicintegrity.org/politics/gun-lobbys-money-and-power-still-holds-sway-over-congress/.

"Don't Tread on Me." The flag was often carried in rallies by men who wore the three-cornered colonial era hats, signs of pitch forks and in some cases actual pitchforks and sticks symbolizing the American Revolutionary War era.

Tea Party rallies often ridiculed President Obama, questioning his citizenship with racist lampooning of his race as an African from Kenya, (the birthplace of his father), and challenging his birthplace in the United States. It was the beginning of *birtherism* [16]that was latched on to by the hard right talk show hosts. Celebrity Billionaire Donald Trump also fanned the flames in multiple public comments questioning Obama's citizenship. The one final common characteristic was the almost exclusive white makeup of the tea party members, made up of rural and small-town activists, supposedly fed up with the new federal government and its new proposed mandates for universal health care that they were completely rejecting as "socialism."

With the battle for the stimulus bill now behind him, Obama and his Vice President who led the effort were still under attack from all sides from those who thought the $819 Billion recovery package was too large, and progressives who felt it was too small. Obama worked hard to continue to advance his next major legislative agenda, Universal Health Care coverage for all Americans. It proved to be an even more bruising political battle with over a year of loud and boisterous Tea Party protest and disruptions at town hall meetings across the country. After 37 legislative votes and multiple attempts by Republicans and their Tea PARTY to defeat the bill, the Affordable Care Act, a.k.a. Obamacare was passed into law on March 23, 2010.[17]

Even while Democrats celebrated the decades' long goal of passing health care reform, many operatives in the party feared that the issue might cause the Democrats to lose seats in the upcoming 2010 congressional elections. Pundits predicted that the midterms would produce a traditional loss of seats for the party in power, even without the Obamacare battle. Their predictions proved to be true as Republicans regained control of the U.S. House of Representatives in November of 2010 while Democrats maintained their control of the U.S. Senate but lost 6 critical votes going from a 57 to a slim 51-seat majority.[18] The resound-

---

16 "birtherism," Oxford Learner's Dictionary, (n.d.) accessed March 22, 2022, https://www.ox fordlearnersdictionaries.com/us/definition/english/birtherism.

17 "Affordable Care Act (ACA) & Health Care and Education Reconciliation Act of 2010 (HCERA)," University of Minnesota Law Library, last modified January 26, 2022, https://lib guides.law.umn.edu/c.php?g=125769&p=906254.

18 "2010 United States House of Representatives elections," Wikipedia, last modified March 23, 2022, https://en.wikipedia.org/wiki/2010_United_States_House_of_Representatives_elec tions.https://en.wikipedia.org/wiki/2010_United_States_House_of_Representatives_elections

ing success of Republicans in the 2010 elections sent shock waves through the democratic party and the White House. With the wind in their sails, Republicans now set their sights on the 2012 elections as their best chance to retake the U.S. Senate majority and the White House.

Republicans for their part nominated a well-known moderate former Massachusetts Governor Mitt Romney. He had run twice before in 2004 and 2008 with no luck, barely making it past the first tier of candidates and primaries. On his 2012 bid Romney invested millions of his own resources to ensure his success the third time around. He was also able to build a more robust campaign apparatus than John McCain, the party's 2008 nominee, and attempted to appeal to more moderate Democrats who may have thought Obama had gone too far left for the party. The Tea Party had also grown quite strong by 2012, still reeling from the Obamacare battles and starting to see the importance of taking back the US Senate that was only barely in control of the Democratic party.

While Black leaders were actively engaged in preparing for the 2012 election, Republicans continued their voter suppression legislative efforts in key battleground states that President Obama had won in 2008. In 2011, Ohio Republicans led General Assembly passed a draconian voter suppression bill, HB 194 that rolled back most of the recent reforms enacted by the previously Democratic controlled legislature.[19] An effort was undertaken by the former Democratic Ohio Secretary of State Jennifer Brunner to lead a statewide referendum against the new law. Brunner asked me to serve as campaign manager for the coalition Fair Election Ohio which coordinated the signature collection effort to repeal the law. The broad-based coalition included the Ohio chapter of the Obama For America (OFA) grassroots organization labor leaders, clergy, civil rights, and other advocacy groups. The repeal effort gained support in every region of the state, both urban and rural including deep red counties that had strong republican support. After gaining the necessary 303,000 signatures to get the measure repealed by voters, the republican legislature repealed most of the provisions of its own law in early 2012 fearing a backlash at the polls in November. It marked the first time in Ohio history that a bill subject to a referendum was repealed by the legislature before taking effect.[20]

In North Carolina, the legislature repealed the voter reforms from 2007 that expanded early vote and created same day voter registration at polling locations.

19 "Ohio Election Law Veto Referendum (2012)," Ballotpedia, (n.d.) accessed March 22, 2022, https://ballotpedia.org/Ohio_Election_Law_Veto_Referendum_(2012)https://ballotpedia.org/Ohio_Election_Law_Veto_Referendum_(2012)

20 "Ohio repeals HB 194, lawsuit likely," Ballotpedia, last modified May 15, 2012, https://ballotpedia.org/Ohio_repeals_HB_194,_lawsuit_likely.

The rollbacks included adding new photo ID requirements, the repeal of a modified Election Day Registration and shortening of early voting days.[21] In Wisconsin the Republican Legislature and Governor also tightened photo ID restrictions in Wisconsin by requiring that student IDs could no longer be acceptable as a form of ID to vote.[22] This was a deliberate attempt to reduce the number of students who were still registering in record numbers at the University of Wisconsin in Milwaukee, Madison, and other college towns from across the state. Efforts to challenge both the North Carolina and Wisconsin measures were not successful.[23]

Despite these voter suppression efforts, there was another historic turnout of Black voters in the 2012 general election. Black voter turnout also reached a historic milestone as 66.2% of African Americans voted compared to 64.1% for non-Hispanic white voters. It would mark the first time in US history that Black voters voted in a higher percentage than whites.[24] Obama was able to hold on to most of the states he won in 2008, but fell short in North Carolina, and Indiana, aided by their new restrictive photo ID and rollback of recent voter reforms.[25] While these two states reverted back to their red state status, Ohio came through again despite predictions of its return to its historical red state tradition. Once again, the turnout in Ohio was high at 70.5% even slightly higher than the 69.9% turnout in 2008.[26] Obama was again elected by a comfortable margin of the popular vote over former Governor Mitt Romney, 51–47% and an electoral vote landslide of 332 to 206.[27]

---

21 Barry Yeoman, "Court Rules NC Voting Rights Rollback to Stay In Place Until After Midterm Elections," The America Prospect, last modified August 15, 2014, https://prospect.org/power/court-rules-nc-voting-rights-rollback-stay-place-midterm-elections/.

22 "Wisconsin voter identification requirements and history," Ballotpedia, (n.d.) accessed March 22, 2022, https://ballotpedia.org/Wisconsin_voter_identification_requirements_and_history.

23 Ibid.

24 Sarah Wheaton, "For First Time on Record, Black Voting Rate Outspaced Rate for Whites in 2012," The New York Times, last modified May 8, 2013, https://www.nytimes.com/2013/05/09/us/politics/rate-of-black-voters-surpassed-that-for-whites-in-2012.html.

25 Yeoman, "Court Rules NC Voting Rights Rollback to Stay In Place Until After Midterm Elections," The America Prospect, last modified August 15, 2014, https://prospect.org/power/court-rules-nc-voting-rights-rollback-stay-place-midterm-elections/.

26 "Voter turn out in General Elections," Frank LaRose – Ohio Secretary of State, (n.d.) accessed March 22, 2022, https://www.ohiosos.gov/elections/election-results-and-data/historical-election-comparisons/voter-turnout-in-general-elections/.

27 "2012 United States presidential election," Wikipedia, last modified March 11, 2022, https://en.wikipedia.org/wiki/2012_United_States_presidential_election.

The Black voter mobilization in Ohio, Michigan, Wisconsin and other midwestern states once again proved to be a big factor, but now joined by an overwhelming support from Hispanic, LGBTQ, Jewish and young voters 18 – 24 from across the country who all voted heavily democratic in the 2012 elections. It was also the year when Black women voted in a higher rate than any other racial, gender or ethnicity for the first time in American history.[28] Black women had a turnout rate of 70 % due in large part to the voter mobilization effort Melanie Campbell's Black Women's Roundtable, an expansive coalition of sororities, professional women associations, Black Church networks, labor unions and other community based organizations. The winning electoral coalition had been preserved and for a fleeting moment it began to feel like we had the wind against our back. The hard right Tea Party had failed to convert their rage into electoral success in 2012, leading many of the progressive activists and leaders of advocacy groups to believe that they were permanently defeated in electoral politics. History would soon prove them wrong.

---

28 Maya Harris, "Women of Color: A Growing Force in the American Electorate," American Progress, last modified October 30, 2014, https://www.americanprogress.org/article/women-of-color/.

Chapter 14
The Shelby Decision and the Battle to Restore the VRA

Throughout many of the 50 years since the passage of the spell out "Voting Rights Act" with new chapter VRA, litigation had been filed by the NAACP-LDF, the ACLU, the Lawyers Committee for Civil Rights Under Law, the Mexican American Legal Defense Fund, the Brennen Center at NYU, and other litigators to defend the various provisions of the act. Most litigation had been challenged by states and, in some instances, counties, which were often in charge of implementing the federal statutes within their jurisdictions. One of those jurisdictions was Shelby County, Alabama.

A legal challenge to the Voting Rights Act had been launched by Shelby County (Shelby County v. Holder), challenging its requirement to still be forced into pre-clearance based on the existing formula of Section 4(b) of the VRA. On June 25, 2013, the Supreme Court, led by Bush appointee Justice John Roberts, ruled 5 – 4 that the VRA's pre-clearance formula was outdated and had to be updated by Congress.[1] The landmark decision was the first major legal challenge and setback for the Voting Rights Act in the US Supreme Court since its enactment in 1965. Suddenly, with just one Supreme Court decision, a major cornerstone of the Voting Rights Act that had survived for almost 50 years was gone. The fight to restore the act's strength was just the beginning of the resistance that would continue in Congress and across the US. The great groundbreaking expansion of the electorate that we had helped to build over several decades was facing its most serious challenge ever. The battle to restore the VRA in Congress was now added to the battles already taking place in states against voter suppression bills and even within the very process of the fair administration of elections.

For over 50 years, the VRA and its subsequent amendments were all passed by the US Congress on a bipartisan basis, gaining the support of both Republicans and Democrats. The VRA had been amended or reauthorized several times, in 1970, 1975, 1982, 1992, and 2006.[2] In each instance, a strong bipartisan wall of

---

1 "Shelby County v. Holder," Brennan Center for Justice, last modified August 4, 2018, https://www.brennancenter.org/our-work/court-cases/shelby-county-v-holder.https://www.brennancenter.org/our-work/court-cases/shelby-county-v-holder

2 Richard A. Williamson, "The 1982 Amendments to the Voting Rights Act: A Statutory Analysis of the Revised Bailout Provisions," *Washington University Law Review* 62, no. 1 (1984): 1–77.

https://doi.org/10.1515/9783110742473-017

support helped to sustain the act and its implementation in states over the years by election officials of both parties working together at the federal, state, and local levels. This bipartisan support in implementation was essential to ensuring that all the new VRA provisions were fully enforced. The Shelby decision ruled that VRA's Section 4(b), which spelled out the formula for selecting states requiring pre-clearance of changes to state election-related laws, was unconstitutional and in need of revision by Congress.[3]

The original jurisdictions covered were primarily Southern states with a number of counties and sub-jurisdictions across the US.[4] As a result of the ruling, states with a history of voter disenfranchisement could now enact restrictive state laws as of June 25, 2013, without the full protection of the VRA.[5] Although the Supreme Court had dismantled Section 4(b), it called on Congress to update the formula to ensure that it reflected the most current data related to voting restrictions being undertaken by states. However, since 2014, numerous pieces of legislation introduced into Congress, designed to update the formula, have all been stalled due to hyper-partisan political wrangling.

The Shelby decision sent shock waves through the civil rights and voting rights community. Suddenly, all the optimism and excitement that had followed the re-election and second inauguration of President Obama six months earlier was replaced by despair and great uncertainty over what the decision could mean. We would discover the answer within days, as North Carolina introduced new voter suppression legislation within hours of the Shelby decision, followed by Texas and Georgia days later. The proverbial leash had been taken off states as the Department of Justice and federal courts were no longer able to preview a flurry of new election procedures to ensure they did not violate the Voting Rights Act. Since the VRA was enacted, it had stopped thousands of state and local proposed regressive election-related bills from ever being enacted into law.[6] That longstanding pre-emptive protection against voter dilution schemes was now gone.

---

3 "Shelby County v. Holder," Ballotpedia, (n.d.) accessed March 22, 2022, https://ballotpedia.org/Shelby_County_v._Holder.

4 "Jurisdictions previously covered by section 5," U.S. Department of Justice, last modified November 29, 2021, https://www.justice.gov/crt/jurisdictions-previously-covered-section-5.

5 Hearings (Kristen Clarke), "Testimony, Continued Challenge to the Voting Rights Act Since Shelby v. Holder, House Judiciary Committee, June 25, 2019," U.S. House Committee On The Judiciary, last modified June 25, 2019, https://judiciary.house.gov/calendar/eventsingle.aspx?EventID=2259.

6 Ibid.

The only remaining recourse for civil rights litigators was for each law or procedure to be challenged in court under Section 2 of the Voting Rights Act, but only *after* the provision had been enacted into law. This was a process that often took many years of litigation and worked *only* if there was conclusive evidence that the law had a discriminatory *intent* or *impact*. Suddenly, the great promise that our democracy had shown in the 2008 and 2012 elections gave way to the despair that was soon to follow as the Supreme Court rolled back the clock on voting rights in 2013. The next few months following the decision set off a flurry of activity in state capitols, with bills being introduced or re-introduced going back to 2011, when Republicans, in the aftermath of the 2010 elections, gained control of many state legislatures. By the end of 2013, multiple states had introduced or enacted new restrictive bills into law. Once again, the civil rights community sprang into action, holding press conferences, rallies, public policy forums, and even candlelight visuals for the Voting Rights Act.[7]

The Lawyers Committee for Civil Rights Under Law (LCCR), led by its president Barbara Arwine, formed a National Commission on Voting Rights that scheduled a series of hearings across the country to gather testimony and build a body of evidence indicating that there were still cases of voter suppression and intimidation that would warrant the need for a new VRA Section 4 formula. Hearings were held in 25 cities across the US to collect testimony about voting discrimination and election administration challenges and successes. Hundreds of voters, advocates, and expert witnesses shared personal experiences and research highlighting both the obstacles to fully accessing the ballot as well as opportunities for reform.[8] Many of the hearings began with Arwine displaying her updated "Map of Shame" that showed all the states where restrictive voting laws had been either introduced or passed by the state legislatures.[9] Based on the testimony that the hundreds of witnesses provided, the commission issued a national report highlighting multiple cases of US citizens being adversely impacted by how elections were being run in their communities.[10]

---

7 Wade Henderson, *VRA Today Issue Brief* (Leadership Conference on Civil and Human Rights, 2014).

8 Stanley Augustin, "New Report Released by National Commission on Voting Rights: More Work Needed to Improve Registration and Voting in the U.S.," Lawyers Committee, last modified September 22, 2015, https://www.lawyerscommittee.org/new-report-released-by-national-commission-on-voting-rights-more-work-needed-to-improve-registration-and-voting-in-the-u-s/.

9 Ibid.

10 "Highlights Of Hearings Of The National Commission On The Voting Rights Act 2005," The National Commission on the Voting Rights Act, last modified February, 2006, https://www2.ohchr.org/english/bodies/hrc/docs/ngos/lccr3.pdf.

On September 22, 2014, the Commission on Voting Rights released its long-awaited findings and report, which summarized the 25 hearings that had been held in every region of the country. The hearings had taken testimony from over 400 witnesses who recounted problems and barriers they had encountered in registering to vote, casting a vote, or having their vote counted, or issues related to the administration of elections. The report highlighted the successes as well as the challenges and concluded by stating "the need for state and local election administrators to increase efforts to improve the voter experience by removing obstacles to both registering and casting a ballot.[11] Key Recommendations from the report included:

– Voter registration needs to be easier to include online and same-day voter registration.
– States should comply with all federal voter registration laws and halt (regressive) rollbacks on voter reforms.
– Long lines at the polls could be reduced by the use of more poll worker recruitment and training, better use of secured technology, and early planning by election administrators.
– End excessive restrictive voter ID laws that disproportionly impact students, low-income, and people of color.
– Provide more funding for election administration to update old and malfunctioning voting equipment.
– Provide relief for voters with disabilities who continue to face accessibility problems with voting equipment.
– Provide federal and state legislative relief for people with felony convictions who face multiple voting barriers after release, with a maze of confusing state rules and regulations on the restoration of their voting rights.[12]

Despite the gravity of the 25 hearings convened by the Commission on Voting Rights, where voter suppression efforts were revealed in great detail with live witnesses, they received little national media attention. Nonetheless, with the commission's report as its new ammunition, civil rights groups continued to regard the restoration of the Voting Rights Act as its top priority. Once again, Congressman John Conyers took the lead on the VRA as Ranking Member on the House Judiciary Committee. Rep. John Lewis, congressional leaders and leading civil rights groups were well aware of the pitfalls of the last battle to restore the VRA in 2006. It had been passed on a bipartisan basis in both houses, but not

---

11 Ibid.
12 Ibid.

without the clear warning from many Republicans, including then-Senator Jeff Sessions of Alabama. Sessions and Republicans on the Senate Judiciary Committee argued that the formula for deciding pre-clearance was outdated and would one day be challenged at the Supreme Court. Those predictions turned out to be accurate.

Democratic staffers on the Judiciary Committee, led by Keenan Keller, Ted Kalo, and Perry Applebaum, worked to fashion a bipartisan bill that would not only get the support of a sufficient number of Republicans but would also withstand a constitutional challenge from the U.S. Supreme Court. Conyers, Keller, Kalo, and the committee's chief counsel, Perry Applebaum, began working with the Judiciary Committee's Republican chairman, Jim Sensenbrenner, and his leading staff on a bipartisan bill, the Voting Rights Amendment Act (VRAA), which was introduced on January 16, 2014.[13] The new bill's key provisions were spelled out in clear although somewhat technical terms: Key Provisions of the VRAA:

1. Re-asserted the principle that federal courts would retain jurisdiction for an appropriate period to prevent the commencement of new devices to deny or abridge the right to vote.
2. Expanded the types of violations triggering the authority of a court to retain preclearance jurisdiction.
3. Revised requirements for determining which states and political subdivisions were covered subject to the requirements for making such a coverage if 5 or more voting rights violations occurred in the state during the previous 15 years.
4. Prescribed new transparency requirements, including reasonable public notice, regarding any changes to: (1) voting prerequisites, standards, or procedures; (2) polling place resources; or (3) demographics and electoral districts.
5. Modified (expanded) authority to assign federal observers, including authorizing the assignment of observers to enforce bilingual election requirements.
6. Revised requirements for injunctive relief, including its scope and the persons authorized to seek relief.
7. Excluded from the list of violations triggering jurisdiction the imposition of a requirement that an individual provides photo identification as a condition of receiving a ballot; and

---

13 "Glossary of Legislative Terms – bill summary," Congress.gov, (n.d.) accessed March 22, 2022, https://www.congress.gov/help/legislative-glossary#glossary_billsummary.

8. Specified application of such new coverage requirements to any specific political subdivision if: (A) 3 or more voting rights violations occurred in it during the previous 15 calendar years; or (B) 1 or more voting rights violations
   occurred in it during the previous 15 calendar years **and** (C) the subdivision
   had persistent, extremely low minority turnout during that period.[14]

The final two provisions were major concessions to Sensenbrenner and the Republicans, who for years had sought to impose strict photo ID requirements in
states. Excluding photo ID laws from the list of violations that would trigger
pre-clearance provided an escape hatch for a number of non-Southern states
that had recently imposed strict ID requirements, including Sensenbrenner's
home state of Wisconsin, Indiana, Missouri, and other Midwestern states. The
final provision specifying the number of violations during a 15-year period
that would trigger pre-clearance coverage also provided a caveat that the state
or sub-division would have to have had "extremely low minority turnout during
that period." The massive Black turnout for Obama in 2008 and 2012 in states
across the US provided another *front door* for states to exit from the requirement
of pre-clearance coverage. Under the new VRAA, only five states would fall into
the category of being initially covered—dramatically lower than the nine states
and 56 jurisdictions that had required pre-clearance under the old formula,
which had been declared unconstitutional by the 2013 Supreme Court ruling.[15]

The bill with the new criteria for coverage of states was more technical and
nuanced than past VRA reauthorization bills. It had been carefully crafted by
Conyers' and Sensenbrenner's Judiciary Committee lead staff counsel to pick
up Republican votes in the House and Senate. They openly expressed the need
for the proposed bill to pass the constitutional tests in the federal courts that
had not looked favorably upon voting rights cases in recent years. Nonetheless,
the Conyers-Sensenbrenner bipartisan approach was embraced by Rep. John
Lewis, congressional leaders and Wade Henderson, President of the Leadership
Conference on Civil and Human Rights. The LCCHR was also working with key
members of Congress on a comprehensive immigration reform bill and President
Obama's stalled judicial nominations that were piling up. All required a bipartisan approach that would be able to secure the six to eight Republicans needed to
get to 60 votes.

The urgency of the timing was not lost on Henderson, his longtime legislative director Nancy Zirkin, or his Vice President for Field Operations Ellen Buch-

---

14 Ibid.
15 Ibid.

man. They saw the upcoming 2014 elections as a potential political turning point for getting major legislation passed into law during the second term of the Obama Administration. While Democrats controlled the Senate 54 – 46, several Senate seats were up in November and were considered toss-ups that could threaten the Democratic majority. Getting the VRAA passed was the top priority of the LCCHR, the Congressional Black Caucus, and the civil rights community. All were united in their belief that the VRAA had to be passed before formerly covered states expanded their voter suppression efforts in the run-up to the 2014 mid-term and 2016 presidential elections. But they were not all united in their approach toward the legislation, which many organizations and CBC members thought did not go far enough.

Splits in the coalition were reminiscent of the reluctance of the former Democratic Majority Leader George Mitchell during the NVRA legislative battles. The civil rights groups continued to list passage of a fix to the VRA as their top priority and urged Senate leaders to move the Senate version of the VRAA that had been introduced by Judiciary Chairman Pat Leahy in January 2014. The Sensenbrenner/Conyers house version of VRAA, H.R. 3899, had garnered 177 co-sponsors including 17 Republicans,[16] making it the only bipartisan voting rights vehicle that stood any chance of being voted out of the still Republican-controlled House. Despite the bipartisan nature of the bill, the new chairman of the House Judiciary Committee, David Goodlette, a conservative Republican from rural southwest Virginia, refused to schedule the bipartisan bill being co-sponsored by Sensenbrenner, an intra-party rival and the former chairman of the committee.

Goodlette consistently ignored repeated calls from Representative Sensenbrenner, his ranking member Conyers, the 205 members of the LCCHR, the entire civil rights community, and even constituents from his own district to hold a hearing on the bill.[17] The resistance of Goodlette and the House Republican leadership to even bring the bill up for a hearing sent the clear signal that Republicans were not interested in passing the bill, even with bipartisan support. Their continued resistance guaranteed that the state voter suppression actions that were being highlighted by the Commission on Voting Rights hearings would continue unabated. With only a few months before the midterm elections and two years before a presidential election, the failure of Congress to act on fixing the

---

16 "Cosponsors – H.R.3899 – 113th Congress (2013 – 2014): Voting Rights Amendment Act of 2014," Congress.gov, last modified March 20, 2014, https://www.congress.gov/bill/113th-congress/house-bill/3899/cosponsors.

17 Wade Henderson, *VRA Today Issue Brief* (Leadership Conference on Civil and Human Rights, 2014).

VRA was taking its toll in multiple states. The failure to pass VRAA placed millions of Black and Latino voters in danger of being disenfranchised without all the protections of the Voting Rights Act for the first time in 50 years.

While there was unified support for a hearing within the civil rights and voting rights community, the bipartisan bill had not been fully embraced by all elements of the civil rights community. The VRAA carved out an exception for states that imposed restrictive photo ID laws as a trigger for pre-clearance. Minority language provisions were also weaker than advocates had hoped for. On the positive side, the bill expanded opportunities for more states to be bailed into pre-clearance coverage. The new bail-in was based on a look back at voting rights violations over a 15-year period for states. This new bail-in formula began with a smaller number of southern states and jurisdictions being bailed in initially, but also an unprecedented opportunity for more states outside the South to be bailed into pre-clearance for the first time. The struggle against voter suppression was no longer a phenomenon of just the South. It was now taking place in northern states like Ohio, Wisconsin, Missouri, and Indiana. But it was hard to shine the spotlight on states outside the South when so much attention was being paid to how many of the Southern states would initially be covered.

In late February 2014, the LCCHR convened a national gathering of over 150 advocates to plan a national strategy for passage. While planning the steps needed to advance the VRAA among the grassroots, NAACP State Conference presidents and a vocal number of local civil rights advocates from many of the previously covered Southern states of Georgia, Texas, Mississippi, and North Carolina raised reservations and even objections to supporting the VRAA in its present form. One of the leading concerns was that the new formula would not even initially cover all of the previously covered southern states, including Alabama, the state of the Shelby decision. Voting rights litigators also called for a stronger bill that would stand a better chance of expanding the list of initially bailed-in states and strengthened language that would ensure full protection for language minorities and people with disabilities. Conyers supported adding each of the issues raised through amendments that would be made in the committee markup, or on the floor of the House. However, the growing opposition to the original version of the Sensenbrenner/Conyers VRAA halted the momentum that had been building for swift passage of a bill before the Shelby decision anniversary in June.

Supporters of a stronger VRAA bill redirected their energies toward the drafting of a new bill that would address all the missing elements of the Sensenbrenner/Conyers bill. According to an analysis undertaken by Ari Berman of The Nation magazine, the new bill would begin with a formula revising Sections 4 and 5 of the VRA by requiring states with 15 voting violations over the past 25 years, or

10 violations if one was statewide, to submit future election changes for pre-clearance federal approval.[18] This new formula would initially cover 13 states: Alabama, Arkansas, Arizona, California, Florida, Georgia, Louisiana, Mississippi, New York, North Carolina, South Carolina, Texas, and Virginia. (The original Voting Rights Amendment Act of 2014 fully covered only Georgia, Louisiana, Mississippi, and Texas.) Coverage would last for 10 years."[19]

With the anniversary of the Shelby decision and being one year out from the 50th anniversary of the Voting Rights Act, the coalition now looked to a new legislative leader, Representative Terri Sowell, a native of Selma and a representative from the very state of the Shelby decision, as the lead sponsor. She was joined in introducing the bill by the legendary John Lewis from Georgia, another covered state that would be directly impacted by the passage of the new Voting Rights *Advancement* Act (VRAA). Representatives Sowell and Lewis introduced the new VRAA, H.R. 2867, on June 24, 2014, on the eve of the first anniversary of the Shelby decision.[20] The Voting Rights "Advancement" Act was renamed to show distinction between the original Conyers-Sensenbrenner Voting Rights "Amendment" Act. They were intentionally made to sound similar by legislators to try and maintain support A companion bill, S. 1659, was also introduced on the same day by Senate Judiciary Committee Chairman Pat Leahy. In an interview with The Nation's Ari Berman, Leahy noted: "The previous bill we did in a way to try and get bipartisan support—which we did. We had the Republican majority leader of the House [Eric Cantor] promise us that if we kept it like that it would come up for a vote. It never did. We made compromises to get [Republican] support and they didn't keep their word. So, this time I decided to listen to the voters who had their right to vote blocked, and they asked for strong legislation that fully restores the protections of the VRA."[21]

The new bill now had the full support of the civil rights community, the CBC, the Democratic Party, and a new cadre of progressive advocates across the board. However (unlike the earlier, Conyers-Sensenbrenner version), it lacked any Republican support, marking the first time in the history of the Voting Rights Act

---

18 Ari Berman, "Congressional Democrats Introduce Ambitious New Bill to Restore the Voting Rights Act," The Nation, last modified June 24, 2015, https://www.thenation.com/article/archive/congressional-democrats-introduce-ambitious-new-bill-to-restore-the-voting-rights-act/.
19 Ibid.
20 "Glossary of Legislative Terms – bill summary," Congress.gov, (n.d.) accessed March 22, 2022, https://www.congress.gov/help/legislative-glossary#glossary_billsummary.
21 Berman, "Congressional Democrats Introduce Ambitious New Bill to Restore the Voting Rights Act," The Nation, last modified June 24, 2015, https://www.thenation.com/article/archive/congressional-democrats-introduce-ambitious-new-bill-to-restore-the-voting-rights-act/.

that the bill did not have bipartisan support. As chair of the Senate Judiciary Committee, Leahy was able to hold a hearing on the anniversary of the Shelby decision with the new bill highlighted as the vehicle to fully restore and even expand the protection of the Voting Rights Act. It would be the only hearing held on the VRAA, as House Judiciary Committee Chairman Goodlette continued to refuse to hold a hearing in the House. Barbara Arwine's "Map of Shame" had grown in the months since the original Voting Rights Amendment Act was first introduced. With a record number of voter suppression laws continuing to be passed in states, the time, energy, and political capital spent on other reform bills, like a constitutional amendment to reform campaign finance laws, seemed less urgent or meaningful to many in the civil rights community.

In early 2013 the fervor for action on getting big money out of politics was very strong in the donor community and among a number of progressive good government advocacy groups like Citizens Action, Every Voice, Common Cause, and a number of major environmental and climate action groups including the Sierra Club and Greenpeace. They formed a new coalition called the Democracy Initiative and threw their full support behind a constitutional amendment strategy and pushed hard for the U.S. Senate to take up a bill to finally address the issue. The bill they coalesced behind was *The Constitutional Amendment to Overturn Citizens United Decision and Corporate Citizenship for Purposes of Political Activity, (H. Res. 311)*.[22] After several months of drafting and deliberations among an increasingly large Money in Politics coalition, a bill was introduced by New Mexico Democratic Senator Tom Udall on June 18, 2013.[23] It was a spirited and serious legislative effort to do what had not been done since 1971 with the passage of the 26th Amendment granting 18-year-olds the right to vote. One week later, the Supreme Court would rule on the landmark Shelby v Holder decision that changed the entire landscape of legislative priorities. Instantly all of our efforts in the civil rights community turned to accessing the impact of the decision and strategizing about what next steps needed to be taken.

---

22 "Actions – S.J.Res.19 – 113th Congress (2013 – 2014): A joint resolution proposing an amendment to the Constitution of the United States relating to contributions and expenditures intended to affect elections," Congress.gov, last modified September 11, 2014, https://www.congress.gov/bill/113th-congress/senate-joint-resolution/19/all-actions.

23 "S.J.Res.19 – 113th Congress (2013 – 2014): A joint resolution proposing an amendment to the Constitution of the United States relating to contributions and expenditures intended to affect elections," Congress.gov, last modified September 11, 2014, https://www.congress.gov/bill/113th-congress/senate-joint-resolution/19.

Virtually every Democratic member of the U.S. Senate signed on as a co-sponsor or supporter.[24] However not a single republican even gave the bill any support or serious consideration. Despite this widespread support it enjoyed among Democrats, the bill had very little awareness or public support within the African American community. I was personally supportive of the effort having seen firsthand the debilitating role that big money played in advancing several major legislative initiatives. However, I also knew that even if passed by the US Senate, it would have taken years to be ratified by three-fifths (i.e., 38) states.

After a spirited debate on the Senate floor to end cloture, Senator Harry Reid gave in to pressure from advocacy groups and scheduled a vote on the Senate Floor. Surprisingly, Republicans did not invoke cloture or threaten to filibuster the bill. On September 11, 2014, the Senate vote for the amendment was 54–42, a clear majority of the senate, but well short of the 67 votes needed to pass a constitutional amendment.[25]

For its part, the media shifted its focus away from both the Money in Politics battle and the struggle to fix the VRA in light of the Shelby decision. Instead, they turned their focus to the political battle for control of the US House and Senate, which showed Republicans rapidly gaining ground. Voting rights rallies and hearings were covered only tangentially, without making clear connections between the laws that were being modified across the country since the Shelby decision and the upcoming 2014 election. The infighting among the supporters of voting rights over the two VRAA bills had been costly in terms of burning down the time needed to get the bill through the House and Senate.

The failure to pass any fix to the Voting Rights Act, the continued voter suppression efforts in states, and the influx of unprecedented amounts of big money flooding into the political system produced a perfect storm of support for Republicans at the ballot box in the fall. On November 4, 2014, Republicans retained control of the US House of Representatives and won control of the US Senate, upending the Democratic majority for what would be the last two years of the Obama Administration.[26] Republicans won a net gain of nine Senate seats—the largest Senate gain for either party since the Reagan Revolution election of 1980. Republicans won a net gain of thirteen seats in the US House of Represen-

---

24 "Cosponsors – S.J.Res.19–113th Congress (2013–2014): A joint resolution proposing an amendment to the Constitution of the United States relating to contributions and expenditures intended to affect elections," Congress.gov, last modified September 11, 2014, https://www.congress.gov/bill/113th-congress/senate-joint-resolution/19/cosponsors.
25 Ibid.
26 "Senate Election Results," The New York Times, last modified December 17, 2014, https://www.nytimes.com/elections/2014/results/senate.

tatives, giving them their largest majority since the onset of the Great Depression in the 1930s.[27] In state elections, Republicans flipped control of ten state legislative chambers. These victories were aided by their ability to take full advantage of the 2011 redistricting process in light of their major gains in the 2010 elections across the US.[28] These gains were further aided by the U.S. Supreme Court's dual campaign finance constitutional rulings on the *Citizens United v. Federal Election Commission (FEC)* decision on January 21, 2010 which took caps off of contributions to Political Action Committees, and the April 2, 2014 *McCutcheon vs FEC* decision which took aggregate spending caps off individual political contributions to candidates and PACs.[29] These two new campaign finance rules were fully operational in the 2014 elections and led to the unprecedented fundraising levels and expenditures reaching a record $3.7 billion in the midterm election.[30] It would become the most expensive political campaign expenditure in US history. Despite overwhelming spending by both political parties, the 2014 election also saw the lowest turnout since 1942, with just 36.4% of eligible voters voting.[31]

The loss of the Senate meant more than Democrats losing chairmanships of all the major committees at the start of the new Congress in January 2015. Under pressure to get President Obama's federal judges and presidential appointees around the filibuster, Majority Leader Harry Reid utilized what was known as the "nuclear option" and changed the Senate rules to weaken the filibuster.[32] While Democrats and progressives had praised this as a bold move when Democrats had control of the Senate, it now meant that the new Republican majority, and a potentially new Republican president, could fill vacancies in the federal court on a simple majority vote, *with Democrats powerless to stop them*. McConnell had warned Democrats that were they to eliminate the filibuster for federal judges, he would raise the stakes and remove it for filling Supreme Court vacancies. "Be careful what you wish for," he had repeatedly warned from the floor of

27 "2014 United States Elections," Wikipedia, last modified March 8, 2022, https://en.wikipedia. org/wiki/2014_United_States_elections#:~:text=House.
28 Ibid.
29 "McCutcheon, et al. v. FEC," Federeal Election Commission – United States of America, (n.d.) accessed March 22, 2022, https://www.fec.gov/legal-resources/court-cases/mccutcheon-et-al-v-fec/.
30 "2014 United States Elections," Wikipedia, last modified March 8, 2022, https://en.wikipedia. org/wiki/2014_United_States_elections#:~:text=House.
31 Ibid.
32 Molly E. Reynolds, "What is the Senate filibuster, and what would it take to eliminate it?," Brookings, last modified September 9, 2020, https://www.brookings.edu/policy2020/votervital/ what-is-the-senate-filibuster-and-what-would-it-take-to-eliminate-it/.

the Senate. His words of caution, which had been dismissed as partisan rhetoric, now became reality.

The major downside to Democrats reforming the filibuster was the possibility that Senate Democrats would one day be in the minority and unable to stop federal judges nominated by a future Republican president from being appointed. Democrats would not be able to use the filibuster the way the Republicans had done to block scores of federal judicial appointments that had become vacant during President Obama's eight years in office. At the beginning of Obama's term there were 44 district vacancies and a total of 88 by the end of the term. This represented a 100% increase in the number of vacancies—unprecedented for a modern day two term presidency. [33] This could have a profound impact on a plethora of new Obama era laws that had been passed. It also would be the courts that would be ruling on the remaining provisions of the VRA, as future cases against restrictive state voter laws would have to work their way through the federal courts.

In the closing days of December 2014, during the lame-duck session of Congress, one bright spot ended an otherwise disastrous year in voting rights. After over four years of being unable to conduct official business with a full complement of confirmed commissioners, Senate Democrats were able to muster the votes to confirm the Obama Administration's stalled nominations to the US Election Assistance Commission (EAC) and the Federal Election Commission (FEC).[34] In the closing weeks of the 114th Democratic-controlled Senate, I worked with the newly formed pro-democracy group, Democracy Initiative, to circulate a letter to Rules Committee Chairman Chuck Schumer and Majority Leader Harry Reid, making an impassioned plea to advance the appointments of the two EAC nominees, Democrat Ben Hovland and Republican Doug Palmer. Both were confirmed on December 16, paving the way for the U.S. Election Assistance Commission to be able to fully function for the first time in over four and a half years since 2010.[35] With the upcoming Presidential election in 2016, this was the best news in an otherwise dark December as Democrats prepared to relinquish control of the Senate and Republicans prepared to seize control of both chambers of Congress for the first time during the Obama presidency.

---

33 Barry J. McMillion, "U.S. District Court Vacancies at the Beginning and End of the Obama Presidency: Overview and Comparative Analysis," Federation of American Scientists, last modified January 31, 2017, https://sgp.fas.org/crs/misc/IN10570.pdf.
34 Ibid.
35 Rick Hasen, "Breaking: Senate Confirms 3 Commissioners to the Election Assistance Commission," Election Law Blog, last modified December 16, 2014, https://electionlawblog.org/?p=69221.

By mid-year 2015, we had gone two years without the full protections of the Voting Rights Act, with multiple states having now passed restrictive voting laws and with scores of vacancies in the federal judiciary. The prospects for passing either version of the VRAA ended with the loss of the Senate to Republicans in the last two years of President Obama's term. Given the Republicans' track record of supporting voter suppression bills and opposition to electoral reform efforts, our major concern was no longer just passing the new Voting Rights Act. It would now become even more important to develop strategies to stop new federal anti-voting rights legislation from being passed into law.

At this point, I began to have private reservations about weakening the filibuster. I had always believed that the filibuster was an anathema to democracy, in which the majority rules. I knew all too well how it had plagued our over-five-year battle to pass the NVRA every step of the way and how it had been used against major civil rights bills in the past. However as a numerical racial minority and now a political minority, I was skeptical of eliminating a procedure that would *strengthen the power of the majority* and *weaken the power of political and even racial minorities*. I was also aware of several inconsistencies in past years when Democrats had rightfully filibustered hard-right judicial appointments like Judges Robert Bork and Clarence Thomas to the US Supreme Court.[36] Democrats had also threatened Republican leaders with filibusters of bills to overturn reproductive (abortion) rights, Repeal of Obamacare and abolish agencies like the Energy Department in years past period. In recent years advocates had urged Democrats to filibuster multiple Republicans bills to abolish and/or defund the U.S. Election Assistance Commission.

The Senate filibuster, for all its racist origins, was the only tool Democrats would now have in Congress to stop REPUBLICANS' hard-right legislative initiatives. While there were many democratic advocates and colleagues of mine who privately held this view, few felt comfortable articulating it publicly. The occasion of having a Democratic president was the only protection against hard right republicans' legislative overreaches being enacted into law. But even that was up for a vote in 2016, with no guarantees that Democrats would retain the White House. However, given the Filibuster's long history of use by enemies of civil rights and African American progress, our best hope remained in mobilizing Black voters to vote in great numbers.

---

36 Noah Feldman, "When Democrats Blocked an 'Out of the Mainstream' Justice," Bloomberg Opinion, last modified January 26, 2017, https://www.bloomberg.com/opinion/articles/2017-01-26/when-democrats-blocked-an-out-of-the-mainstream-justice.

With all these concerns in mind, I began feeling guilty that I had abandoned my post in leading national mobilizations of Black voters in multiple key battleground states during the 2014 elections as I had done in past election cycles since the 1980s. Instead, I felt the fight to pass the VRAA in Washington, DC was at a critical stage and needed my help. I had worked hard following the 2012 elections trying to re-ignite a major national Black Civic Engagement Initiative voter mobilization collaboration in conjunction with Black legacy organizations. After the crushing defeat of the 2014 elections, we could not afford for the 2016 elections to be a further step back from all the progress we had made over the past 8 years with President Obama and earlier efforts going back to passage of the NVRA in the 1990s. We knew that Obama would not be on the ballot in 2016 and that the mobilization of Black voters was severely threatened by the loss of the VRA. The lack of a well-funded national Black voter mobilization or infrastructure increased the sense of urgency for passing any version of the VRAA while there was still time before the 2016 elections.

* * *

March 2015 marked the 50th anniversary of the Voting Rights Act and the 50th anniversary of the Selma, Alabama "Bloody Sunday" march across the Edmund Pettis Bridge. This offered the best opportunity to place the nation's attention back on Congress' failure to fix the Voting Rights Act. While strongly supportive of the act's passage, the Obama White House staff had not been fully engaged with the legislative process to ensure its swift passage. With stalled federal judgeships, attacks on Obamacare, his groundbreaking international global work to pass a major climate accord pending, and a nuclear arms containment deal with Iran, the Obama Administration was otherwise preoccupied. It was next to the last year of his term, and he had to contend with a Republican-controlled House and now a Republican Senate that was opposing him on every front. So, when the president announced that he was going to Selma for the 50th Anniversary commemoration, our hopes rose that this would launch a full-court press to pass the new and improved Voting Rights Advancement Act.[37]

On March March 7, 2015, over 80,000 people converged on the small town of Selma, Alabama to mark the historic occasion.[38] A usual commemoration in years past would have drawn 5,000 to 10,000 people. With the 50th anniversary

37 Chris Kromm, "Selma and voting rights: Commemoration or legislation?," Facing South, last modified March 6, 2015, https://www.facingsouth.org/2015/03/selma-and-voting-rights-commemoration-or-legislati.html.
38 "Obama in Selma: "Our march is not yet finished"," CBS News, last modified March 7, 2015, https://www.cbsnews.com/news/obama-selma-alabama-50th-anniversary-bloody-sunday/.

and a major address to be given by President Obama, supporters came from far and wide to be part of it. For the 50th anniversary there were two other previous presidents in attendance who had signed major voting rights legislation, President George W. Bush who signed the VRA reauthorization in 2006 and Bill Clinton who signed the NVRA in 1993.[39] They marched alongside Obama and a broad cross section of Americans who had joined the pilgrimage across the Edmund Pettis Bridge.

Flights for this historic gathering had been booked solid weeks in advance, so I decided to drive down with my wife Jean for the festivities from DC. We got a late start and stopped over in Atlanta the night before, rather than driving all the way over to Selma, which had only a handful of hotels. The decision proved to be a bad one, as cars from throughout the region clogged the lone Highway 40 leading into Selma. By early Saturday afternoon, when most of the major commemoration activities were underway, we were still in our car 5 miles outside Selma, on a highway that soon turned into a parking lot. For hours, nothing moved into the town due to the thousands of cars trying to enter Selma and find parking in a city that could not accommodate more than a few hundred cars. The safety procedures for moving the President of the United States through the small city made this already chaotic situation even more congested and chaotic. We ended up hearing the president's speech from my car radio. It was a well-delivered and glowing speech about the historical journey of African Americans to obtain the right to vote. It was proceeded by impassioned speeches by Congressman John Lewis, John Conyers, Congresswoman Terri Sowell, Rev. Al Sharpton, Martin Luther King, III, Rev. Jesse Jackson, and so many other legendary and up and coming leaders.

For those few days when we were all in Selma, it felt like the whole world was watching and the VRAA battle was finally getting the full attention of the president and members of Congress from both parties who had come down to be part of the commemoration. And finally, the media, which had all but ignored past rallies and marches over the past few years since the Shelby decision, was paying attention and writing stories and editorials about the importance of passing the act. But that attention was not long-lived. The political leaders all returned to Washington on Sunday evening, leaving the small city of Selma to clean up after what looked like a New Year's Eve celebration.

Longtime Bloody Sunday Commemoration March organizer Rose Sanders had lost her voice completely, as she often did after her annual commemorations. This was by far the biggest ever and she wondered out loud how many

---

39 Ibid.

days and weeks it would take for them to get the city back into regular operations after everyone had left. In many ways, it was the same for me. After the 50th anniversary commemoration, and after the thousands of people marching under the banner of passing the VRAA, there was an eerie silence. Just a week after the big anniversary, there were few floor speeches in Congress, no more committee hearings, no more presidential meetings or speeches calling on Congress to act. Washington, it seemed, was moving on to the next big thing.

Having returned from Selma still energized, I met my old friend, Wade Henderson, at his favorite spot, the St. Regis hotel lounge, along with his vice president for field operations, Ellen Buchman. To regain some of the momentum from the big Selma commemoration, they proposed pulling together a campaign to hold a major voting rights rally in Congressman Bob Goodlette's district in Roanoke, Virginia on the 2nd anniversary of the Shelby decision on June 25. Wade and Ellen asked me to take on as an additional assignment with the LCCHR. We had hoped to build upon the EAC support campaign with activities around the second anniversary of the Shelby decision. The major rally we were planning would be not in Selma or Washington, DC but, rather, in rural southwest Virginia, in Congressman Goodlette's own backyard.

I thought the effort would need the full support of the LCCHR. We were already deeply involved with efforts on the hill in support of the stalled appointments to the US Election Assistance Commission and opposing Republican efforts to defund and abolish the commission. We agreed that I would reach out to all of the allied groups that made up the new coalition, the Democracy Initiative (DI), where I was already working to help build convergence between voting rights groups and money in politics advocates. In late spring, I decided that this would be my last attempt to help jump-start some legislative action on the VRAA. It would be late June—still enough time to get out of Washington, DC and refocus my efforts on voter mobilization. Only a small window of time was left to build a quality program that could make a difference in the November elections. But I did not want to leave before we put the maximum amount of pressure on Republicans in Congress to pass this or any version of the VRAA. We began meeting with several allies, trying to figure out how to build upon the momentum from Selma. Our primary strategy for the march in Roanoke was to place the focus on the resistance of the one man, Congressman Goodlette, who was singlehandedly preventing the VRAA from even getting a hearing in the US House of Representatives.

The LCCHR, the Democracy Initiative Coalition, and NAACP local branch president Barbara Hale worked hard with me for several months to plan the June 25 Shelby second anniversary march. The coalition focused on filling-chartered buses with a growing and diverse blend of multi-racial and multi-issue partners including postal workers' unions, climate change and climate justice advocates, LGBTQ activists, and food justice groups, who joined with the more traditional civil rights and now, money in politics groups.

On June 25, 2015, several hundred marchers gathered in front of the Roanoke Library. The event was rare for the sleepy Southwest Virginia town. It took place just a few blocks from Goodlette's congressional office.[40] In addition to the buses from DC, Virginia NAACP activists converged on the town with buses and vans from Tidewater, Virginia, led by Cynthia Downs-Taylor, and from as far away as Raleigh, North Carolina, led by the increasingly popular Rev. William Barber, president of the North Carolina NAACP. As we had hoped, the event shone a bright light on Goodlette's resistance to the bill for his constituents in Southwest Virginia. Many of the local residents—and even media outlets that attended the rally—were completely unaware of Goodlette's resistance to the VRAA bill. It was rare for such a high-profile political event to take place in Goodlette's own backyard.

Despite the several hundred people who attended the spirited rally, Goodlette was not moved to take any action to move the bill. Having run for re-election several times with no Democratic opposition, he felt little political pressure, being from a solidly gerrymandered Republican district. Despite large marches in Selma and his home district, Goodlette vowed that the VRAA would never get its hearing in the Judiciary Committee as long as he was chairman.

After the early Selma 50th anniversary commemoration and march, we knew the Roanoke rally on the anniversary of the Shelby decision could be our last chance to turn the tide for the bill before the 2016 presidential elections. It had been a long struggle for voting rights, and Roanoke's name was now added to the list of small Southern towns where the right to vote was fought. The local media and some national media covered the event but not to the level that we had hoped. We wanted to make this grassroots effort the next big thing in moving the voting rights bill forward. However, in the days leading up to the march, the next big thing was happening far north of Roanoke.

---

40 "Voting Rights Act Rally," The Roanoke, last modified June 25, 2015, https://roanoke.com/photo/voting-rights-act-rally/collection_a8bac487-229a-5c8e-bef0-b5b8bdfde7a4.html.

Chapter 15
The Rise of Trump and the Movement for Black Lives

That next big thing took place nine days before our rally, on June 16, 2015, in New York City as "Celebrity Apprentice" reality television host Donald Trump came down the escalators of his Trump Tower and announced his run for President of the United States.[1] Suddenly, the political and media world stopped in its tracks and turned its full attention to the prospects of Donald Trump being a serious candidate for president. The "self-proclaimed" billionaire whose only claim to political fame was his years-long questioning of President Obama's US citizenship, completely captured the attention of the media and, subsequently, the nation. His opening announcement speech was laced with racist and offensive language against Mexican Americans, as well as a litany of insults against the political systems of both parties.[2]

Trump's campaign represented a combination of the Tea Party, the Obama birtherism movement, and whistle blowing the ghost of white supremacy. It was a clear signal and a throwback to the former separatist Alabama governor and presidential candidate, George Wallace.[3] Trump was seeking to launch a new era of what former President Richard Nixon described as "the silent majority" emerging from the crevices that our country had struggled so hard to forget.[4] Trump shot to the top of the opinion polls among Republican voters, far outpacing 11 other well-known and well-established Republican candidates. Among them was Florida Governor Jeb Bush, the son and brother, respectively, of the last two former Republican presidents, and other big-name leading candidates like Mitt Romney, the 2012 Republican Party nominee, Florida Senator Marco Rubio, an up-and-coming star among the Tea Party, and former New Jersey Governor Chris Christie, long rumored to be a frontrunner for the nomination. De-

---

1 Rupert Neate, "Donald Trump announces US presidential run with eccentric speech," The Guardian, last modified June 16, 2015, https://www.theguardian.com/us-news/2015/jun/16/donald-trump-announces-run-president.
2 Ibid.
3 "George Wallace," Wikipedia, last modified March 9, 2022, https://en.wikipedia.org/wiki/George_Wallace.
4 "Silent majority," Wikipedia, last modified March 2, 2022, https://en.wikipedia.org/wiki/Silent_majority.

https://doi.org/10.1515/9783110742473-018

spite spending unprecedented millions of dollars during the Republican primaries against him, they were not able to slow down the Trump momentum.[5]

The Democratic Party establishment initially laughed off Trump's candidacy, with Hillary Clinton even proclaiming, amid her famous laugh, that she relished the thought of running against Donald Trump. Progressive activists and donors were also thrilled at the prospect of running against Trump as a major way to mobilize their base across the country by labeling Trump as a racist and political buffoon. Cable news media outlets on both sides of the political spectrum gave wall-to-wall coverage to the Trump campaign, covering his every move and analyzing every word of his daily tweets. It was the lowest-cost media coverage ever given to a presidential candidate, even surpassing the exceptional coverage of the historic campaign of Barack Obama. Trump took the political, media, and social media world by storm. The need to pass a fix to the Voting Rights Act, voter suppression battles and the money in politics reforms were pushed to the back burner even further. All now took a back seat to the Trump phenomenon and the national obsession that followed.

★ ★ ★

While the mainstream and cable news media gave episodic coverage to the ongoing and systemic crisis of Black men and women being killed in the streets by police, the Movement for Black Lives held its first national convention in Cleveland, Ohio in the summer of 2015.[6] I attended as part of my effort to reconnect myself and our national Black Civic engagement plans to what was happening outside Washington, DC with the new and emerging generation of Black Lives Matter (BLM) leaders from around the country. The movement had grown exponentially since the murders of Trayvon Martin in Florida, Michael Brown in Ferguson, Missouri, Eric Garner in New York, Sandra Bland in Texas, Freddie Gray in Baltimore, Tamir Rice in Cleveland and so many others. The initial Black Lives Matter demonstrations and the first national convening were in response to these and other police killings in a number of cities across the US. It had quickly grown into a protest movement that focused on police accountability and criminal jus-

---

5 "2016 Republican Presidential Nomination," RealClear Politics, (n.d.) accessed March 22, 2022, https://www.realclearpolitics.com/epolls/2016/president/us/2016_republican_presidential _nomination-3823.html.
6 Jane Morice, "Thousands of 'freedom fighters' in Cleveland for first national Black Lives Matter conference," Cleveland.com, last modified July 25, 2015, https://www.cleveland.com/metro/ 2015/07/thousands_of_freedom_fighters.html.

tice reform in the aftermath of police officers not being held accountable for their actions.[7]

Young people—Black, white, and Brown—gravitated toward this movement as the one that was finally speaking truth to power. Unlike the civil rights movement and partisan political party leaders who spoke in platitudes, BLM spoke directly to the needs and aspirations of a generation desperately looking for someone or something that could relate to *them*. Every level of engagement that they had seen or heard thus far from politicians began with an appeal for their vote, for their financial contribution, or for them to join an existing social or political organization that they could not really relate to.

On the second day of the convening of the Movement for Black Lives, the gathering debated a plethora of issues related to police accountability, but soon expanded into issues related to identity politics, support for the burgeoning movement for transgender rights, and the need to build a new movement for social justice and Black economic empowerment. Speaker after speaker launched a full assault on American crony capitalism and other race and gender cultural issues that had seldom been raised as publicly and as forcefully in American society. It was a free flow of expression that was high-octane energy throughout, often breaking out into the spoken word poetry, hip-hop music, and liberation dancing in the aisles of the auditorium. It was unlike any political convention I had ever attended!

After several hours had passed, the conference got back on schedule and returned to the many workshops that had been set up to have more detailed group discussions on policies and topics based on a pre-selected survey of participants according to their areas of interest. I was scheduled to facilitate a concurrent workshop on civic participation and political empowerment. With an approaching presidential election already underway, I anticipated that there would be great interest on the part of the delegates in moving BLM from street protest to political empowerment. However, I was shocked to learn that my workshop had scored close to the bottom in terms of interest on the part of the delegates attending.

Out of the over 1,500 delegates who had attended the gathering, only 12 showed up for the political engagement workshop. Once we went around the room, it was clear that over half of the participants had no interest in, or little appreciation for, the importance of political engagement. Most of the gathering was very cynical about getting involved in electoral politics at all. They viewed

---

7 "Movement for Black Lives," Wikipedia, last modified March 9, 2022, https://en.wikipedia.org/wiki/Movement_for_Black_Lives.

American politics and elected officials as a big part of the problem, not the solution. Their justifiably cynical view of civic engagement was seen as something that would divert their attention away from the protest movement underway in the streets. Expending the energy and "voting for them" (politicians) was not the way to solve the problem. In fact, some said that their non-participation in the political process was itself a statement of protest against the political system. It was an honest and eye-opening dialogue between two very divergent viewpoints of how best to build Black political power. As a person who had committed their life to increasing civic participation, this was a particularly hard and sobering pill for me to swallow.

Trayvon Martin had been killed simply for walking home from a store; Eric Garner choked to death by New York City police simply for selling single cigarettes in front of a neighborhood store. Freddie Gray was killed en route to being arraigned at a Baltimore police station. Police officers gave no consideration to Gray's wellbeing after he was stuffed into a steel paddy wagon and tussled to death on his way to being booked. For many of the young people who saw their friends and neighbors gunned down, the Voting Rights Act and the Democrats controlling the US Congress or White House was the furthest thing from their minds. I left the convening still committed to building a Black political mobilization campaign, but it was clear that the BLM movement would be the dominant effort that would capture the imagination and attention of our young and upcoming generation of Black leadership.

* * *

The presidential primary election season in 2016 was dramatic for both parties. The battle between Hillary Clinton and Senator Bernie Sanders was a surprisingly bold and powerful progressive challenge to the Democratic Party's favorite to win the nomination. Large segments of the Democratic Party, most notably young and more progressive constituency groups, gravitated to Bernie Sanders' campaign. Sanders was an unabashed Democratic Socialist who had a very dedicated and energized following throughout the US. Most had not been involved in Democratic Party politics and were getting engaged with the Democratic Party primary for the sole purpose of supporting Sanders' campaign for president.

For her part, Clinton enjoyed strong support from African Americans, women, and traditional Democratic Party regulars: three major constituencies with a strong ability to impact the primaries. Clinton outpaced Sanders in key Southern and Midwestern states with large urban and rural Black populations. Women voters were with Hillary and the important glass ceiling breakthrough as the potential first woman Democratic nominee and president. But the gap between her support among women and Donald Trump in the general election was surprisingly smaller than the campaign had hoped—particularly among white women. Clinton won women voters 54–42%.[8] Clinton's support among African Americans was overwhelming at 88%, but this was far less than the 93% support that Obama had received in 2012.[9] The gap in her support among young voters 18–24 was abysmal, with over 65% having supported Sanders in the primaries over Clinton and only winning 54% of young voters to Trump's 37%[10] Yet her support among African Americans in key primary states was enough to propel the Clinton Campaign to the Democratic nomination. This was followed by a *play it safe* fall campaign that limited the outreach of the candidate to a handful of battleground states where her core constituencies could be mobilized. While launching a full-scale campaign, many Democratic party operatives mistakenly viewed the Trump campaign as a fringe, polarized, and unorganized campaign that would not be taken seriously by the American people.

By late fall, the Clinton Campaign's post-convention failure to campaign in states like Michigan and Wisconsin had a major impact on voter turnout. In Ohio and other toss-up states, the race between Clinton and Trump was very close, with Trump leading in states like Florida, Arizona, and North Carolina, though within the margin of error. Polling suggested that Clinton was in striking distance and in a similar position as Obama in 2008. With a massive turnout from labor unions, single women, and African American voters, Clinton's campaign believed that it could win in the major battleground states, including Ohio—the one state that every Republican nominee who went on to be elected president had to win.[11] Because no Republican had ever been elected president without winning Ohio, it meant that investing in the state was the best insurance policy against a potential Trump victory. Despite the campaign's private belief that Ohio was somewhat a lost cause, I joined a chorus of voices calling for more investment in Ohio from donors and supporters who wanted to have a real impact on the 2016 elections. Ohio also stayed in the spotlight because the Republicans had decided to hold their national convention in Cleveland. It

---

8 Aamna Mohdin, "American women voted overwhelmingly for Clinton, except the white ones," Quartz, last modified November 9, 2016, https://qz.com/833003/election-2016-all-women-voted-overwhelmingly-for-clinton-except-the-white-ones/.

9 Alec Tyson and Shiva Maniam, "Behind Trump's victory: Divisions by race, gender, education," Pew Research Center, last modified November 9, 2016, https://www.pewresearch.org/fact-tank/2016/11/09/behind-trumps-victory-divisions-by-race-gender-education/.

10 Ibid.

11 Kyle Kondik, *The Bellwether: Why Ohio Picks the President* (Athens: Ohio University Press, 2016).

was the polar opposite of the Movement for Black Lives convening that took place there one year ago!

Having a program up and running in 2016 in Ohio was important to show that progressive and civil rights organizations would not be abandoning Ohio. Even with my being on the ground, it was hard to tell how much the campaigns were doing to shore up support from grassroots voters. Hundreds of millions of dollars were being spent by both sides on wall-to-wall television political ads. National polling showed that both Trump and Hillary Clinton were viewed unfavorably among their most likely voters. It was unprecedented in gallop polling. In both parties, there was a large contingent of non-believers among their respective party nominees.[12]

On the Democratic side, many strong supporters of presidential candidate Bernie Sanders were tepid in their support of Hillary Clinton after a long and bitter primary campaign. Sanders himself said and did all the things that are traditionally done by a losing presidential candidate. He attended rallies with Clinton, urged his supporters to give their full support to her, and even worked out a compromise party platform that was viewed as the most progressive party platform ever adopted. But many of his most staunch supporters in Ohio had rejected Sanders' pleas and refused to endorse the Clinton Campaign after the Democratic Convention.[13] It was a decision that had major ramifications on the voter turnout for Clinton and the Democratic Party on Election Day in Ohio and other key battle grounds states like Michigan and Wisconsin.

On the Republican side, Trump had trounced all of the more traditional candidates for president early in the primaries. By late spring, he was the presumptive Republican nominee despite misgivings about his personal and controversial lifestyle and his politically polarizing campaign rhetoric. Trump regularly took shots against both the Democratic and Republican parties. Although he enjoyed daily wall-to-wall news coverage, the media was still somewhat dismissive of Trump's chances until very late in the campaign. Most political analysts still saw the race as Clinton's to lose. National polls showed a close race with most placing Hillary Clinton a few points ahead in the popular vote, although still

---

12 Lydia Saad, "Trump and Clinton Finish With Historically Poor Images," Gallup, last modified November 8, 2016, https://news.gallup.com/poll/197231/trump-clinton-finish-historically-poor-images.aspx.

13 Jacob Pramulk, "'Nothing' will make me vote Clinton: Some Bernie backers hold firm as DNC starts," CNBC, last modified July 25, 2016, https://www.cnbc.com/2016/07/25/nothing-will-make-me-vote-clinton-some-bernie-backers-hold-firm-as-dnc-starts.html.

neck and neck in all of the battleground states.[14] Partly driven by polls and partly by overconfidence, the Clinton Campaign narrowed her direct candidate outreach to the handful of battleground states where the race was close. In the more traditionally Democratic-leaning states like Michigan, Wisconsin, and Minnesota, the campaign made a series of fateful decisions of not sending the candidate there in the fall, believing that they were secure enough to devote more time to purple and red states like Arizona, North Carolina, and Florida, which showed some promise of turning blue.[15]

Key to each of the aforementioned states was the level of Black and Hispanic voter turnout. In the Midwest, the Black turnout was THE deciding factor in states that were geographically made up of conservative rural areas that voted heavily Republican. A large turnout of Black voters in major urban centers like Cleveland, Ohio, Detroit, Michigan, and Milwaukee, Wisconsin was the only thing that kept the states in the blue column. Wisconsin, like Michigan, was also heavily rural but with a strong tradition of independent-minded Democratic voting.[16] In addition to the cities of Milwaukee, Racine, and Madison were the University of Wisconsin and smaller campuses and college towns that were peppered throughout the state. This made Wisconsin a state that had leaned blue in past presidential elections. However, the 2016 presidential campaign saw Trump making strong inroads among white and rural voters across the states, including the surrounding suburbs of Milwaukee, Cleveland, Minneapolis, and other Midwestern cities.[17]

The Republican-led legislature and Republican Governor Scott Walker in Wisconsin had recently signed into law a bill that would no longer allow college students to use their university IDs as acceptable identification for voting. The law went into full effect in mid-2015 after being challenge by voting rights groups but upheld by the US Supreme Court. [18] As a result, literally thousands of young

---

14 Andrew Mercer, Claudia Deane, and Kyley McGeeney, "Why 2016 election polls missed their mark," Pew Research Center, last modified November 9, 2016, https://www.pewresearch.org/fact-tank/2016/11/09/why-2016-election-polls-missed-their-mark/.

15 Ronald Brownstein, "How the Rustbelt Paved Trump's Road to Victory," The Atlantic, last modified November 10, 2016, https://www.theatlantic.com/politics/archive/2016/11/trumps-road-to-victory/507203/.

16 Ibid.

17 Ibid.

18 "Wisconsin voter identification requirements and history," Ballotpedia, (n.d.) accessed March 22, 2022, https://ballotpedia.org/Wisconsin_voter_identification_requirements_and_history.

voters were not able to cast their votes as they had in previous elections. That one act alone was enough to tip the scale in Wisconsin. In Detroit Michigan, there were reports of widespread discrepancies related to voting machine counts on Election Day. Post-election audits would reveal that 248 or 37% of Detroit's 662 precincts had ballot tabulation counts that did not match the voting machine scanners.[19] It was an odd anomaly that raised red flags among election protection and voting rights activists in Detroit. The Michigan race was decided by just over 10,700 votes despite the massive support from the city of Detroit where Clinton was winning 95% of the vote.[20]

In Ohio, there were no such anomalies this year as there were in 2004. There was another high turnout among voters across the state. In the Obama campaigns of 2008 and 2012, that increase in turnout was led by African American voters. However, in 2016, the 71.3% turnout surge was predominantly among white male voters who increased their level of participation in rural areas of Ohio and other states across the US.[21] The turnout in the rural areas was so overwhelming that it threw off all the pre-election modeling done by the America Votes Ohio state table and the newly established For Our Future super PAC. Progressive activists had met most of the numeric voter turnout goals, knocking on over 2 million doors in the lead up to the election. As one of America Votes' and For Our Future's affiliate partners in Ohio, our program knocked on 206,000 African American Household doors across the State of Ohio in Cleveland, Columbus, Cincinnati, Akron, and Dayton. With additional resources and support from the Potomac Coalition, we formed the Ohio Voter Fund Political Action Committee to coordinate out voter mobilization efforts. Statewide field efforts were led by our most experienced team of Dave Holt, Jesse Jenkins, Carolyn Perkins, Reginald Holt, Charlie Bibb, Kate Harshman, Regina Smith and Jackie Williams. While I was proud of this being the largest field operation we had ever run in Ohio, knocking on over 200,000 doors in just 10 weeks, we did not reach the levels of historic high turnout in the rural and exurban areas of the state that traditionally voted heavily republican.

The same would hold in other states that worked hard to turn out the vote, but, as in Ohio, the Black voter mobilization underperformed its turnout levels

---

19 Joel Kurth and Jonathan Oosting, "Records: Too many votes in 37% of Detroit's precincts," The Detroit News, last modified December 13, 2016, https://www.detroitnews.com/story/news/politics/2016/12/12/records-many-votes-detroits-precincts/95363314/.
20 Ibid.
21 Rob Griffin, Ruy Teixeira, and John Halpin, "Voter Trends in 2016," American Progress, last modified November 1, 2017, https://www.americanprogress.org/article/voter-trends-in-2016/.

from 2008 and 2012.[22] This was also the case in Michigan and Wisconsin, the same states that we had targeted for a major Black civic engagement voter mobilization plan that had collapsed in late 2015 due to a lack of funding. On election night, the national cable news media reported on the developments across the US and began to see Trump's support staying competitive in states as the night wore on. States like Pennsylvania, Michigan, Wisconsin, and even Minnesota, once thought to be reliably Democratic, teetered back and forth all night between Trump and Clinton.

In Ohio, the lead for Trump began early in the night and never subsided. As I had done on past presidential election nights, I traveled to the post-election party in Columbus for allied groups, being hosted by America Votes. The mood in the room was far from festive. In the end, Ohio had been heavily invested in by labor as an "insurance policy" state that could still block a Trump victory. No Republican had ever been elected president in US history without winning Ohio. If all else failed, Ohio could still stop the seemingly improbable election of Donald Trump.

As the night wore on, the Trump lead in Ohio grew—from 2 to 4 to 6 to 8% by the end of the night. His lead was larger in Ohio than it was in Texas and other longtime Republican states. I was briefly able to join the huddle of America Votes and FOF data and political strategists in the back of the tavern. They were going back and forth over the modeling and data targets. They had concentrated the vast majority of their time and resources on the eight urban counties among Ohio's 88 counties, with a focus on African Americans and labor union members. It was a massive undertaking that invested tens of millions of dollars into a turnout that they had projected would overtake whatever support Trump was picking up from the predominantly rural counties.

In many of the urban counties, the coalition had met its turnout projection targets, which had been carefully calculated. However, the overperformance of Trump voters in even some of the blue counties took data strategists by surprise. The larger surprise was the unprecedented overwhelming turnout and support that Trump was getting from counties that progressive groups had never touched. It was a playbook that had worked for Democrats in 2008 and 2012 but collapsed in 2016. Many of the same voters in the same counties that had voted for Obama twice were now voting for Trump by large margins, with numbers that shocked even the most seasoned political observers.[23]

---

22 Ibid.
23 Ibid.

I also began to feel guilty again that I had left my role as a national voter mobilization leader to focus on efforts in only one state. The Black Civic Engagement Initiative (BCEI) efforts had targeted those very states of Michigan and Wisconsin that were now being lost by just a handful of votes. Had we pushed harder, had we spoken out louder about being defunded, or had we not disbanded and drifted our separate ways, we could have easily made up the difference in the 44,000 votes in Michigan and Wisconsin that would have turned the election in the opposite direction.[24]

Like Al Gore in 2000, Clinton was winning the popular vote even more decisively, by over two million votes. But once again, the antiquated electoral college system would award those electoral voters to Donald Trump. As the long night wore on the networks still had the races too close to call. Ohio was called early in the evening, so the focus remained on the states of Michigan, Wisconsin, and Pennsylvania, where all the major networks considered the races "too close to call."

By 1:30 AM, the bar where the watch party was being held began to close down. A handful of campaign operatives remained, glued to their phones or to the TV screen in disbelief. *This cannot be happening again* was the general expression throughout the room. I kept telling my longtime friend Dave Holt who had joined me for the election party that the night was not over. There was still time for Clinton to pull out a win. I just could not believe that this country would ever elect a man like Donald Trump as president. In the back of my mind, I knew this was wishful thinking. As the watch party winded down and people started to go home, I left feeling distraught and checked into the nearest downtown hotel.

The streets of Columbus were foggy and silent as it approached 2:00 AM. I listened on the car radio as Clinton's campaign chairman, John Podesta, announced to all the campaign workers assembled at the Javits Center in New York that Hillary Clinton would not be coming down to address them. She would have more to say in the morning. He urged them to go home and await more information after they had a chance to look at the numbers and sort things out. It was not the most inspiring message and signaled that the campaign was not confident about how the night was going.

By the time I got to the Holiday Inn downtown, I was feeling even more anxious. Almost an hour had passed since I had last checked the cable news. As I turned on the television, I saw Donald Trump walking on stage with his family, clapping to the cheers of the crowd. I first thought that Clinton had made a mistake in not coming out to address her supporters as Trump was now doing. I

---

24 Ibid.

switched the channels to see what the other new stations were covering. All of them had the same images of Trump, walking out and clapping. And then I saw the caption that CNN ran beneath the image in large red letters: BREAKING NEWS, CNN PROJECTS DONALD TRUMP ELECTED PRESIDENT OF THE UNITED STATES.

My heart sank and I plopped on the bed in disbelief. Clinton had a clear lead in the popular vote, and her lead had seemed to go up from the last time I saw the totals. She was ahead by over 1.5 million votes. *Based on the purest definition of a functioning democracy, she had been elected by the majority of the American people to be President of the United States.* But in the Electoral College vote, the numbers showed that Trump had crossed the 270 electoral vote threshold needed to be elected president. I kept switching channels to find another station that would still show the race as "too close to call." However, by this point, in addition to Ohio, they had all gone with the projections that Trump had won Michigan, Wisconsin, and Pennsylvania and had prevailed in the Electoral College.[25]

I soon found myself in tears sitting on the bed as I stared into the television screen. This was not like the hurt I had felt in 2000, or 2004. It was much more painful. And they were not the tears of joy I had shed in 2008 at the election of the country's first Black president. These were tears of frustration and anguish that we had lost so badly in Ohio and had lost so closely in Michigan and Wisconsin. These were tears that were soon replaced by anger that the country and the democracy I had fought so hard for, for so many years, would elect a man like Donald Trump as president. That anger then turned to the Clinton Campaign for taking the states of Wisconsin and Michigan for granted and not even bothering to campaign in them. My anger then turned to my home state of Ohio, which went from voting for President Obama twice to making a 180-degree turn and voting for his political and moral opposite, Donald Trump. And it was not even close, with Trump winning by over 8-percentage points![26]

My disbelief of how this could happen soon turned to the very sobering realities that I had witnessed over the last three years that gave me the clear answer as to why. The Trump victory and Clinton loss were aided by our failure to pass the Conyers/Sensenbrenner Bipartisan Voting Rights Amendment Act back in 2014 and 2015, while we had the chance. It was aided by the failure of many donors to trust and invest in African American legacy organizations that had a proven record of registering and turning out Black voters over the years.

---

25 Ibid.
26 "2016 United States presidential election in Ohio," Wikipedia, last modified February 7, 2022, https://en.wikipedia.org/wiki/2016_United_States_presidential_election_in_Ohio.

The election of 2016 would go down as one of the most defining and decisive elections, attributed to Trump's new counter-cultural messaging and the "silent majority" of white voters who rose in response to it. But the election is seldom, if ever, attributed to the small missteps that shaved votes from African Americans, students, and working people, who could have made a difference in the handful of states that would have produced a different result.

> What if the election protection and legal support programs that I had helped put in place at the DNC in 2006 had actually been fully activated?
>
> What if the Clinton Campaign and DNC had kept their promise to "count every vote" in Michigan and other close states—before the party's presidential nominee conceded?
>
> What if the North Carolina voting reforms from 2007 had not been repealed after the Obama 2012 election victory in the days following the Shelby decision?
>
> What if we had worked harder to hold together the Black voter engagement coalition which would have been able to increase the Black turnout in Michigan, Wisconsin, and Ohio?
>
> And most importantly, what if we had pressed harder to convince our more strident and progressive allies that the Bipartisan Conyers-Sensenbrenner version of the Voting Rights Amendment Act of 2014–even with its limitations on initially covered states–could have prevented most of the states' voter suppression efforts which were put in place after the Shelby v. Holder Supreme Court ruling?

The Shelby decision, as feared, literally eviscerated the longstanding preclearance provisions of the 1965 Voting Rights Act. Having been an integral part of all these recent voting rights battles over the years, I found it hard to not internalize the results. It was hard to not feel at least somewhat responsible for not fighting harder to enact and implement these pro-democracy and voter registration reforms that we had worked so hard to secure. We had worked for many years, even decades, to provide more funding for Black voter mobilization, but we were never able to be fully funded to build the sustainable capacity that was needed.

> What if we had taken a harder stand in the face of the mounting political obstacles and indifference from politicians, political operatives, their consultants, and vendors?
>
> What if more people who had the means to do more were not misguided in how they had devalued the importance of the Black vote in this and many other elections?
>
> What if all the progressive activists who could not stomach Hillary Clinton after the primary battle with Bernie Sanders had saw the urgency of the moment and not let perfect be the enemy of the good?

The election of Donald Trump as president would lead to a new era of efforts to further suppress the votes of African Americans, Latinos, young people, and other disenfranchised Americans who had fought for decades to break through the barriers of participation in our democracy. In 2008, we had seen the apex of our political strength break the exclusive 219-year dominance of the US Presidency by White Anglo-Saxon males. We had succeeded in electing an African American president by record-level turnouts and galvanizing our allies in labor, the Latino community, young people, the LGBTQ community, Millennials, Asian Americans, Native Americans, and white progressives. However, the political and racial backlash it unleashed in the United States was fierce and redefined the perception of many that the United States had indeed turned the corner on race. Whether perceived or real, it was the reality that haunted me and so many others who had fought so hard for so long.

Epilogue
Why We Still Can't Wait: To Fulfill the Promise of Democracy

For over 150 years, the United States Congress enacted a myriad of laws and procedures designed to stop African Americans from registering and voting in numbers proportional to their population. Voter registration laws would become a central part of that strategy of disenfranchisement. We fought a six-year battle to change the voter registration laws of our country so that it was easier for people to become a part of this system they call a democracy. But the real battle was much longer and bloodier, from the Bill of Rights, through the 15th Amendment in the aftermath of the Civil War in the mid-1800s, through the women's suffrage movement near the turn of the century, to the fight for the Voting Rights Act in Selma, Alabama in 1965. It continued through the student anti-war movement that would usher in the 26th Amendment, granting 18-year-olds the right to vote in the early 1970s.

The two historic Jackson for President Campaigns in the 1980s helped reveal many hidden barriers to voting and helped usher in the reforms of our voter registration laws in the 1990s. The NAACP's and NAACP-National Voter Fund's historic Black voter registration and mobilization campaigns of 2000 and 2004 helped usher in a new era of more advanced data-centered Black voter mobilization and election protection techniques. The final push to secure the reauthorization of the Voting Rights Act in 2006, coupled with the collective and continuous mobilization efforts, helped pave the way for the historic election of America's first Black president in 2008. These were the movements, the very democratic tenets, which would change the course of our nation's history and redefine our democracy as we entered the 21st century.

After all the battles I had waged as a national student activist, all the voter registration drives with Rev. Jackson, the six-year legislative battle to pass the NVRA as a voting rights advocate and Congressional staffer, and the endless tasks of monitoring and advocating for full implementation of the law, I thought I was pretty much done with my work in this area of voting rights. However, like the other longtime advocates of voter reform, I (and the rest of the country) would soon discover the harsh reality of the new expanded democracy that we had fought so hard to create. In the aftermath of the 2000 Bush vs Gore election debacle and all the election administration malfunctions of the 2004 election in Ohio, it became painstakingly and abundantly clear that our struggle to expand and protect this right to vote was not coming to an end; rather yet an-

https://doi.org/10.1515/9783110742473-019

other phase of the struggle was now beginning. After all these years, I am now convinced that the battle for our democracy might, in fact, be never-ending. It will always be challenged and weakened by those who have not (yet) embraced the same democratic principles that we had embraced and supported over the years.

The reforms that we were successful in enacting into law now face their most fierce challenge. The Voting Rights Act remains under attack at the US Supreme Court. The VRA legislative fix remains stalled in Congress. Republican-controlled states continue to intensify their efforts to actively roll back voting rights with measures making it harder to cast a vote and even count our votes. At the same time, Democratic-controlled states are actively advancing voting rights and breaking down long-standing administrative barriers to voting. It is a tug of war to open the doors of our democracy wider against those forces that seek to close the door and restrict the right to vote and the voices of the most disenfranchised.

There was never any evidence to suggest that our nation's jails were over-flowing with people who have been accused and convicted of voting twice. Our problem was never with people who were voting twice; it was with those who were not voting even once. Even some of the strongest supporters of voter reform were skeptical of its true impact after all the modifications that were made to the original motor voter bill. Many believed that it was not polit-ically possible to pass and that, if it did pass, it would not be properly imple-mented without federal funding and strict enforcement. We had proven the skep-tics wrong in 2008 and 2012. The electorate of our nation dramatically expanded, and when it did, we were able to make our federal, state, and local governments more diverse and representative of their populations.

At the end of the day, I had seen a number of things prevent the expansion of our democracy. All along the way, there was always some politician, some party, some force that stood in the way as we worked to move our democracy forward. Why was there so much opposition to the people being able to take the lead in public policy under a system of one person, one vote? There was cer-tainly a rational political reason for opposition when it came to some, mostly Re-publican lawmakers not wanting to empower young people or African Ameri-cans who voted heavily Democratic. But there was often great opposition from politicians who represented rural and poor white people in their districts. Even these communities, which in many ways were just as dependent on govern-ment programs and assistance, could become more actively involved in the proc-ess through the implementation of the NVRA. Yet many of their elected leaders opposed this new law that would give their constituents a greater voice in polit-ical decision-making.

We the people, the millions of disenfranchised Black, Brown, and young voters, seemed like intruders within our own democratic home. This was America and we sought nothing more than what was first enshrined by Thomas Jefferson in the Declaration of Independence and that resurfaced in so many of the constitutional amendments and statutes creating the democracy we were taught in our history books. When we tried to make it apply more universally, more democratically, opponents cried *foul*—or, more literally, they cried *fraud*. They believed that the more they opened the process to young people and people of color, the more restrictions they had to put in place on the newly enfranchised people who were being empowered by it. Opponents to reform viewed the expansion of democracy as anathema to their own political power and control over the political process. Their fervent battles against our efforts to expand our democracy are always present and they seldom back down from their opposition.

Throughout my involvement in passing the motor voter bill and mobilizing Black and young voters across the US, I saw more and more that the focus of too many politicians was not trust, service, or accountability. The central focus —the central theme—was raising money and getting elected and re-elected. It took money, (and lots of it), to run for office, and you had to bring money into the district to be successful. The measure of a person's worth and qualifications for a position was not the conviction of their ideas, but the size of their campaign war chest. News outlets would cover only candidates who had the "money" to endure the presidential primaries. Candidates of all races with little money were, and continue to be, dismissed as a "novelty." They were often called "spoilers," "fringe radicals," or, on a good day, "independents."

At one time in our democracy, political parties seemed to play a critical role in determining the political direction of the country. More and more, I saw that even political parties becoming an increasingly smaller part of the political makeup and could be easily overtaken by idealogues or misguided political leaders. Candidates' decisions are now, for the most part, driven by campaign consultants, super PACs (political action committees) and their pollsters, and cable news network personalities. They have essentially turned our system of political engagement into a cable television reality show and an online spectator sport for most younger Americans. The participation of regular, everyday people in the decision-making process regarding who runs for and wins elected office is often reduced to a few well-connected individuals who sort through and choose the winners before the people have much of a chance to provide real input. Essentially, in contrast to the adage saying that politics drives money (i.e., helps determine fiscal priorities), it is, in fact, money that drives politics. Inter-party rivalries are seen as mere intramural battles among two competing political power sources for control of Washington. Unfortunately, as important as this battle is, I discovered through all my years of advocacy that hyper-partisan politics has often little relevance to the daily lives of most Americans and certainly most African Americans.

Our political process has been taken over by all these forces, and the expansion of the electorate is the only way to give the people a true voice again. However, to do that, we had to break down the barriers to voter registration and give everyday citizens a chance to assert their true political strength. That did not begin to happen until we were able to register the tens of millions of Americans who were not registered before 1995 and who had no entrée into the political system. In the first year after the NVRA took effect, less than 50% of all Americans voted in the 1996 presidential elections. *Clearly, half of our electorate was completely left out of the political decision-making process of our country.* This, in essence, was the broken promise of our democracy.

It was the failure of our government to take those necessary steps to ensure that all of its citizens have the right and ability to participate in the governing process. While the nation boasted of a government based on "one person, one vote," this was rarely fully practiced at any level of government. There were always restrictions on people who could and couldn't vote:

Were you registered?
Did you live at a different address since the last time you voted?
Had your name changed?
Had your party changed?
Did you respond to the last mailing we sent asking you to verify that you were a voter?

Failure to answer the mail from the Board of Election to "confirm" that you were "still" an eligible voter would translate into the assumption that you were "not" still eligible. The burden of proof regarding your right to vote was, and remains, on the voter and not the government. *It seems (to me at least) that if America or any democratic nation is a land where the accused are innocent until proven guilty, then the burden to affirm my right to vote should fall on the state to prove that I am* **not** *an eligible voter, and not on me, the citizen voter, to prove that I* **am.**

In the system that existed before motor voter, that responsibility was placed fully upon the individual citizen. The main function of the government was to remove your name from the voter rolls. It was the responsibility of the voter to add their name and constantly re-affirm their voting eligibility throughout the entire voting process. This one requirement alone led to the disenfranchisement of millions of American citizens for many decades. Year after year, tens of millions of dollars were spent by state and county governments to *remove* citizens from voter lists while a pittance was spent on *adding* people to the voter list. For many decades, the task of registering voters was left to financially crippled non-profit good government groups, advocacy organizations, and fringe candidates for office.

An honest inquiry into both political parties' top priority in the 1990s would reveal that their ultimate operational goal was not 100% registration of all the people, but "clean voter lists." The priority before 1993 was measured based on not how many people had been registered, but on how much "dead weight" was removed or "how clean voter list were." How often and how effectively they removed voters from the list was, and in many cases remains, the central measure of success. The result was that the cleaner the voter lists, the lower the level of voter turnout. In essence, restrictive voter registration laws and voter roll purges for decades proved to be among the biggest obstacles to achieving a full representative form of government. While many of these same conditions existed in the post-motor voter era, the rulemaking for adding, removing, and cleaning voter lists had no federal standards prior to 1993, leaving many states free to implement the most restrictive rules at will. This was why many local politicians, particularly in those resistant states, resisted the intervention of the federal government and its mandates, believing that the NVRA and HAVA and in the south even the VRA, was interfering in what they felt was their state's eminent domain.

Yes, this was where the true broken promise of our democracy began to unravel: not on the battlefields overseas and not even in the halls of Congress or behind the walls of the White House. *The promise of democracy was also broken before 1993, when data managers and list vendors could restrict one of our most precious rights—without federal standards for voter registration procedures and voter list maintenance.* Voter registration maintenance had been carried out by a collaboration of election administrators and private industry vendors who had unfettered control over who did and did not vote in America. The more partisan elected officials fought the new federal bill, the more I saw why they were so concerned about election procedures. They literally wanted to control the process of counting the votes in every election. It was in the interest of politicians and even political parties to keep this process under their control and not the control of the federal government or the people whom they claimed to represent.

Despite the different levels of concern among both advocates and election administrators, the battle was significant in the national redefinition of the role of the federal government in US elections. Advocates of the Voting Rights Act, the National Voter Registration Act, and the Help America Vote Act all fought for national remedies to address these issues. We viewed low voter participation as a national problem and a barrier to full democratic participation. This was not a problem that could be resolved solely by advocates and litigators who had to fight case by case at the state and county levels. A national remedy was necessary if the fulfillment of the cherished "one person, one vote" constitutional guarantee was ever to be realized for all Americans.

By the mid-1990s, nearly 30 years after the passage of the Voting Rights Act, the United States was quickly becoming an endangered democracy—even in the midst of worldwide "democratic movements" across the globe. At the end of the Cold War, which had consumed Americans and Europeans for years, this threat to America's democratic process had not come about because of an outside threat from the Soviet Union/Russia, China, Iran, or any other nation seeking to overthrow our democratic system of government. On the contrary, this threat to our democracy was arising out of internal neglect—in essence, our inability to modernize our own democratic and elections machinery.

This threat had also come about because of very deliberate attempts on the part of the political power brokers in the past who had erected longstanding barriers designed to limit the influence of African Americans, people of color, women, the economically disadvantaged, and young people on the political process. This was done through state and local laws that were passed that produced inaccessible registrars, dual registration requirements, restrictions on deputy registrars, voter role purges, restrictions on registration sites, the denial of voting rights to students, or formally incarcerated citizens. These efforts alone or in combination, reduced the political impact of these constituencies for many generations throughout the nation's recent history. These were all the battles that we have fought over a 35-year period, and in many cases continue to fight even today.

Like the 1950s and 1960s, which witnessed the civil rights struggle, the 1990s and early 2000s would go down as being decades of democratic reform in the US and around the world. We argued that with less than 51% participation in our national elections, the US could not stand idly by while the world struggled to build democracies that expanded the participation of all their citizens. The United States itself needed a pro-democracy movement. The voter registration and electoral reform movements of the 1990s and early 2000s were the closest we came to advancing this effort forward since the struggle to pass the Voting Rights Act of 1965.

By the same token, those who opposed voter registration reform and push for voter suppression laws were sending a very negative signal to the world. That signal said, "A true democracy does not have to be open to all its citizens. It's all right to erect artificial barriers that make it difficult for ethnic minorities, poor people, and young people to be enfranchised." The US was practicing or facilitating all of these restrictions, yet still expecting to be called *the world's greatest democracy!* As we moved toward the democratization of nations throughout the world, we saw many similarities between those who opposed democratic reforms around the world and those who opposed making voter registration and voting easier here in the US. In fact, many were working overtime to erect more barriers after many of the long-fought-for voting rights reforms had been made.

This drive to "protect the integrity of the vote" by restricting the franchise was often led by old-guard politicos who mistakenly believed that they were protecting the best interest of the state against "fraud", that was in reality extremely rare or non-existent. Given all the voting rights battles I had experienced in the early 1990s, I found it hard to not make the comparison between voting rights opponents in the US and hard-liners in Eastern Europe who fought democratic reforms there. While only one side embraced democratic principles, even some reformists feared democratization and the massive participation of citizens in the political process. As the Berlin Wall came down and former Soviet Union states began to unravel across Eastern Europe, many hardliners opposed democratization efforts that would allow universal voting rights: "one person, one vote." They rationalized their opposition by saying that they were *protecting* the nation-state and political system against outside influences.

Some who were moved by our arguments for change began to spout rhetoric that supported democratic participation in the US, but still clung to their opposition when it came down to actually enacting or implementing voter reforms. Whether reluctant or willing opponents of electoral reform, they became as big of a threat to democracy as the soldiers who, on orders, stood guard at the Berlin Wall for years before it came down. The only difference was that in the US, these barriers were not erected to keep people from *getting out*; they were erected to keep people from *entering* the democratic process.

Many of the little-known yet heroic battles for the right to vote that took place over these last three decades, and that this book has described, never made it to daily newspaper front pages, the evening news, or cable news television shows. They were never captured by social media and may even seem irrelevant or out of place in today's hyper-partisan battles. *But the battles that we fought and won over these 30+ years proved to be the necessary ingredients for strengthening our nation's democracy and preventing it from collapsing during one of its most critical moments and challenges in recent years.*

The historic voter turnout of 2020 at the polls was part of this historic legacy of voting rights, innovative election administration and citizen mobilization. It was a historic turnout election held in the aftermath of the George Floyd senseless murder in Minnesota and the massive national and international Black Lives Matter movement that grew out of it. Administering our elections in a time of national crisis or upheaval would be the next phase of a generational battle to expand our democracy—one that continued through an international Covid-19 pandemic and cyber security threats to our election systems. The unprecedented emergency measures undertaken in election administration were carried out to ensure that every citizen had the right to *safely* vote absentee during an international pandemic. The massive expansion of absentee voting ushered in one of the largest turnouts in US history as 66.8% of eligible citizens voted in the 2020 presidential elections, according to the US Census.[1] By utilizing many of the provisions of the Voting Rights Act of 1965, the National Voter Registration Act of 1993, and the Help America Vote Act of 2002, the US was able to conduct a free, fair, and safe election and ensured that our democracy was preserved during one of the most challenging times in our nation's history. Without the enactment of these three landmark laws, this would not have been the case.

The 26th Amendment, NVRA, and HAVA were all necessary reforms that were the offspring of the Voting Rights Act of 1965. The voting rights crusades to pass them were won through the blood, sweat, and tears of voting rights champions for 50 years. Looking back over all these years, I find it important to note—and acknowledge—that ALL the major federal voting rights and electoral reform bills *that were actually passed into law* had one major distinguishing characteristic: *They were passed on a bipartisan basis.* The federal-level reforms that were strictly partisan, introduced by only one party, failed to be enacted into law, with very few exceptions. Likewise, Republican partisan efforts to repeal these major federal voting rights reforms over the years were defeated or never saw the light of day. Were these reforms repealed or never enacted, the results of the 2020 elections might have been decidedly different.

On January 6, 2021, the United States survived one of the greatest challenges to its democracy since the Civil War and Reconstruction. Our democracy withstood the challenge despite the forces led by Donald Trump who sought to undermine this democracy by perpetrating "the big lie" about the results of the 2020 election. The election administration system properly certified that Joe Biden had been elected President of the United States, winning the popular vote 51.3% to 46.9% by over seven million votes, and the Electoral College vote by a margin of 306–232.[2] The US witnessed one of the highest voter turnouts ever, with Joe Biden winning over 81.2 million votes—the most votes ever

---

1 Jewel Jordan, "2020 Presidential Election Voting and Registration Tables Now Available," U.S. Bureau of the Census, last modified April 29, 2021, https://www.census.gov/newsroom/press-releases/2021/2020-presidential-election-voting-and-registration-tables-now-available.html.
2 "2020 United States presidential election," Wikipedia, last modified March 17, 2022, https://en.wikipedia.org/wiki/2020_United_States_presidential_election.

cast for a presidential candidate.[3] The false narrative that the election was stolen has been aided by political opportunism, manufactured political hatred, and, ultimately, violence on January 6 carried out by people who subscribed to or were led to believe this false and misguided notion. Instead, American democracy prevailed on Election Day, November 3, 2020, and on Inauguration Day, January 20, 2021, despite all the attempts to undermine on January 6, 2021 the will of the American people in a democratic process.

*Congress's continued failure to pass a new formula for the Voting Rights Act is not a failure of **our democracy**, but a failure of **Congress** to do what has been done for over 50 years—work on a bipartisan basis to pass voting rights legislation.* It is vitally important for both parties to embrace any meaningful or sustainable voting rights bill. This approach is important not just in its bipartisan *passage* but also, and even more critically, in its bipartisan *implementation*. After so many years of fighting for the expansion of this democracy, I have concluded that this is the only way our election administration system can properly function. Hyper partisan politics has no place in Election Administration, period. Hyper-partisan electoral reform bills, no matter how meritorious or onerous, will always be challenged for their legitimacy—on both sides. This book has clearly documented just some of the many struggles that I witnessed in seeking to move this democratic experiment forward. It was never easy and remains a challenge as we continue fighting to preserve the laws that we have passed and move forward to expand our democracy even more in the years to come.

I am mindful of all the efforts being made to roll back the clock on voting rights—efforts that take place in states across the US to this very day. In the aftermath of the political fallout of the contentious 2020 elections, Georgia, Texas and over 40 other state legislatures have passed or accelerated their march toward restrictive voting laws with no protections from the VRA to prevent their enactment. Our only protection lies with utilizing the still existing Section 2 provisions of the VRA that "prohibits voting practices or procedures that discriminate on the bases of race, color or membership in one of the language minority groups."[4] As important as this section is, it only provides for legal challenges after the laws have taken effect.[5]

Unfortunately, former President Donald Trump and his supporters have fanned the flames of distrust in our electoral system, causing an acceleration of voter suppression bills at the state level. These voter suppression antics will

---

3 Ibid.
4 "Section 2 of the voting rights act," The United States Department of Justice, (n.d.) accessed March 22, 2022, https://www.justice.gov/crt/section-2-voting-rights-act#sec2.
5 Ibid.

not end with the passage of any one federal law or even one lawsuit—no matter how well-crafted it is. The forces who oppose the expansion of our democracy will continue to fight back. That is why our fight must always continue at the state and even local levels. As this battle rages on, one fact remains true: Despite all its flaws, *our democracy is stronger and more resilient* than many current political leaders and cable news commentators would lead us to believe.

The challenges to our democracy that we are witnessing now are not new. They have been going on for years and even decades. Those of us who have worked for years to defend this democracy have never given up on its strength and vitality...and we never will. That can happen only if we give up on ourselves and on the importance of our critical role in preserving and expanding this great democratic experiment.

It was a privilege to be part of all these movements over a 30-year period and to be blessed by God to live long enough to share these many stories that might otherwise not have been told. All of us who worked for years on reforming our nation's restrictive voter registration laws and the ongoing struggle to break down barriers to voting never believed that the reforms we fought for would, by themselves, be the end to politics as we know it. However, the struggle continues as we fight on in the hopes that we will move our nation closer to finally establishing the representative democracy that America always promised but has yet to fulfill. As the failed January 6, 2021 "insurrection" so graphically proved, it is no longer a question of whether we can fix our broken democracy. It is now a question of whether we can save it.

References

20C History Project. "L.A. Riots: President Bush's reaction." Youtube. Last modified October 19, 2015. https://www.youtube.com/watch?v=KD_3NOIEk-0.

ABC News Internet Venture. "Florida Secretary of State Rejects Counties' Appeal For More Time." Last modified November 12, 2000. https://web.stanford.edu/class/polisci179/ABC NEWS_com%20%20Secretary%20of%20State%20Rejects%20Recount%20Appeal.htm.

Adams, J. Christian. "Legal Memorandum: A Primer on "Motor Voter": Corrupted Voter Rolls and the Justice Department's Selective Failure to Enforce Federal Mandates." The Heritage Foundation. Last modified September 25, 2014. http://thf_media.s3.amazonaws.com/2014/pdf/LM139.pdf.

Amadeo, Kimberly. "Obama's Stimulus Package and How Well It Worked." The Balance. Last modified December 31, 2021. https://www.thebalance.com/what-was-obama-s-stimulus-package-3305625.

Amistad Digital Resource. "Black Politics." Accessed March 22, 2022 (n.d.). https://www.amistadresource.org/the_future_in_the_present/black_politics.html.

Amistad Digital Resource. "Social and Economic Issues of the 1980s and 1990s." Accessed March 22, 2022 (n.d.). https://www.amistadresource.org/the_future_in_the_present/social_and_economic_issues.html.

Ancheta, Angelo N. "Language Accommodation and The Voting Rights Act ". In *Voting Rights Act Reauthorization of 2006*, edited by Ana Henderson, 293 – 325. Berkeley Public Policy Press: University of California, Berkeley, 2007.

Apple Jr., R. W. "The 1989 Elections; Black Success With Measured Approach." The New York Times. Accessed March 22, 2022 (1989). https://www.nytimes.com/1989/11/08/us/the-1989-elections-black-success-with-measured-approach.html.

Augustin, Stanley "New Report Released by National Commission on Voting Rights: More Work Needed to Improve Registration and Voting in the U.S." Lawyers Committee. Last modified September 22, 2015. https://www.lawyerscommittee.org/new-report-released-by-national-commission-on-voting-rights-more-work-needed-to-improve-registration-and-voting-in-the-u-s/.

Ballotpedia. "Majority-minority districts." Accessed March 22, 2022 (n.d.). https://ballotpedia.org/Majority-minority_districts.

Ballotpedia. "Ohio Election Law Veto Referendum (2012)." Accessed March 22, 2022 (n.d.). https://ballotpedia.org/Ohio_Election_Law_Veto_Referendum_(2012).

Ballotpedia. "Ohio repeals HB 194, lawsuit likely." Last modified May 15, 2012. https://ballotpedia.org/Ohio_repeals_HB_194,_lawsuit_likely.

Ballotpedia. "Primary election: Background." Accessed March 22, 2022 (n.d.). https://ballotpedia.org/Primary_election#Background.

Ballotpedia. "Shelby County v. Holder." Accessed March 22, 2022 (n.d.). https://ballotpedia.org/Shelby_County_v._Holder.

Ballotpedia. "Voter caging and purging." Accessed March 22, 2022 (n.d.). https://ballotpedia.org/Voter_caging_and_purging.

Ballotpedia. "Wisconsin voter identification requirements and history." Accessed March 22, 2022 (n.d.). https://ballotpedia.org/Wisconsin_voter_identification_requirements_and_history.

https://doi.org/10.1515/9783110742473-020

Bebbington, Jim, and Laura Bischoff. "Blackwell rulings rile voting advocates." MIT. Accessed March 22, 2022 (n.d.). http://www.mit.edu/people/fuller/peace/league_women_voters. htm.

Benson, Jocelyn , and Michael T. Morley. "The Twenty-Sixth Amendment." National Constitution Center. Accessed March 22, 2022 (n.d.). https://constitutioncenter.org/inter active-constitution/interpretation/amendment-xxvi/interps/161.

Berke, Richard L. "50.16% Voter Turnout Was Lowest Since 1924." The New York Times. Accessed March 22, 2022 (1988). https://www.nytimes.com/1988/12/18/us/50.16-voter-turnout-was-lowest-since-1924.html.

Berlow, Alan , and Gordon Witkin. "Gun lobby's money and power still holds sway over Congress." The Center for Public Integrity. Last modified May 1, 2013. https://publi cintegrity.org/politics/gun-lobbys-money-and-power-still-holds-sway-over-congress/.

Berman, Ari. "Congressional Democrats Introduce Ambitious New Bill to Restore the Voting Rights Act." The Nation. Last modified June 24, 2015. https://www.thenation.com/ar ticle/archive/congressional-democrats-introduce-ambitious-new-bill-to-restore-the-voting-rights-act/.

Berman, Ari. "How the 2000 Election in Florida Led to a New Wave of Voter Disenfranchisement." The Nation. Last modified July 28, 2015. https://www.thenation. com/article/archive/how-the-2000-election-in-florida-led-to-a-new-wave-of-voter-disen franchisement/.

BIll of Rights Institute. "Jimmy Carter and the Iran Hostage Crisis." Accessed March 22, 2022 (n.d.). https://billofrightsinstitute.org/essays/jimmy-carter-and-the-iran-hostage-crisis.

Blount, Devetta. "How former Indiana representative Katie Hall made the Martin Luther King Jr. holiday day happen." WHAS-TV. Last modified January 20, 2020. https://www.whas11. com/article/news/history/king-holiday-katie-hall-indiana-ronald-reagan/417-f4cce98d-c6a9-4351-9d77-1ef7276e3a18.

Boyd, Thomas M., and Stephen J. Markman. "The 1982 Amendments To The Voting Rights Act: A Legislative History " Washington and Lee Law Review 40, no. 4 (1983): 1347–1428.

Brennan Center for Justice. "Shelby County v. Holder." Last modified August 4, 2018. https:// www.brennancenter.org/our-work/court-cases/shelby-county-v-holder.

Brownstein, Ronald "How the Rustbelt Paved Trump's Road to Victory." The Atlantic. Last modified November 10, 2016. https://www.theatlantic.com/politics/archive/2016/11/ trumps-road-to-victory/507203/.

Cave, Damien, and Darcy Eveleigh. "In 1968, a 'Resurrection City' of Tents, Erected to Fight Poverty." The New York Times. Last modified February 18, 2017. https://www.nytimes. com/2017/02/18/us/martin-luther-king-resurrection-city.html.

CBS News. "Obama in Selma: "Our march is not yet finished"." Last modified March 7, 2015. https://www.cbsnews.com/news/obama-selma-alabama-50th-anniversary-bloody-sunday/.

Cha, Mijin. "Registering Millions: The Success and Potential of the National Voter Registration Act at 20." Demos. Last modified May 20, 2013. https://www.demos.org/re search/registering-millions-success-and-potential-national-voter-registration-act-20.

Chandler, D. L. "Little Known Black History Fact: Operation Push Boycotts." Black America Web. Accessed March 22, 2022 (n.d.). https://blackamericaweb.com/2014/08/10/little-known-black-history-fact-operation-push-boycotts/.

CIRCLE (The Center for Information and Research on Civic Learning and Engagement). "Featured: Voter Turnout Among Young Women and Men in the 2008 Presidential Election." Last modified October 29, 2010. https://archive.civicyouth.org/featured-voter-turnout-among-young-women-and-men-in-the-2008-presidential-election/.

CIRCLE (The Center for Information and Research on Civic Learning and Engagement). "Youth Turnout Rate Rises to at Least 52%." Last modified November 7, 2008. https://archive.civicyouth.org/youth-turnout-rate-rises-to-at-least-52/.

Clerk – United State House of Representatives. "Roll Call 194 | Bill Number: S. 250." Accessed March 22, 2022 (1992). https://clerk.house.gov/Votes/1992194.

Clinton, William Jefferson "Statement on the Implementation of the National Voter Registration Act of 1993." Govinfo. Accessed March 22, 2022 (1994). https://www.govinfo.gov/content/pkg/WCPD-1994-09-19/pdf/WCPD-1994-09-19-Pg1758-2.pdf.

Coleman, Milton. "Jackson Begins Crusade For More Black Voters." The Washington Post. Accessed March 22, 2022 (1983). https://www.washingtonpost.com/archive/politics/1983/05/11/jackson-begins-crusade-for-more-black-voters/85322183-0622-4a49-815a-4a8ac97d2fae/.

Coleman, Milton "Jackson Launches 1984 Candidacy." The Washington Post. Accessed March 22, 2022 (1983). https://www.washingtonpost.com/archive/politics/1983/11/04/jackson-launches-1984-candidacy/3a977116-21c5-4516-9f9e-15bb5798173b/.

Congress.gov. "Actions – H.R.2 – 103rd Congress (1993–1994): National Voter Registration Act of 1993." Accessed March 22, 2022 (1993). https://www.congress.gov/bill/103rd-congress/house-bill/2/all-actions?overview=closed#tabs.

Congress.gov. "Actions – H.R.9 – 109th Congress (2005–2006): Fannie Lou Hamer, Rosa Parks, and Coretta Scott King Voting Rights Act Reauthorization and Amendments Act of 2006." Last modified July 26, 2006. https://www.congress.gov/bill/109th-congress/house-bill/9/all-actions?overview=closed#tabs.

Congress.gov. "Actions – H.R.17 – 101st Congress (1989–1990): Universal Voter Registration Act of 1989." Accessed March 22, 2022 (1989). https://www.congress.gov/bill/101st-congress/house-bill/17/actions?r=20&s=1.

Congress.gov. "Actions – H.R.2190 – 101st Congress (1989–1990): National Voter Registration Act of 1989." Accessed March 22, 2022 (1990). https://www.congress.gov/bill/101st-congress/house-bill/2190/all-actions?q=%7B%22roll-call-vote%22%3A%22all%22%7D.

Congress.gov. "Actions – H.R.3295 – 107th Congress (2001–2002): Help America Vote Act of 2002." Last modified October 29, 2002. https://www.congress.gov/bill/107th-congress/house-bill/3295/all-actions?overview=closed#tabs.

Congress.gov. "Actions – S.250 – 102nd Congress (1991–1992): National Voter Registration Act of 1992." Accessed March 22, 2022 (1992). https://www.congress.gov/bill/102nd-congress/senate-bill/250/all-actions.

Congress.gov. "Actions – S.622 – 106th Congress (1999–2000): Hate Crimes Prevention Act of 1999." Last modified March 24, 1999. https://www.congress.gov/bill/106th-congress/senate-bill/622/actions?r=4&s=1.

Congress.gov. "Actions – S.J.Res.19 – 113th Congress (2013–2014): A joint resolution proposing an amendment to the Constitution of the United States relating to contributions and expenditures intended to affect elections." Last modified September 11, 2014. https://www.congress.gov/bill/113th-congress/senate-joint-resolution/19/all-actions.

Congress.gov. "All Info – H.R.15 –101st Congress (1989 –1990): National Voter Registration Act of 1989." Accessed March 22, 2022 (1989). https://www.congress.gov/bill/101st-con gress/house-bill/15/all-info?r=75&s=1.

Congress.gov. "Cosponsors – H.R.3899 –113th Congress (2013 –2014): Voting Rights Amendment Act of 2014." Last modified March 20, 2014. https://www.congress.gov/bill/113th-congress/house-bill/3899/cosponsors.

Congress.gov. "Cosponsors – S.J.Res.19 –113th Congress (2013 –2014): A joint resolution proposing an amendment to the Constitution of the United States relating to contributions and expenditures intended to affect elections." Last modified September 11, 2014. https://www.congress.gov/bill/113th-congress/senate-joint-resolution/19/co sponsors.

Congress.gov. "Glossary of Legislative Terms – bill summary." Accessed March 22, 2022 (n.d.). https://www.congress.gov/help/legislative-glossary#glossary_billsummary.

Congress.gov. "H.R.2 –103rd Congress (1993 –1994): National Voter Registration Act of 1993." Accessed March 22, 2022 (1993). https://www.congress.gov/bill/103rd-congress/house-bill/2.

Congress.gov. "H.R.9 –109th Congress (2005 –2006): Fannie Lou Hamer, Rosa Parks, and Coretta Scott King Voting Rights Act Reauthorization and Amendments Act of 2006." Last modified July 27, 2006. https://www.congress.gov/bill/109th-congress/house-bill/9.

Congress.gov. "H.R.3295 –107th Congress (2001 –2002): Help America Vote Act of 2002." Last modified October 29, 2002. https://www.congress.gov/bill/107th-congress/house-bill/3295.

Congress.gov. "H.R.3950 –100th Congress (1987 –1988): Universal Voter Registration Act of 1988." Accessed March 22, 2022 (1988). https://www.congress.gov/bill/100th-congress/house-bill/3950?s=1&r=55.

Congress.gov. "S.2104 –101st Congress (1989 –1990): Civil Rights Act of 1990." Accessed March 22, 2022 (1990). https://www.congress.gov/bill/101st-congress/senate-bill/2104.

Congress.gov. "S.J.Res.19 – 113th Congress (2013 –2014): A joint resolution proposing an amendment to the Constitution of the United States relating to contributions and expenditures intended to affect elections." Last modified September 11, 2014. https://www.congress.gov/bill/113th-congress/senate-joint-resolution/19.

Congressional Budget Office US Congress. "Letter Honorable Paul D. Coverdell United States Senate." Accessed March 22, 2022 (1995). https://www.cbo.gov/system/files/104th-con gress-1995-1996/costestimate/53745-motor-voter-act.pdf.

Congressional Quarterly Almanac 1992. *Bush Rejects 'Motor Voter' Legislation.* 48 ed. Washington, DC: Congressional Quarterly, 1993.

Constitution Center. "10th Amendment: Rights Reserved to States or People." Accessed March 22, 2022 (n.d.). https://constitutioncenter.org/interactive-constitution/amend ment/amendment-x.

Cooley, Aaron. "War on Poverty " Encyclopedia Britannica. Last modified February 18, 2020. https://www.britannica.com/topic/War-on-Poverty.

Daily Kos. "Ohio rejects 1000s of voter registration applications due to paper weight." Last modified September 27, 2004. https://www.dailykos.com/stories/2004/9/27/53984/-.

Desilver, Drew. "In past elections, U.S. trailed most developed countries in voter turnout." Pew Research Center. Last modified November 3, 2020. https://www.pewresearch.org/

fact-tank/2020/11/03/in-past-elections-u-s-trailed-most-developed-countries-in-voter-turn
out/.

Duffin, Erin. "Youth voter turnout in presidential elections in the U.S. 1972 – 2020." statista.
Last modified March 19, 2021. https://www.statista.com/statistics/984745/youth-voter-
turnout-presidential-elections-us/.

Eidenmuller, Michael E. "Jesse Jackson 1984 Democratic National Convention Address."
American Rhetoric. Last modified January 6, 2022. https://www.americanrhetoric.com/
speeches/jessejackson1984dnc.htm.

Encyclopedia Britannica. "Bush v. Gore." Last modified December 5, 2021. https://www.bri
tannica.com/event/Bush-v-Gore#ref1046312.

Encyclopedia Britannica. "United States presidential election of 1968." Last modified October
29, 2021. https://www.britannica.com/event/United-States-presidential-election-of-1968.

Exner, Rich. "2004 Ohio presidential election results; George W. Bush defeats John Kerry
(photo gallery)." Cleveland.com. Last modified January 11, 2019. https://www.cleveland.
com/datacentral/2016/06/2004_ohio_presidential_electio.html.

Federal Election Commission. "The Impact of the National Voter Registration Act of 1993 on
the Administration of Federal Elections." Last modified June, 1997. https://www.fec.gov/
about/reports-about-fec/agency-operations/impact-national-voter-registration-act-1993-
administration-federal-elections-html/.

Federeal Election Commission – United States of America. "McCutcheon, et al. v. FEC."
Accessed March 22, 2022 (n.d.). https://www.fec.gov/legal-resources/court-cases/
mccutcheon-et-al-v-fec/.

Feldman, Noah. "When Democrats Blocked an 'Out of the Mainstream' Justice." Bloomberg
Opinion. Last modified January 26, 2017. https://www.bloomberg.com/opinion/
articles/2017 – 01 – 26/when-democrats-blocked-an-out-of-the-mainstream-justice.

File, Thom, and Sarah Crissey. "Voting and Registration in the Election of November 2008."
U.S. Census Bureau. Last modified July 30, 2012. https://www.census.gov/history/pdf/
2008presidential_election-32018.pdf.

Find Law. "Shaw v. Reno." Accessed March 22, 2022 (n.d.). https://caselaw.findlaw.com/us-
supreme-court/509/630.html.

Frank LaRose – Ohio Secretary of State. "Voter turn out in General Elections." Accessed
March 22, 2022 (n.d.). https://www.ohiosos.gov/elections/election-results-and-data/his
torical-election-comparisons/voter-turnout-in-general-elections/.

George W. Bush Archives. "President Bush Addresses NAACP Annual Convention." Last
modified July 20, 2006. https://georgewbush-whitehouse.archives.gov/news/releases/
2006/07/20060720.html.

Glass, Andrew. "Ron Brown elected as head of DNC, Feb. 10, 1989." Politico. Last modified
February 10, 2017. https://www.politico.com/story/2017/02/ronald-brown-elected-as-
head-of-dnc-feb-10-1989-234705.

GovTrack. "On the Cloture Motion S. 250." Accessed March 22, 2022 (1991). https://www.gov
track.us/congress/votes/102-1991/s134.

Green II, Robert. "The 1983 March on Washington and the Age of Reagan." Society for U.S.
Intellectual History. Last modified June 29, 2014. https://s-usih.org/2014/06/the-1983-
march-on-washington-and-the-age-of-reagan/.

Griffin, Rob, Ruy Teixeira, and John Halpin. "Voter Trends in 2016." American Progress. Last modified November 1, 2017. https://www.americanprogress.org/article/voter-trends-in-2016/.

Harris, Maya. "Women of Color: A Growing Force in the American Electorate." American Progress. Last modified October 30, 2014. https://www.americanprogress.org/article/women-of-color/.

Hasen, Rick. "Breaking: Senate Confirms 3 Commissioners to the Election Assistance Commission." Election Law Blog. Last modified December 16, 2014. https://electionlaw blog.org/?p=69221.

Hearings (Kristen Clarke). "Testimony, Continued Challenge to the Voting Rights Act Since Shelby v. Holder, House Judiciary Committee, June 25, 2019." U.S. House Committee On The Judiciary. Last modified June 25, 2019. https://judiciary.house.gov/calendar/even tsingle.aspx?EventID=2259.

Heinemann, Kenneth J. "Students and the Anti-War Movement." Bill of Rights Institute. Accessed March 22, 2022 (n.d.). https://billofrightsinstitute.org/essays/students-and-the-anti-war-movement.

History. "19th Amendment." Last modified March 9, 2022. https://www.history.com/topics/womens-history/19th-amendment-1.

History. "The 26th Amendment." Last modified April 23, 2021. https://www.history.com/top ics/united-states-constitution/the-26th-amendment.

History. "Civil rights leader Medgar Evers is assassinated." Last modified June 10, 2020. https://www.history.com/this-day-in-history/medgar-evers-assassinated.

History. "Hurricane Katrina." Last modified August 9, 2019. https://www.history.com/topics/natural-disasters-and-environment/hurricane-katrina#political-fallout-from-hurricane-ka trina.

History. "Riots erupt in Los Angeles after police officers are acquitted in Rodney King trial." Last modified April 27, 2021. https://www.history.com/this-day-in-history/riots-erupt-in-los-angeles.

History. "Voting Rights Act of 1965." Last modified January 11, 2022. https://www.history.com/topics/black-history/voting-rights-act#.

History, Art, & Archives, U.S. House of Representatives. "GRAY, William Herbert, III." Accessed March 22, 2022 (n.d.). https://history.house.gov/People/Detail/14072.

History, Art, & Archives, U.S. House of Representatives. "Suffrage for 18-Year-Olds." Accessed March 22, 2022 (n.d.). https://history.house.gov/Records-and-Research/Listing/c_016/.

Holmes, Steve A. "The 1994 Election: Voters; Did Racial Redistriction Undermine Democrats." The New York Times. Accessed March 22, 2022 (1994). https://www.nytimes.com/1994/11/13/us/the-1994-election-voters-did-racial-redistricting-undermine-democrats.html.

Jennings, Jerry T. "Voting and Registration in the Election of November 1990." U.S. Bureau of the Census. Accessed March 22, 2022 (1991). https://www.census.gov/library/publications/1991/demo/p20-453.html#

Jennings, Jerry T. "Voting and Registration in the Election of November 1992." U.S. Bureau of the Census. Accessed March 22, 2022 (1993). https://www.census.gov/library/pub lications/1993/demo/p20-466.html.

Jennings, Jerry T. "Voting and Registration in the Election of November 1992." U.S. Bureau of the Census. Accessed March 22, 2022 (1992). https://www.census.gov/content/dam/Cen sus/library/publications/1993/demo/p20-466.pdf.

Jordan, Jewel. "2020 Presidential Election Voting and Registration Tables Now Available." U.S. Bureau of the Census. Last modified April 29, 2021. https://www.census.gov/news room/press-releases/2021/2020-presidential-election-voting-and-registration-tables-now-available.html.

Justice.gov. "Case 3:11-cv-00470-JJB -DLD." Last modified July 12, 2011. http://www.justice.gov/crt/about/vot/nvra/la_nvra_comp.pdf.

Kasdan, Diana. "State Restrictions on Voter Registration Drives." Brennan Center for Justice, 2012. https://www.brennancenter.org/media/310/download.

King Institute Stanford University. "Voter Education Project (VEP)." Accessed March 22, 2022 (n.d.). https://kinginstitute.stanford.edu/encyclopedia/voter-education-project-vep.

Kondik, Kyle. *The Bellwether: Why Ohio Picks the President*. Athens: Ohio University Press, 2016.

Kornacki, Steve. "1988: Jackson mounts a serious challenge, but a loss in one state ends the quest." nbc News. Last modified July 29, 2019. https://www.nbcnews.com/politics/elec tions/1988-jackson-mounts-serious-challenge-loss-one-state-ends-quest-n1029601.

Kromm, Chris. "Selma and voting rights: Commemoration or legislation?" Facing South. Last modified March 6, 2015. https://www.facingsouth.org/2015/03/selma-and-voting-rights-commemoration-or-legislati.html.

Kurth, Joel, and Jonathan Oosting. "Records: Too many votes in 37% of Detroit's precincts." The Detroit News. Last modified December 13, 2016. https://www.detroitnews.com/story/news/politics/2016/12/12/records-many-votes-detroits-precincts/95363314/.

Legal Information Institute – Cornell Law School. "Young v. Fordice (95 – 2031), 520 U.S. 273 (1997)." Accessed March 22, 2022 (n.d.). https://www.law.cornell.edu/supct/html/95-2031.ZO.html.

Lewis, Jerry M., and Thomas R. Hensley. "The May 4 Shootings at Kent State University: The Search for Historical Accuracy." Kent State University. Accessed March 22, 2022 (1970). https://www.kent.edu/may-4-historical-accuracy.

Liptak, Adam. "Voting Problems in Ohio Set Off an Alarm." The New York Times. Last modified November 7, 2004. https://www.nytimes.com/2004/11/07/politics/campaign/voting-problems-in-ohio-set-off-an-alarm.html.

Lobrary of Congress. "Voting Rights for African Americans ". Accessed March 22, 2022 (n.d.). https://www.loc.gov/classroom-materials/elections/right-to-vote/voting-rights-for-african-americans/.

Los Angeles Times. "Richard Austin; Pioneered 'Motor Voter' Law." Last modified April 26, 2001. https://www.latimes.com/archives/la-xpm-2001-apr-26-me-55842-story.html.

McMillion, Barry J. "U.S. District Court Vacancies at the Beginning and End of the Obama Presidency: Overview and Comparative Analysis." Federation of American Scientists. Last modified January 31, 2017. https://sgp.fas.org/crs/misc/IN10570.pdf.

Mercer, Andrew, Claudia Deane, and Kyley McGeeney. "Why 2016 election polls missed their mark." Pew Research Center. Last modified November 9, 2016. https://www.pe wresearch.org/fact-tank/2016/11/09/why-2016-election-polls-missed-their-mark/.

Merriam-Webster. "superdelegate." Accessed March 22, 2022 (n.d.). https://www.merriam-webster.com/dictionary/superdelegate.

Michigan.gov. "General Election Voter Registration/Turnout Statistics." Accessed March 22, 2022 (n.d.). https://www.michigan.gov/sos/0,4670,7-127-1633_8722-29616-,00.html.

Mohdin, Aamna. "American women voted overwhelmingly for Clinton, except the white ones." Quartz. Last modified November 9, 2016. https://qz.com/833003/election-2016-all-women-voted-overwhelmingly-for-clinton-except-the-white-ones/.

Morice, Jane. "Thousands of 'freedom fighters' in Cleveland for first national Black Lives Matter conference." Cleveland.com. Last modified July 25, 2015. https://www.cleveland.com/metro/2015/07/thousands_of_freedom_fighters.html.

NAACP Legal Defence and Educational Fund, INC. "At-Large Voting Frequently Asked Questions." Accessed March 22, 2022 (n.d.). https://www.naacpldf.org/wp-content/uploads/At-Large-Voting-Frequently-Asked-Questions-1.pdf.

National Archives. "19th Amendment to the U.S. Constitution: Women's Right to Vote ". Last modified August 3, 2021. https://www.archives.gov/historical-docs/19th-amendment.

National Archives. "Congress and the Voting Rights Act of 1965." Accessed March 22, 2022 (n.d.). https://www.archives.gov/legislative/features/voting-rights-1965.

National Constitution Center. "On this day, Bush v. Gore settles 2000 presidential race." Last modified December 12, 2019. https://constitutioncenter.org/blog/on-this-day-bush-v-gore-anniversary.

National Geographic. "The Black Codes and Jim Crow Laws." Accessed March 22, 2022 (n.d.). https://www.nationalgeographic.org/encyclopedia/black-codes-and-jim-crow-laws/#:~:.

nbc News. "Kerry lawyers scrutinize voting in Ohio." Last modified August 4, 2012. https://www.nbcnews.com/id/wbna6460869.

Neate, Rupert "Donald Trump announces US presidential run with eccentric speech." The Guardian. Last modified June 16, 2015. https://www.theguardian.com/us-news/2015/jun/16/donald-trump-announces-run-president.

Nesmith, Bruce F., and Paul J. Quirk. "Triangulation: Positioning and Leadership in Clinton's Domestic Policy ". In *42: Inside the Presidency of Bill Clinton*, edited by Michael Nelson, Barbara A. Perry and Russell L. Riley, 46–76. Ithaca: Cornell University Press, 201.

New Vision. "US may probe Gore, Bush Florida vote." Accessed March 22, 2022 (n.d.). https://www.newvision.co.ug/news/1018269/us-probe-gore-bush-florida-vote.

O'Neill, Aaron. "Voter turnout in U.S. midterm elections by ethnicity 1966–2018." Statista. Last modified July 30, 2020. https://www.statista.com/statistics/1096123/voter-turnout-midterms-by-ethnicity-historical/.

Orlando Sentinel. "Election Digest." Last modified December 5, 2000. https://www.orlandosentinel.com/news/os-xpm-2000-12-06-0012060211-story.html.

Oxford Learner's Dictionary. "birtherism." Accessed March 22, 2022 (n.d.). https://www.oxforddlearnersdictionaries.com/us/definition/english/birtherism.

Paul, Taylor. "Dukaikis Wins N.Y. Primary." The Washington Post. Accessed March 22, 2022 (1988). https://www.washingtonpost.com/archive/politics/1988/04/20/dukakis-wins-ny-primary/b6294ae1-f5fd-4f8c-8f1f-25ededc01946/.

Perlstein, Rick. "Jimmy Carter Tried to Make It Easier to Vote in 1977. The Right Stopped Him With the Same Arguments It's Using Today." Time. Last modified August 20, 2020. https://time.com/5881305/president-carter-election-reform/.

Peters, Gerhard , and John T. Woolley. "1988 Democratic Party Platform." The American Presidency Project – UC Santa Barbara. Accessed March 22, 2022 (1988). https://www.presidency.ucsb.edu/documents/1988-democratic-party-platform.

Pew Reserach Center. "Dissecting the 2008 Electorate: Most Diverse in U.S. History." Last modified April 30, 2009. https://www.pewresearch.org/hispanic/2009/04/30/dissecting-the-2008-electorate-most-diverse-in-us-history/.

Philpot, Tasha S., Daron R. Shaw, and Ernest B. McGowen. "Winning the Race: Black Voter Turnout in the 2008 Presidential Election " *The Public Opinion Quarterly* 75, no. 5 (2009): 995 – 1022.

Piven, Frances Fox , and Richard A. Cloward. *Why Americans Don't Vote.* New York: Pantheon Books, 1988.

Pramulk, Jacob. "'Nothing' will make me vote Clinton: Some Bernie backers hold firm as DNC starts." CNBC. Last modified July 25, 2016. https://www.cnbc.com/2016/07/25/nothing-will-make-me-vote-clinton-some-bernie-backers-hold-firm-as-dnc-starts.html.

Prothero, P. Mitchell. "Florida Supreme Court orders recount of undervotes." United Press International. Last modified DEcember 8, 2000. https://www.upi.com/Archives/2000/12/08/Florida-Supreme-Court-orders-recount-of-undervotes/5410880151053/.

Ray, Michael. "Tea Party movement." Encyclopedia Britannica. Last modified February 7, 2022. https://www.britannica.com/topic/Tea-Party-movement.

RealClear Politics. "2016 Republican Presidential Nomination." Accessed March 22, 2022 (n.d.). https://www.realclearpolitics.com/epolls/2016/president/us/2016_republican_presidential_nomination-3823.html.

Reynolds, Maura. "Boxer Poses a Challenge, Briefly." The Los Angeles Times. Last modified January 7, 2005. https://www.latimes.com/archives/la-xpm-2005-jan-07-na-electoral7-story.html.

Reynolds, Molly E. "What is the Senate filibuster, and what would it take to eliminate it?" Brookings. Last modified September 9, 2020. https://www.brookings.edu/policy2020/votervital/what-is-the-senate-filibuster-and-what-would-it-take-to-eliminate-it/.

Rogers, Estelle H. "The National Voter Registration Act: Fifteen Years On." American Constitution Society. Last modified November 18, 2009. https://www.acslaw.org/issue_brief/briefs-2007 – 2011/the-national-voter-registration-act-fifteen-years-on/.

Rothman, Lily. "The Failed Strategy That Created Super Tuesday." Time. Last modified March 1, 2016. https://time.com/4234474/super-tuesday-history/.

Saad, Lydia. "Trump and Clinton Finish With Historically Poor Images." Gallup. Last modified November 8, 2016. https://news.gallup.com/poll/197231/trump-clinton-finish-historically-poor-images.aspx.

Senate.gov. "Civil War Amendments." Accessed March 22, 2022 (n.d.). https://www.senate.gov/artandhistory/history/common/generic/CivilWarAmendments.htm.

Shane, Peter M. "Disappearing Democracy: How Bush v. Gore Undermined the Federal Right to Vote for Presidential Electors." *Florida State University Law Review* 29, no. 2 (2001): 535 – 585.

Shuler, Peter. "Ken Blackwell's Disgraceful Election Machinations." CityBeat. Last modified December 8, 2004. https://www.citybeat.com/news/ken-blackwell-s-disgraceful-election-machinations-12229108.

Smith, Ralph. "The 'Winner-Take-All' Primary: Rationale and Strategy for It's Abolition." *National Black Law Journal* 2, no. 2 (1972): 130 – 149.

Solomon, Danyelle, Connor Maxwell, and Abril Castro. "Systematic Inequality and American Democracy." Center for American Progress. Last modified August 7, 2019. https://www.americanprogress.org/article/systematic-inequality-american-democracy/.

Strom, Stephanie. "On Obama, Acorn and Voter Registration." The New York Times. Last modified October 10, 2008. https://www.nytimes.com/2008/10/11/us/politics/11acorn.html.

The Columbus Dispatch. "Experts confounded: Turnout higher in Ohio in 2004." Last modified November 7, 2008. https://amp.dispatch.com/amp/23962130007.

The Green Papers. "Preserving Democracy: What Went Wrong in Ohio." Last modified January 5, 2005. https://www.thegreenpapers.com/G04/ohiostatusrept1505.pdf.

The National Archives. "Confrontations for Justice." Accessed March 22, 2022 (n.d.). https://www.archives.gov/exhibits/eyewitness/html.php?section=2.

The National Commission on the Voting Rights Act. "Highlights Of Hearings Of The National Commission On The Voting Rights Act 2005." Last modified February, 2006. https://www2.ohchr.org/english/bodies/hrc/docs/ngos/lccr3.pdf.

The New York Times. "The 1992 Campaign; President Vetoes the 'Motor-Voter' Measure." Accessed March 22, 2022 (1992). https://www.nytimes.com/1992/07/03/us/the-1992-campaign-president-vetoes-the-motor-voter-measure.html.

The New York Times. "Barack Obama's Remarks to the Democratic National Convention." Last modified July 27, 2004. https://www.nytimes.com/2004/07/27/politics/campaign/barack-obamas-remarks-to-the-democratic-national.html.

The New York Times. "Senate Election Results." Last modified December 17, 2014. https://www.nytimes.com/elections/2014/results/senate.

The Roanoke. "Voting Rights Act Rally." Last modified June 25, 2015. https://roanoke.com/photo/voting-rights-act-rally/collection_a8bac487–229a-5c8e-bef0-b5b8bdfde7a4.html.

The United States Department of Justice. "Section 2 of the voting rights act." Accessed March 22, 2022 (n.d.). https://www.justice.gov/crt/section-2-voting-rights-act#sec2.

The Washington Post. "Althea Simmo NAACP Official Dies." Accessed March 22, 2022 (n.d.). https://www.washingtonpost.com/archive/local/1990/09/15/althea-simmons-naacp-official-dies/4356515f-16ba-4fde-9ecb-04fb3bc3c7b8/.

Track Bill. "US Congress S2061 Universal Voter Registration Act of 1988." Accessed March 22, 2022 (n.d.). https://trackbill.com/bill/us-congress-senate-bill-2061-universal-voter-registration-act-of-1988/205425/.

Tyson, Alec, and Shiva Maniam. "Behind Trump's victory: Divisions by race, gender, education." Pew Research Center. Last modified November 9, 2016. https://www.pewresearch.org/fact-tank/2016/11/09/behind-trumps-victory-divisions-by-race-gender-education/.

U.S. Bureau of the Census. "Table 2. Reported Voting and Registration, by Race, Hispanic Origin, Sex and Age, for the United States and Regions." Accessed March 22, 2022 (1988). https://www2.census.gov/programs-surveys/cps/tables/p20/440/tab02.pdf.

U.S. Bureau of the Census. "Voting and Registration in the Election of November 1968." Accessed March 22, 2022 (1969). https://www.census.gov/library/publications/1969/demo/p20–192.html.

U.S. Bureau of the Census. "Voting and Registration in the Election of November 1974." Accessed March 22, 2022 (1976). https://www.census.gov/library/publications/1976/demo/p20–293.html#:~:text=The%20voter%20turnout%20in%20the,off%2Dyear%20election%20since%201946.

U.S. Bureau of the Census. "Voting and Registration in the Election of November 1976." Accessed March 22, 2022 (1978). https://www.census.gov/content/dam/Census/library/publications/1978/demo/p20–322.pdf.

U.S. Commission on Civil Rights. "Voting Irregularities in Florida During the 2000 Presidential Election: Chapter 9 Findings and Recommendations". Accessed March 22, 2022 (n.d.). https://www.usccr.gov/files/pubs/vote2000/report/ch9.htm.

U.S. Commission on Civil Rights. "Voting Irregularities in Florida During the 2000 Presidential Election: Executive Summary." Accessed March 22, 2022 (n.d.). https://www.usccr.gov/files/pubs/vote2000/report/exesum.htm.

U.S. Department of Justice – Civil Rights Division Disability Rights Section. "The Americans with Disabilities Act and Other Federal Laws Protecting the Rights of Voters with Disabilities." Last modified September, 2014. https://www.ada.gov/ada_voting/ada_voting_ta.htm.

U.S. Department of Justice. "About Language Minority Voting Rights." Last modified January 4, 2022. https://www.justice.gov/crt/about-language-minority-voting-rights.

U.S. Department of Justice. "Jurisdictions previously covered by section 5." Last modified November 29, 2021. https://www.justice.gov/crt/jurisdictions-previously-covered-section-5.

U.S. Department of Justice. "National Voter Registration Act of 1993 (NVRA)." Last modified March 11, 2020. https://www.justice.gov/crt/national-voter-registration-act-1993-nvra.

U.S. History Online Textbook. "The Expansion of the Vote: A White Man's Democracy." Accessed March 22, 2022 (n.d.). https://www.ushistory.org/us/23b.asp.

Unitarian Universalist Association. "James Reeb and the Call to Selma." Accessed March 22, 2022 (n.d.). https://www.uua.org/re/tapestry/adults/river/workshop5/175806.shtml.

United State Senate. "Roll Call Vote 102nd Congress – 2nd Session." Accessed March 22, 2022 (n.d.). https://www.senate.gov/legislative/LIS/roll_call_votes/vote1022/vote_102_2_00226.htm.

United States Courts. "History – Brown v. Board of Education Re-enactment." Accessed March 22, 2022 (n.d.). https://www.uscourts.gov/educational-resources/educational-activities/history-brown-v-board-education-re-enactment.

United States Senate. "Roll Call Vote 103rd Congress – 1st Session." Accessed March 22, 2022 (n.d.). https://www.senate.gov/legislative/LIS/roll_call_votes/vote1031/vote_103_1_00117.htm.

United States Senate. "Roll Call Vote 111th Congress – 1st Session." Accessed March 22, 2022 (n.d.). https://www.senate.gov/legislative/LIS/roll_call_votes/vote1111/vote_111_1_00061.htm.

University of Minnesota Law Library. "Affordable Care Act (ACA) & Health Care and Education Reconciliation Act of 2010 (HCERA)." Last modified January 26, 2022. https://libguides.law.umn.edu/c.php?g=125769&p=906254.

USA Election Atlas. "1976 Presidential General Election Results." Accessed March 22, 2022 (n.d.). https://uselectionatlas.org/RESULTS/national.php?year=1976.

Volcker, Paul. "What Led to the High Interest Rates of the 1980s?" PBS News. Last modified May 29, 2009. https://www.pbs.org/newshour/economy/what-led-to-the-high-interest.

Wallach, Philip A. "The Fall of Jim Wright—and the House of Representatives." The American Interest. Last modified January 3, 2019. https://www.the-american-interest.com/2019/01/03/the-fall-of-jim-wright-and-the-house-of-representatives/.

Wheaton, Sarah. "For First Time on Record, Black Voting Rate Outspaced Rate for Whites in 2012." The New York Times. Last modified May 8, 2013. https://www.nytimes.com/2013/05/09/us/politics/rate-of-black-voters-surpassed-that-for-whites-in-2012.html.

Wikipedia. "1972 United States presidential election." Last modified March 19, 2022. https://en.wikipedia.org/wiki/1972_United_States_presidential_election.

Wikipedia. "1980 United States presidential election." Last modified March 19, 2022. https://en.wikipedia.org/wiki/1980_United_States_presidential_election.

Wikipedia. "1988 United States presidential election." Last modified March 22, 2022. https://en.wikipedia.org/wiki/1988_United_States_presidential_election.

Wikipedia. "1992 Los Angeles riots." Last modified March 21, 2022. https://en.wikipedia.org/wiki/1992_Los_Angeles_riots.

Wikipedia. "1992 United States House of Representatives elections." Last modified March 21, 2022. https://en.wikipedia.org/wiki/1992_United_States_House_of_Representatives_elections.

Wikipedia. "1994 United States House of Representatives elections." Last modified February 16, 2022. https://en.wikipedia.org/wiki/1994_United_States_House_of_Representatives_elections.

Wikipedia. "1994 United States Senate election in Virginia." Last modified October 13, 2021. https://en.wikipedia.org/wiki/1994_United_States_Senate_election_in_Virginia.

Wikipedia. "1996 United States presidential election." Last modified March 18, 2022. https://en.wikipedia.org/wiki/1996_United_States_presidential_election#.

Wikipedia. "2000 United States presidential election in Florida." Last modified March 3, 2022. https://en.wikipedia.org/wiki/2000_United_States_presidential_election_in_Florida.

Wikipedia. "2010 United States House of Representatives elections." Last modified March 23, 2022. https://en.wikipedia.org/wiki/2010_United_States_House_of_Representatives_elections.

Wikipedia. "2012 United States presidential election." Last modified March 11, 2022. https://en.wikipedia.org/wiki/2012_United_States_presidential_election.

Wikipedia. "2014 United States Elections." Last modified March 8, 2022. https://en.wikipedia.org/wiki/2014_United_States_elections#:~:text=House.

Wikipedia. "2016 United States presidential election in Ohio." Last modified February 7, 2022. https://en.wikipedia.org/wiki/2016_United_States_presidential_election_in_Ohio.

Wikipedia. "2020 United States presidential election." Last modified March 17, 2022. https://en.wikipedia.org/wiki/2020_United_States_presidential_election.

Wikipedia. "Amendments to the Voting Rights Act of 1965." Last modified February 13, 2022. https://en.wikipedia.org/wiki/Amendments_to_the_Voting_Rights_Act_of_1965.

Wikipedia. "Bill Thomas." Last modified January 1, 2022. https://en.wikipedia.org/wiki/Bill_Thomas.

Wikipedia. "Bipartisan Campaign Reform Act." Last modified March 16, 2022. https://en.wikipedia.org/wiki/Bipartisan_Campaign_Reform_Act.

Wikipedia. "Brooks Brothers riot." Last modified January 25, 2022. https://en.wikipedia.org/wiki/Brooks_Brothers_riot.

Wikipedia. "George Wallace." Last modified March 9, 2022. https://en.wikipedia.org/wiki/George_Wallace.

Wikipedia. "Harold Washington Party." Last modified February 23, 2022. https://en.wikipedia.org/wiki/Harold_Washington_Party.

Wikipedia. "Hurricane Katrina." Last modified February 5, 2022. https://en.wikipedia.org/wiki/Hurricane_Katrina.

Wikipedia. "Minority language." Last modified March 3, 2022. https://en.wikipedia.org/wiki/Minority_language.

Wikipedia. "Movement for Black Lives." Last modified March 9, 2022. https://en.wikipedia.org/wiki/Movement_for_Black_Lives.

Wikipedia. "National Rifle Association." Last modified March 15, 2022. https://en.wikipedia.org/wiki/National_Rifle_Association.

Wikipedia. "Organizing for America." Last modified March 19, 2022. https://en.wikipedia.org/wiki/Organizing_for_America.

Wikipedia. "Silent majority." Last modified March 2, 2022. https://en.wikipedia.org/wiki/Silent_majority#:.

Wikipedia. "Troubled Asset Relief Program." Last modified February 18, 2022. https://en.wikipedia.org/wiki/Troubled_Asset_Relief_Program.

Williamson, Richard A. "The 1982 Amendments to the Voting Rights Act: A Statutory Analysis of the Revised Bailout Provisions." *Washington University Law Review* 62, no. 1 (1984): 1–77.

Yeoman, Barry. "Court Rules NC Voting Rights Rollback to Stay In Place Until After Midterm Elections." The America Prospect. Last modified August 15, 2014. https://prospect.org/power/court-rules-nc-voting-rights-rollback-stay-place-midterm-elections/.

Zinn Education Project. "Aug. 4, 1964: Civil Rights Workers Bodies Found." Accessed March 22, 2022 (n.d.). https://www.zinnedproject.org/news/tdih/civil-rights-workers-found/.

Zinn Education Project. "May 15, 1970: Jackson State Killings." Accessed March 22, 2022 (n.d.). https://www.zinnedproject.org/news/tdih/jackson-state-killings/.